I0808134

Cougar
INDY 500
FIREHAWK

Cobra Jet

Rob Kinnan and Diego Rosenberg

The History of Ford's Greatest High-Performance Muscle Cars

CarTech®

CarTech®

CarTech®, Inc.
838 Lake Street South
Forest Lake, MN 55025
Phone: 651-277-1200 or 800-551-4754
Fax: 651-277-1203
www.cartechbooks.com

Edit by Wes Eisenschenk
Layout by Hailey Samples

ISBN 978-1-61325-378-6
Item No. CT612

Library of Congress Cataloging-in-Publication Data

Names: Kinnan, Rob, 1965- author. | Rosenberg, Diego, 1971- author.
Title: Cobra Jet : the history of Ford's greatest high-performance muscle cars / Rob Kinnan and Diego Rosenberg.
Description: Forest Lake, MN : CarTech, Inc., [2019] | Includes index.
Identifiers: LCCN 2019032687 | ISBN 9781613253786 (hardcover)
Subjects: LCSH: Mustang automobile--History--20th century. | Muscle cars--United States--History--20th century.
Classification: LCC TL215.M8 K564 2019 | DDC 629.222/2--dc23
LC record available at https://lccn.loc.gov/2019032687

Written, edited, and designed in the U.S.A.
Printed in China
10 9 8 7 6 5 4 3 2 1

End papers photo courtesy RM Auctions.

DISTRIBUTION BY:

Europe
PGUK
63 Hatton Garden
London EC1N 8LE, England
Phone: 020 7061 1980 • Fax: 020 7242 3725
www.pguk.co.uk

Australia
Renniks Publications Ltd.
3/37-39 Green Street
Banksmeadow, NSW 2109, Australia
Phone: 2 9695 7055 • Fax: 2 9695 7355
www.renniks.com

Canada
Login Canada
300 Saulteaux Crescent
Winnipeg, MB, R3J 3T2 Canada
Phone: 800 665 1148 • Fax: 800 665 0103
www.lb.ca

TABLE OF CONTENTS

ACKNOWLEDGMENTS

Rob Kinnan

There are several ways to develop an affection or addiction to anything, including things of the automotive persuasion. It can be either passed down from a family member, taught by a friend who is into the subject, or nurtured on its own within a person after an experience involving something mechanical. Mine is a combination of all that.

I credit my dad with passing down a love of all things mechanical. His career was as a heavy equipment mechanic and manager (think Caterpillar bulldozers), and before I was born he raced go-karts. My first memory of fast cars was hanging out with him and his buddy Jerry Spangler while they worked on Jerry's sprint car in northwest Ohio, and Dad even took me for a few hot laps in the race car while I sat on his lap. I'm sure he just putted around the track in gear, but in my 5-year-old mind we were going 1,000 mph, and that sealed my lifelong desire for speed.

While I begged him to build me a kart or quarter midget of my own by the time I was old enough to talk, it never happened, but he did finance my first car and taught me how to work on it. We tore it down and rebuilt the engine and entire front half of the car before I even had my driver's license.

I credit my mom with my reading and writing abilities (such as they are) since she devoured books and encouraged me to read, which naturally grew into writing. I first picked up a Stephen King book, *Christine*, because it had a 1957 Plymouth on the back cover. So, there's an intersection of both passions right there.

In junior high, bored to death in study hall, I read car magazines instead of actually studying anything, and that also gave me tips on both fronts. In college I was still consumed by *Hot Rod*, *Car Craft*, *PHR*, and *Car & Driver* magazines while my engineering-major roommates were studying thick and boring textbooks. Once I got the job at *Hot Rod*, one of those ex-roommates remarked, "I guess all those times we gave you s—— about reading car mags you were actually studying, huh?" Yep, I'll take that.

I acknowledge Jeff Smith, former editor of *Hot Rod* and my first real boss, for trusting me enough to hire me as a glorified receptionist (editorial assistant was the actual job title), right there on the Sunset Strip in Hollywood. There's an enormously long list of folks I worked with on the editorial, production, and art side who taught me what I needed to know to survive and thrive in the industry. The list is too long to call anyone out specifically, but those people know who they are.

Thanks to my editor at CarTech, Wes Eisenschenk, for roping me into this Cobra Jet project. I was horribly late on my first book with Wes, which was the autobiography of Linda Vaughn (Miss Hurst), but he gave me another shot with this book, which I'm even later on. That leads me to give a special thanks to coauthor Diego Rosenberg, who took the reins to finish this book while my day-to-day job kept me too busy to complete it. Thanks, man. I owe you a beer (or 10).

Finally, thanks to all the folks who helped put this book together. Diego mentions a few of them, but I need to include Jerry Heasley for his help with photos and information and a few tips on surviving the book trade after penning a bunch of automotive books himself. Lump Donald Farr into that mix as well and for being a well-published friend in the Ford world for years. And finally, Evan J. Smith, who put together the last chapter about Ford continuing the Cobra Jet legacy from 2008 to today.

I hope what Diego and I put together here will inform and entertain you. This is the result of several years of research and toil, and we think it is the ultimate authority on Cobra Jet.

Diego Rosenberg

This automotive history could not have happened without the following influences and experts:

Thank you to my mom and dad for being fine parents and feeding my automotive interests when I was a kid (and kudos to my sister Marsha for knowing what a 4-4-2 is). Thanks to my wife Tatiana for being a supporting cast member.

Then, there are the guys who were in the trenches: Marty Schorr, Joe Oldham (RIP), Al Kirschenbaum, and Dave Wallace, Jr. (from back in the day); and Jim Campisano, Don Keefe, Tom Shaw (RIP), Paul Zazarine, Donald Farr, Drew Hardin, Richard Truesdell and Mark Fletcher, Steve Magnante, and Dave Kennedy (from my formative years to today).

Special thanks to Wes Eisenschenk and the cast of CarTech Books for approaching me for my first book, *Selling the American Muscle Car: Mar-*

keting Detroit Iron in the 1960s and 1970s, and to Rob Kinnan for suggesting me as coauthor.

Kevin Marti and Marti Auto Works (https://www.martiauto.com) deserve a mention for the contribution to the documentation and preservation of Ford Motor Company products. Without their hard work, Rob and I couldn't have imparted Cobra Jet history as successfully.

Charlie Morris has been instrumental in sorting through the misinformation in my research and suggesting how things were. He deserves recognition for being an encyclopedia of FoMoCo and era knowledge. Other knowledgeable folks include Robert Day, Richard Fleener, and Scott Hollenbeck.

Gavin Schlesinger, Dennis Pierachini, Michael Banks, and the many other members of the Cougar Club of America stepped up to the plate to make this book better.

Many owners and photographers have kindly contributed imagery in this book. Find them in the photo credits.

While it would be unauthentic to thank Facebook, there are many pages and groups in which I was able to connect with enthusiasts and find answers—sometimes from the 1960s racers themselves.

The possibility of overlooking contributors pains me; so, with apologies, this space is for you.

Dedicated to Terrance Hansler

FOREWORD BY AL JONIEC

The first time I ever heard "Cobra Jet," it was late 1967. I was happily racing my 427 SOHC, fuel injected, altered wheelbase Funny Car when I got a call from the then-new drag race coordinator Chuck Folger. He said that since I was a member of the Ford factory team, they were going to ask us first if we would like to run a new car Ford was going to introduce at the 1968 NHRA Winternationals.

I was curious and said it sounded good but asked if he could tell me more. Chuck then told me that after a couple of years, Ford looked in the mirror and was tired of supporting these crazy Funny Cars we were racing because they were not sold at dealerships. Ford wanted to go back to the new-car showroom "Win on Sunday, sell on Monday"–style of selling cars.

I said that it sounded good to me and asked what kind of car it was going to be. He said it would be a real Mustang that anyone can drive on the street but that it would go like hell. He said Ford was going to put together a combination of hybrid performance parts of the 428 engine and it would be called a Cobra Jet. I then told him that was a great name and sign me up, and that's how I became one of the drivers of the six-car Ford team.

Chuck told me that since Pomona was nearby, the Cobra Jets were all going to be equally prepared at the West Coast Holman-Moody-Stroppe location, so they would be all the same except for automatic and 4-speed transmissions. I could pick up the car there. Obviously, there were many finer points yet to be determined, but we did have a few months to plan the details.

I started to figure out the logistics. The trip involved more than two weeks away from home, so it wasn't easy to get volunteers. I did find Bill Boyce and Ralph Hart, who wanted to go with me on the long journey. Since we now had three drivers, we could shorten up the time away from home by driving nonstop, rotating each guy. One would sleep in the back of the crew cab and two would be up front. We would only stop for fuel, for food, and to pee. We were there 56 hours later—something I would never do again under any circumstances (I still remember the grind of those 56 hours).

We arrived at Holman-Moody-Stroppe's dead tired, and all of the other cars were done and lettered but mine. I had told Chuck that I would be bringing my own artist, Ralph Hart, and he would be lettering the car. If you notice the other five team cars look alike, it's because they were all done by the same guy. Also, because I wasn't there and my car was not lettered, they did public relation pictures without me. Ford had rented a racetrack all week for us to test on, but we had to wait for Ralph to finish the car before we could begin testing. We did work on the car while Ralph was doing his thing.

FOREWORD
(CONTINUED)

As a side note, since the Holman-Moody-Stroppe engine guys were both off-road and NASCAR racers, I guessed that they would most likely be conservative with the cam timing. At any rate, I talked to Crane Cams and brought with me the latest and greatest cam just in case. My hunch proved correct; when I changed the cam, I immediately picked up 2/10s ET and was far and away the fastest Cobra Jet during testing, according to Chuck.

We went right through tech inspection after getting much-needed sleep and rest, and I was feeling good about what we had accomplished so far. I didn't quite understand and/or grasp how important of a race it was for Ford or Chuck Folger, as this was his first big test as the new leader of the team.

Because Super Stock racers can run close to their records, it's all about red lights and/or cutting *great* lights, not just good lights at the start. Redlighting can also be a strategy for a team car to make a faster car run out of its bracket and cause them to lose. To deal with the redlighting issue, Chuck had Al Turner, the Mercury team coordinator, stand about three-quarters of the way down the track as near to the edge as possible for us to look for. If he was waving his arms, that meant the car we were running redlighted (on the handicap system, if you leave first, you could never know if the other car redlighted or not).

During the S/SE class round off, we faced our first crisis. Hubert Platt—also in a Cobra Jet—and I were about to race, and we could easily go way below the national record. If we were racing each other, we would lose any advantage we had by resetting the record. In a frantic last-minute effort, Chuck stuck his head in both my window and Hubert's window while we were buckling up and yelled that whoever was ahead by the end of third gear would win and at that point we should back off.

When we raced, I almost crapped my pants because Hubert was about 1½ car lengths ahead of me when we left the line. I frantically said to myself, "Self, we have to go balls out to catch him by third gear." I started to reel him in, and by third gear I was ahead, but I forgot to back off as planned. When I saw this guy out of the corner of my eye waving his hands and jumping up and down like a crazy man, the light bulb went on. I realized that Hubert redlighted, which was why he was so far ahead of me off the line. I then backed off and won the S/SE class.

For the Super Stock Eliminator, I went on to what appeared to be a sea of Mopars, and they were redlighting too. I assumed the Mopar guys knew we could easily go way below the record if we had to, so they tried to force us out by running too fast to end the advantage we had. It didn't work. Between Al Turner and me cutting great lights, I won S/S Eliminator as well. By the way, this was the very first S/S Eliminator for Ford.

It was a home run. The new Cobra Jet won everything there was to win on its inaugural introduction. Forty years later, when the Cobra Jet was reintroduced at the same Winternationals, Brent Hajek painted four of the new cars with the same paint scheme as the original 1968 Ford team cars. One of the cars was painted like mine. What are the odds that out of all the cars competing that day the one with my name on it would win again? It did, and I was lucky enough to be there to watch it happen. Like they say, lightning strikes twice and/or its like déjà vu all over again.

I'm a lucky guy.

—Al Joniec

CHAPTER ONE

1960–1966: FROM RACING BAN TO THE TOTAL PERFORMANCE YEARS

There is a reason many automotive enthusiasts and racing fans point to the 1960s as the glory days of cars and racing—the decade experienced an explosion in horsepower and speed not seen before or since. One of the quickest and most iconic street cars to come out of the muscle car era was the 428 Cobra Jet Mustang. Yet before we get into 428 Cobra Jet history, we must look at what led to its creation.

Back to the 1940s

World War II made the 1940s a tumultuous time for American automakers. As the war came to a close and American GIs came home, they brought their fledgling passion for small European sports cars, as well as extensive knowledge of mechanics, since many had been thrust into the role of maintaining Jeeps, tanks, airplanes, and any other implements of war. Naturally, they began using their newfound talents and interests to modify indigenous American vehicles and thereby created one of the strongest and longest-enduring hobbies (for lack of a better term) of postwar America.

For many, this meant going back to their prewar hot rodding roots by hopping up the Model A and B Fords that they had left when they went off to war, only now with pockets full of money and all that mechanical knowledge. These men and women began racing on the dry lakes, the streets, and at a few scattered drag strips that had sprung up. The unfortunate result, especially from the view on the street, was the negative reaction toward the increased presence of hot rodders. Much like today's connotation of "street outlaws," hot rodders were perceived (rightly or wrongly) as a group of delinquent troublemakers with no regard to general public safety.

Across the country, dangerous (and sometimes fatal) street racing caught on, and with it the practice of gathering at local hangouts showing off their rides and cruising up and down local pikes at night. These activities became an easy target for public attention that focused increasingly on what was perceived as disconcerting national problems: juvenile delinquency and teenage gangs. As the popularity of hot rods (called "gow jobs" in the beginning) soared, hot rods and hot rodding, along with rock 'n' roll, became symbols for the darker side of American youth. A prime indicator of the hobby and its public image can be seen in any number of hot rod–related films from the 1950s; the characters were usually portrayed as hooligans and delinquents out to prey on the common folk.

SCTA: Sanctioned Racing

There needed to be some common ground in order for hot rodding to exist as a potentially positive thing in the general public's eyes, and that's where the Southern California Timing Association (SCTA, the sanctioning body that ran the dry lakes races at Muroc, El Mirage, and later, Bonneville) came in. In January 1948, the first Hot Rod Exhibition was put on by the SCTA at the National Guard Armory in Los Angeles in an attempt to validate hot rodders and their cars.

The emphasis was on the positive aspects of hot rodding, namely craftsmanship, engineering, and, most of all, safety. The SCTA also partnered with police officers (many of whom were hot rodders as well) and local governmental officials to lend an air of legitimacy, while former Hollywood publicist Robert E. Petersen created the program to the show, called it *Hot Rod*, and sold it on the steps outside the Armory.

So, the fuse was lit. Within two years, *Hot Rod* magazine's circulation crossed the 300,000 mark, and the rest of the country had an insider's look at what was happening on the West Coast, helping hot rodding spread across the country.

Racing Forced to Grow Up

Sadly, just as the hooligan label was starting to leave hot rodders, the racing world saw several brutal accidents with multiple fatalities. Perhaps the worst of them was at the 1955 24 Hours of Le Mans, when Pierre Levegh crashed his Mercedes-Benz into the densely populated grandstands at 150 mph, resulting in a huge end-over-end fireball. Seventy-seven people were killed in the accident. As a result of this disaster, the French government responded to race safety by moving the spectators farther back from the track, and Mercedes-Benz left racing for about two decades.

AMA's Attempted Bans

At a board meeting of the Automobile Manufacturers Association (AMA) in 1957, the president of General Motors, Harlow Curtice, floated the idea that the association ban factory-supported racing in hopes that it would keep the government from imposing racing regulations on the automobile industry. On June 6, 1957, the AMA adopted a resolution and banned race involvement, meaning that manufacturers not only would not support organized racing with new cars but also would stop supplying race cars and doing anything to publicize results or use performance as a selling tool for their new vehicles.

In reality, Ford was the only manufacturer that abided by the ban, as General Motors and Chrysler paid it lip service but continued to build hot cars for the street. Ford quickly noticed the burgeoning market full of younger speed-obsessed new-car buyers. Like-minded people inside Ford eventually got through to the bean counters pulling the strings and, by 1960, began to market to younger performance-minded and style-conscious people who were buying new cars.

Factory 1960s Hot Rods from Ford

Ford introduced the all-new Ford-Edsel (FE) series in 1958, which was initially a 332-ci engine with a 352 variant that offered up to 300 hp. In 1960, when Ford debuted the sleek Starliner (an upscale Galaxie with a bubble top roofline), the marque trailed the lighter and smaller

Chevrolets and Pontiacs but stepped up to the plate with the midyear introduction of the 360-hp 352.

In a memo dated July 11, 1960, Economy and Performance Division manager Dave Evans approved a "lease" of a 360-hp Starliner that came to be known as the "Black Project." The AMA ban was still technically in place, but the Black Project allowed Ford to look into the racing potential of the new car and yet not "break any rules" imposed by the ban. A few of those cars competed in some 1960 NHRA National events and, while they didn't win, they held their own against many of the Chevys.

This was around the same time that Gaspar "Gas" Ronda was racing a 360-hp 352 Starliner and regularly beating up on Chevys at Half Moon Bay Raceway in Northern California. He soon hooked up with Les Ritchey, a high-performance automotive shop owner who had set a ton of records in a Y-block-equipped 1956 Ford. Ford's post-AMA ban effort now was taking flight. Through the pages of *Hot Rod*, folks outside California saw what was going on and tried to either duplicate what the West Coast was doing or do it better, with many choosing 1960 Fords as their platform.

For 1961, the FE was given more cubic inches with a bigger bore and stroke (4.05- and 3.78-inch, respectively) for 390 ci of displacement and 300 hp with a 4-barrel. Soon a performance version became available, offering 375 hp with a 4-barrel on an aluminum intake manifold or 401 horses with a triple 2-barrel induction setup. The magazines began paying attention.

Here are Bob Martin and Jerry Alderman racing their 401-hp 390 Starliner in Super Stock in 1961. (Photo Courtesy Charlie Morris)

Dick Brannan was making a name for himself at the track with his 1960 Galaxie Starliner, racking up a gang of trophies. (Photo Courtesy Charlie Morris)

Dick Brannan raced his street-driven Starliner in Super Stock at NHRA's 1961 Indianapolis event. While he didn't win, he was successful, eventually moving on to become Ford's Drag Coordinator. (Photo Courtesy Charlie Morris)

Dick Brannan's 1962 lightweight Galaxie was located and restored to its original-as-raced appearance. This is one of only three of the original 11 lightweight Galaxies known to exist. (Photo Courtesy Charlie Morris)

Car Craft called the 390/401 "Detroit's Hottest Street Engine" on its October 1961 cover. They somewhat had to, since Fords were beginning to win in the Stock classes at the drag strip.

In 1962, Ford again bumped up the power of the FE by creating the 406, a bored version of the 390 with 385 or 405 hp (with single 4-barrel or three 2-barrels, respectively). Advertising in turn was getting more aggressive, blatantly advertising the performance of Ford vehicles.

Around that time, veteran Dick Brannan was working as the pilot for Romy-Hammes Ford's company airplane. He happened to become friendly with the son of the owner of the South Bend, Indiana, dealership and, through that relationship, he convinced the dealership to buy a 406 Galaxie and go racing. The duo plus a mechanic promptly took over a service bay to prep the Galaxie for NHRA's Super Stock class at Detroit Dragway.

As mentioned in CarTech's book *Total Performers: Ford Drag Racing in the 1960s*, author Charles R. Morris wrote, "Entered in the Super Stock event, Dick proceeded to not only mow down every Chevrolet, Pontiac, and Mopar in sight, but also to knock off the 'factory' Fords of team test drivers Bill Humphries and Len Richter. Having won the event, Dick would not be declared the winner until the car was found to be legal, as some believed there was no way that this kid and his Ford won fair and square. After practically dismantling the entire car, track officials declared it legal in the wee hours of the morning. The crowd, having remained to see the outcome of the tear-down, cheered the underdog who had beaten the big boys."

The Fermier Brothers, out of Jacksonville, Florida, usually won whichever race they entered with this 1962 406 Galaxie. (Photo Courtesy Charlie Morris)

Even Ford brass wasn't convinced that Brannan and his Galaxie were legitimate, so he was invited to bring it to Ford's Romeo, Michigan, test track to prove it (which was foreshadowing a very significant moment in the birth of the 428 Cobra Jet—but more on that later). After Brannan yet again whipped up on Ford factory race cars and drivers, Ford offered Brannan the job of Drag Racing Coordinator in the Experimental Vehicles Department, which was the beginning of a successful relationship between Brannan and Ford that would eventually be called the Ford Drag Council.

Here the Fermier Brothers' 1962 406 Galaxie lays waste to the Jackshaw 1966 Pontiac GTO. (Photo Courtesy Charlie Morris)

Ford Racers

Other Ford racers of note were Phil Bonner, Chuck Martin, and Leon Burt; all raced in both NHRA's Stock classes and purpose-built non-NHRA-legal cars to make money in the hotly contested "match racing" world of the Southeast. During this time, Chevrolet developed a reputation with the 409 engine, which helped prompt the arrival on the scene of a man who would be pivotal in not only Ford drag performance and racing but also the saga of the 428 Cobra Jet: Robert E. Tasca of Tasca Ford in East Providence, Rhode Island.

Tasca had almost had enough of the punk kid driving by his dealership in a 1962 409 Chevy, talking smack about Fords, and leaving in a haze of tire smoke. The dealer instructed his chief mechanic, John Healey, to find out who this kid was (Billy Lawton) and then build a Ford to kick his butt. The weapon of choice became the first of a series of Tasca race cars: a 1962 Ford with a stout 406 engine. Tasca met Lawton at the local drag strip and informed him, "Kid, you just won your last drag race." Healey won the race handily, but Tasca was impressed by Lawton's skill behind the wheel and hired him to drive his future race cars.

In the middle of the 1963 model year, the soon-to-be-legendary 427 debuted. It was a remodel of the 406 with the same 3.78 stroke but a bigger bore of 4.23 inches, plus a more robust bottom-end design. With a single 4-barrel carb, the 427 made 410 hp or 425 with dual Holley 4-barrels, both on an aluminum low-riser, dual-plane intake. Introduced at the same time as the 427 was a sleek semi-fastback roofline, both in time for the 1963 Daytona 500.

At this moment, it was fairly apparent that Ford was all but divorced from the AMA ban on racing, especially after 1963's "Total Performance" assault on global competition. That year saw the creation of several

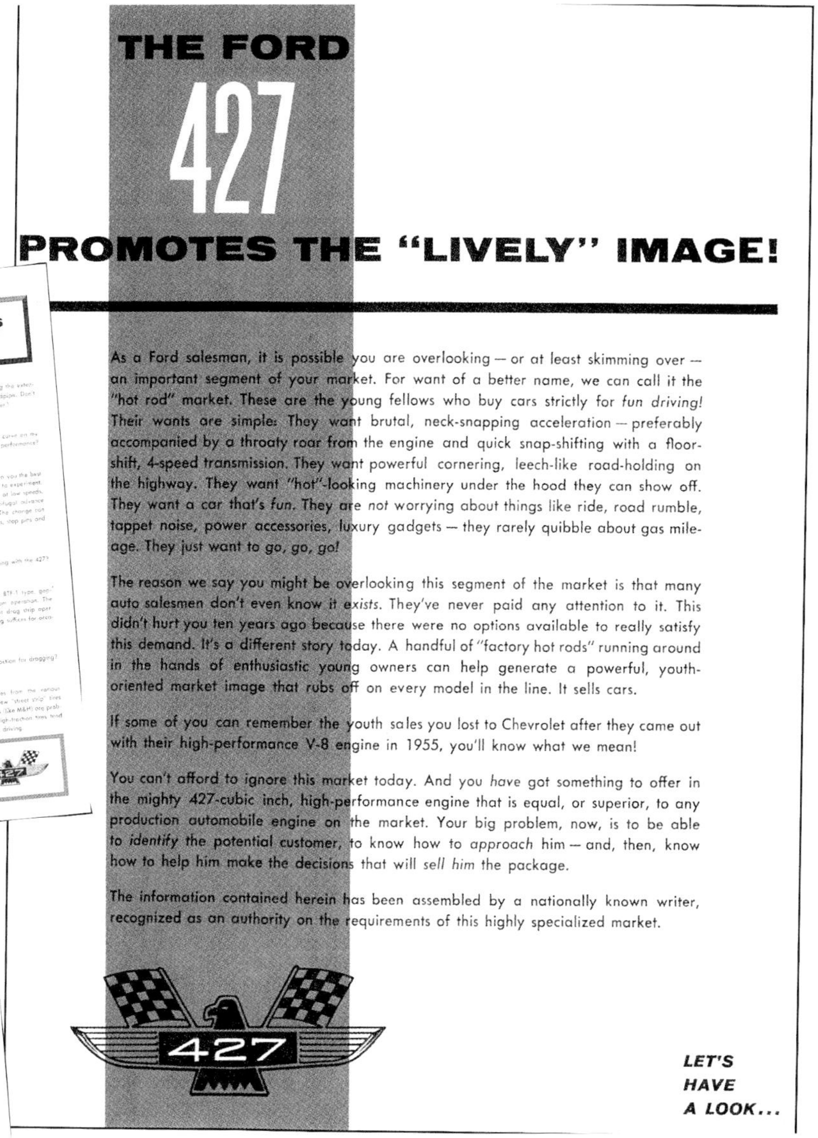
THE FORD
427
PROMOTES THE "LIVELY" IMAGE!

As a Ford salesman, it is possible you are overlooking — or at least skimming over — an important segment of your market. For want of a better name, we can call it the "hot rod" market. These are the young fellows who buy cars strictly for *fun driving!* Their wants are simple: They want brutal, neck-snapping acceleration — preferably accompanied by a throaty roar from the engine and quick snap-shifting with a floor-shift, 4-speed transmission. They want powerful cornering, leech-like road-holding on the highway. They want "hot"-looking machinery under the hood they can show off. They want a car that's *fun.* They are *not* worrying about things like ride, road rumble, tappet noise, power accessories, luxury gadgets — they rarely quibble about gas mileage. They just want to *go, go, go!*

The reason we say you might be overlooking this segment of the market is that many auto salesmen don't even know it *exists.* They've never paid any attention to it. This didn't hurt you ten years ago because there were no options available to really satisfy this demand. It's a different story today. A handful of "factory hot rods" running around in the hands of enthusiastic young owners can help generate a powerful, youth-oriented market image that rubs off on every model in the line. It sells cars.

If some of you can remember the youth sales you lost to Chevrolet after they came out with their high-performance V-8 engine in 1955, you'll know what we mean!

You can't afford to ignore this market today. And you *have* got something to offer in the mighty 427-cubic inch, high-performance engine that is equal, or superior, to any production automobile engine on the market. Your big problem, now, is to be able to *identify* the potential customer, to know how to *approach* him — and, then, know how to help him make the decisions that will *sell him* the package.

The information contained herein has been assembled by a nationally known writer, recognized as an authority on the requirements of this highly specialized market.

LET'S HAVE A LOOK...

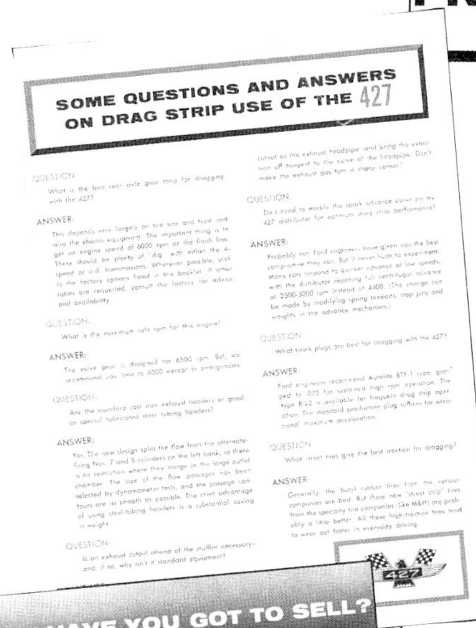
SOME QUESTIONS AND ANSWERS ON DRAG STRIP USE OF THE 427

QUESTION:
What is the best rear axle gear ratio for dragging with the 427?

ANSWER:
This depends very largely on tire size and type and also the chassis equipment. The important thing is to get an engine speed of 6000 rpm at the finish line. There should be plenty of "dig" with either the 4-speed or o.d. transmissions. Wherever possible, stick to the factory options listed in this booklet. If other ratios are requested, consult the factory for advice and availability.

QUESTION:
What is the maximum safe rpm for this engine?

ANSWER:
The valve gear is designed for 6500 rpm. But, we recommend you limit to 6000 except in emergencies.

QUESTION:
Are the standard cast iron exhaust headers as good as special fabricated steel tubing headers?

ANSWER:
Yes. The new design splits the flow from the alternate-firing Nos. 7 and 8 cylinders on the left bank, so there is no restriction where they merge in the large outlet chamber. The size of the flow passages has been selected by dynamometer tests, and the passage contours are as smooth as possible. The chief advantage of using steel-tubing headers is a substantial saving in weight.

QUESTION:
Is an exhaust cutout ahead of the muffler necessary — and, if so, why isn't it standard equipment?

QUESTION:
Do I need to modify the spark advance curve on my 427 distributor for optimum drag strip performance?

ANSWER:
Probably not. Ford engineers have given you the best compromise they can. But it never hurts to experiment. Many cars respond to quicker advance at low speeds, with the distributor reaching full centrifugal advance at 2500-3000 rpm instead of 4400. (The change can be made by modifying spring tensions, stop pins and weights in the advance mechanism.)

QUESTION:
What spark plugs are best for dragging with the 427?

ANSWER:
Ford engineers recommend Autolite BTF-1 type, gapped to .025 for sustained high rpm operation. The type B-22 is available for frequent drag strip operation. The standard production plug suffices for occasional maximum acceleration.

QUESTION:
What street tires give the best traction for dragging?

ANSWER:
Generally, the butyl rubber tires from the various companies are best. But these new "street strip" tires from the specialty tire companies (like M&H) are probably a little better. All these high-traction tires tend to wear out faster in everyday driving.

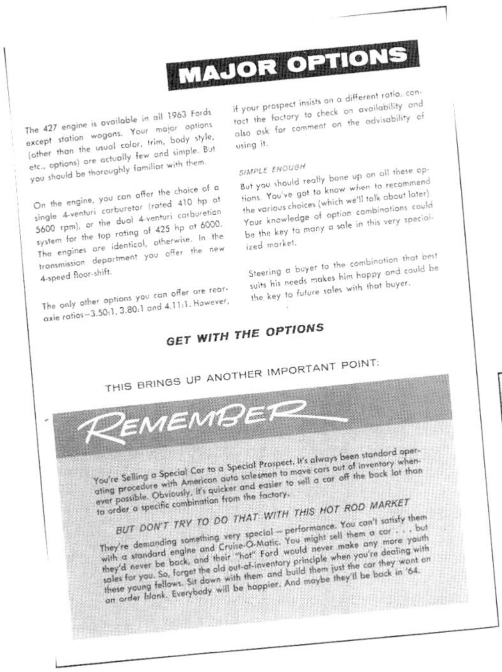
MAJOR OPTIONS

The 427 engine is available in all 1963 Fords except station wagons. Your major options (other than the usual color, trim, body style, etc., options) are actually few and simple. But you should be thoroughly familiar with them.

On the engine, you can offer the choice of a single 4-venturi carburetor (rated 410 hp at 5600 rpm), or the dual 4-venturi carburetion system for the top rating of 425 hp at 6000. The engines are identical, otherwise. In the transmission department you offer the new 4-speed floor-shift.

The only other options you can offer are rear-axle ratios—3.50:1, 3.80:1 and 4.11:1. However, if your prospect insists on a different ratio, contact the factory to check on availability and also ask for comment on the advisability of using it.

SIMPLE ENOUGH

But you should really bone up on all these options. You've got to know when to recommend the various choices (which we'll talk about later). Your knowledge of option combinations could be the key to many a sale in this very specialized market.

Steering a buyer to the combination that best suits his needs makes him happy and could be the key to future sales with that buyer.

GET WITH THE OPTIONS

THIS BRINGS UP ANOTHER IMPORTANT POINT:

REMEMBER

You're Selling a Special Car to a Special Prospect. It's always been standard operating procedure with American auto salesmen to move cars out of inventory whenever possible. Obviously, it's quicker and easier to sell a car off the back lot than to order a specific combination from the factory.

BUT DON'T TRY TO DO THAT WITH THIS HOT ROD MARKET

They're demanding something very special — performance. You can't satisfy them with a standard engine and Cruise-O-Matic. You might sell them a car . . . but they'd never be back, and their "hot" Ford would never make any more youth sales for you. So, forget the old out-of-inventory principle when you're dealing with these young fellows. Sit down with them and build them just the car they want on an order blank. Everybody will be happier. And maybe they'll be back in '64.

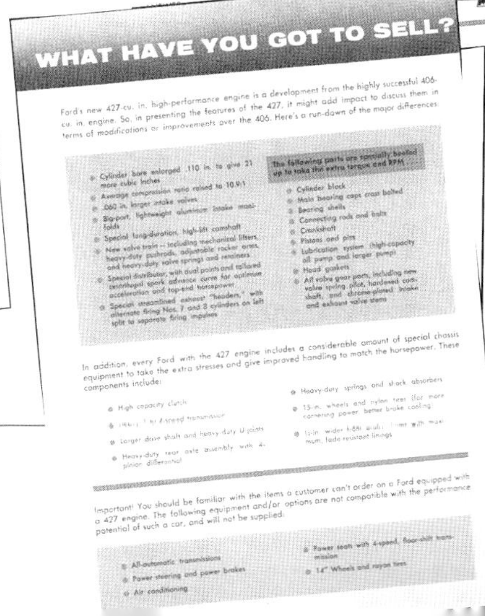
WHAT HAVE YOU GOT TO SELL?

Ford's new 427-cu. in. high-performance engine is a development from the highly successful 406-cu. in. engine. So, in presenting the features of the 427, it might add impact to discuss them in terms of modifications or improvements over the 406. Here's a run-down of the major differences:

- Cylinder bore enlarged .110 in. to give 21 more cubic inches
- Average compression ratio raised to 10.9:1
- .060 in. larger intake valves
- Big-port, lightweight aluminum intake manifolds
- Special long-duration, high-lift camshaft
- New valve train — including mechanical lifters, heavy-duty pushrods, adjustable rocker arms, and heavy-duty valve springs and retainers
- Special distributor, with dual points and tailored centrifugal spark advance curve for optimum acceleration and top-end horsepower
- Special streamlined exhaust "headers," with alternate firing Nos. 7 and 8 cylinders on left split to separate firing impulses

The following parts are specially beefed up to take the extra torque and RPM . . .

- Cylinder block
- Main bearing caps cross bolted
- Bearing shells
- Connecting rods and bolts
- Crankshaft
- Pistons and pins
- Lubrication system (high-capacity oil pump and larger pump)
- Head gaskets
- All valve gear parts, including new valve spring pilot, hardened camshaft, and chrome-plated intake and exhaust valve stems

In addition, every Ford with the 427 engine includes a considerable amount of special chassis equipment to take the extra stresses and give improved handling to match the horsepower. These components include:

- High capacity clutch
- Larger drive shaft and heavy-duty U-joints
- Heavy-duty rear axle assembly with 4-pinion differential
- Heavy-duty springs and shock absorbers
- 15-in. wheels and nylon tires (for more cornering power, better brake cooling)

Important! You should be familiar with the items a customer can't order on a Ford equipped with a 427 engine. The following equipment and/or options are not compatible with the performance potential of such a car, and will not be supplied:

- All-automatic transmissions
- Power steering and power brakes
- Air conditioning
- Power seats with 4-speed, floor-shift transmission
- 14" Wheels and rayon tires

This document is unique because it is an early example of a manufacturer recognizing the role marketing played in selling high-performance cars. No number of race victories would have translated into 427 sales without a knowledgeable sales force.

lightweight, purpose-built Galaxies with the R-code 427 and as little clutter as possible, all in the name of speed—things like sound deadener, carpet, radio, heater, and similar creature comforts were left in the parts bins. Drag Council drivers Gas Ronda and Les Ritchey fielded a two-car team running in Factory Experimental (FX) as the brain trust at Ford put a lot of effort building special race cars for other Drag Council members.

Bob Tasca, always with a pulse on what buyers wanted, made a point in a meeting at Ford that it wasn't fair that the limited number of lightweight Galaxies should only be available to racers, since a buyer who saw one win on Sunday and bought one on Monday (Tasca has been given credit with the "Win on Sunday, sell on Monday" quotation) would be disappointed that his new Galaxie was obviously nowhere near as fast as the car he just watched at the races. When the question came up about who would sell them if Ford were to build more lightweight Galaxies, Tasca stepped up to the plate and ordered 18 of them for his dealership. As for the racing end of it, Gas Ronda ran a 12.07 elapsed time in Super Stock at the 1963 Winternationals with a lightweight Galaxie (which should have given him the win because the Z11 Chevy that defeated him was deemed illegal after the race), while Dick Brannan set 22 track records and won more than 65 races during the 1963 season.

Along Comes the Thunderbolt

Which brings us back to Bob Tasca. In 1963, he once again showed Ford how a fast car could be built with existing production pieces when he put a 427 V-8 under the hood of the intermediate-sized Fairlane and convinced Ford to build a prototype. A 1963 Fairlane was sent to Dearborn Steel Tubing and modified into a race car with Tasca's input. This vehicle featured a domed fiberglass hood to clear the high-riser setup (later cars featured a teardrop hood), front bumper and fenders, and lightweight plexiglass windows.

After Ford evaluated the Fairlane, it was given a go, and Domestic Special Order #33A was established. This, along with paperwork outlining that the cars would go on sale in November 1963 and be covered under Ford's factory warranty, lent some legitimacy to the "factory race car" ruse in order to gain NHRA approval.

Ultimately, the prototype lost its 1963 NHRA Nationals debut when driver Bill Humphrey missed a shift during eliminations; later, with Lawton driving, the Tasca Fairlane set the NHRA A/Factory Experimental MPH record. On the other side of the street performance coin, the economical Falcon received a hot thin-wall 260-ci small-block in the Sprint model, complete with sleeker roofline, *à la* Galaxie 500.

A mighty launch from Jack Whitby's **Total Performer** *Thunderbolt of Wilmington, Delaware. (Photo Courtesy Charlie Morris)*

Dick Brannan posing with the first Thunderbolt,* The Lively One, *in this promotional photo. (Photo Courtesy Charlie Morris)

With the success of the Tasca Fairlane under its belt, Ford decided to unleash 50 competition versions for NHRA Super Stock, now using a 289-powered 1964 Fairlane 500 two-door sedan as the base and having Dearborn Steel Tubing build them. The Super Stock 427 Fairlane was available via special order through the office of the Special Vehicles Manager and would be delivered to the dealer it was ordered from only after the buyer signed what was basically a release of liability and a promise not to register it for the street. The 427 high-riser was making about 500 hp and, off the trailer, Thunderbolts were running low 12s/high 11s in the quarter mile. With tuning and some experience, consistent mid-11s quickly became the norm.

Sure enough, the Thunderbolt scored a win at the 1964 Winternationals when Gas Ronda beat Butch Leal in Mickey Thompson's Thunderbolt, eventually going on to win the class championship that year. Dick Brannan, Len Richter, Phil Bonner, Bill Lawton, and many more T-bolt drivers dispatched the competition throughout 1964, solidifying Ford as a serious player in the horsepower wars.

A look at the Roy Hammes/Dick Brannan 1964 AF/X Falcon, the first of two built by Dearborn Steel Tubing. It was used as a testbed or "mule" to develop parts for the AF/X Mustang for the following year. (Photo Courtesy Charlie Morris)

Al Joniec posing with his **Batcar** ***AF/X Mustang in 1966. The car was formerly called*** **Pegasus** ***but, due to the popularity of the*** **Batman** ***TV show, Joniec changed his marketing plan and reinvented the car. It initially was powered by a 427 high-riser, but Ford soon hooked Joniec up with a SOHC 427 "Cammer" running gasoline, which he eventually modded with mechanical fuel injection stacks running nitromethane. He also switched to an automatic transmission and eventually extended the wheelbase in true AF/X style. (Photo Courtesy Charlie Morris)***

Altered Mustangs

By the time 1965 rolled around (or, more specifically, April 17, 1964), the Mustang was unveiled not just to fanfare but also to insane sales numbers as the car exploded off of magazine pages, television screens, and out of Ford showrooms. The new pony car (as it came to be known) was small, sporty, and reasonably quick for its market position.

When racers saw the little Mustang, they instantly were overcome with an inclination to stuff that big 427 under the hood . . . and the first A/FX Mustangs were born. A/FX cars were basically the forefathers of today's nitro Funny Car, meaning they were race cars with barely a hint of streetability. One of the first successful A/FX Mustangs was owned by Hawkinson Ford and driven by Ron Pellegrini, who had talked Ford out of a new Mustang and then parted out a successful-but-bygone Thunderbolt for its go-fast parts for the Mustang. The car ran 10-second ETs, and Pellegrini won the A/FX class at every race he entered, as well as the title of Overall Stock Eliminator at the US 30 Dragway Meet of Champions on Labor Day Weekend 1964.

The 289-ci Mustangs were also populating Stock classes and doing quite well. Ford performance was solidified in the minds of the public, although Chrysler had been developing its own racing programs just like Ford's and focused slightly more on street performance. General Motors reaffirmed the

Hubert Platt built and ran this Falcon before he made the switch to Mustangs. This is an early incarnation of the vehicle. (Photo Courtesy Charlie Morris)

AMA ban and left racing early in 1963. The Mustang's main competitor in the pony car wars would come to be the 1967 Chevrolet Camaro, which was no slouch with its 350-ci small-block and a true Mustang-beater with the 396 big-block.

Mustang Versus Camaro

Chevrolet's 396 was a durable, well-designed engine that was available in the new Camaro in 325- and solid-lifter 375-hp variants (joined by a 350-hp version in 1968). Known in Bowtie circles as the Mark IV, with origins dating to the "Mystery Motor" from the 1963 Daytona 500, the 396 featured advanced-design cylinder heads that flowed like crazy and earned the name "Porcupine" because of their splayed-valve arrangement. A whole host of high-performance parts was available for the 396 because it was introduced two years earlier for the Corvette and full-size Chevys, which helped make it faster than any production Mustang on the street. Combine that with competition from Chrysler's Street Hemi (installed in intermediates) and the Mustang was hopelessly outpowered when the streetlight turned green.

Ford answered the war cry with a slightly bigger Mustang for 1967 that had an engine compartment that would accept the stalwart 390. The 427 was advertised in 1968 literature but never installed in the Mustang and, as it turned out, the 390 wasn't quite enough. Big-block Camaros could murder a Mustang in the quarter mile by up to a full second, which is a lifetime in drag racing.

Tasca, ever the salesman, recognized this performance gap and the way it impacted his Mustang sales. Once again, he set out to do something about it. The result was the KR-8 Mustang, widely considered to be the godfather of the 428 Cobra Jet.

Gas Ronda lines up against Butch Leal's Mickey Thompson–owned Thunderbolt at the 1964 Hot Rod *Magazine Championship Drag Races at Riverside Raceway. Ronda beat Leal earlier in the year at the NHRA Winternationals. (©MotorTrend Group. All rights reserved.)*

As the AF/X class was morphing into what would eventually be called "Funny Cars," all semblance of "stock" was removed thanks to a full tubular chassis, lift-up fiberglass bodies, and full-race equipment. This is the Denver-based Kenz and Leslie flip-top 1966 Mercury Comet with an injected "Cammer." (Photo Courtesy Charlie Morris)

Bill Lawton poses with his long-nose Mystery 9 AF/X Mustang. Six of these fiberglass precursors to the Funny Car were built by Holman-Moody's shop in Long Beach, California. Sixteen inches were added to the front with a 15-inch setback for the SOHC/C6 automatic combo. (Photo Courtesy Charlie Morris)

CHAPTER TWO

THE TASCA KR-8: THE ONE THAT STARTED IT ALL?

The 428 Cobra Jet story cannot be told without the car that inspired them all: the KR-8 built by Tasca Ford and promoted by *Hot Rod* magazine. It's not a new story; rather, the story has been told in countless books and magazine articles over the five-plus decades of Cobra Jet existence, but it's imperative that we discuss it here in a book about the engine package that this car supposedly inspired.

The Tasca Ford KR-8 Mustang, the predecessor of the Cobra Jet Mustang built by the "Father of the Cobra Jet," Bob Tasca. Here is a very young Bob Tasca Jr. "launching" the car in Tasca Ford's back lot in 1967. (©MotorTrend Group. All rights reserved.)

At the time, Rhode Island's Tasca Ford (the second-largest Ford dealership in the world) replaced the factory 390-ci engine from a 1967 Mustang coupe with a 428 Police Interceptor equipped with 406 heads and other pieces from the Tasca parts department. The car, dubbed "KR-8" for *King of the Road '68*, created a shockingly fast Mustang that could finally hold its own on the street against big-block Camaros, Ram Air GTOs, and even Hemi Mopars.

At the time, Ford still considered its 390-powered Mustang a contender, but those on the mean streets knew better. In Detroit, New York, Chicago, Los Angeles, and elsewhere, Ford 390s were hopelessly outclassed by stronger competition. Bob Tasca understood that all too well, so he developed a Mustang using all factory Ford parts that would stand tall on the street and at the drag strip.

In town for another assignment, *Hot Rod* magazine staff editor Eric Dahlquist learned of Tasca's hot pony and wrote a story on the KR-8 in the November 1967 issue. The opening page to the story was a ballot-style reader's poll instructing them to tell Ford to build the car. And build it they did, in the process creating the 428 Cobra Jet

Eric Dahlquist: In His Words

During a 2013 *Hot Rod* magazine interview, Eric Dahlquist said, "I went back to the East Coast on a road trip for, I think, the Road Runner, and I had been talking to different engineers at Ford in its high-performance area about what it was doing. Ford kind of missed the muscle car era in the beginning. The 390 Fairlane really wasn't anything. Ford should have been right at the forefront, but it wasn't. Bill Holbrook had a group that was putting cars together with truck parts, different blocks, and they worked pretty well, and he told me about a dealer in Rhode Island—Tasca.

"So, I went to see Bob Tasca and his guys, some of whom I'm still in contact with, believe it or not. They showed me something called the King of the Road, and I did a story on their car for *Hot Rod* and showed the pieces that went into it. It went like the hammers and was great, and it turned out Ford had all these pieces in its parts bin but just hadn't put together a car. So, I did the story and talked about what went into the car and the philosophy. In the story, we put a ballot in the magazine and said, if you want a car like this, check this off and send it to Henry Ford II."

The subtitle to the three-page story, just below the "yes/no" checkbox, said, "Circle your choice in the box provided and return to: Mr. Henry Ford II, Dearborn, Michigan 48121. It may be the only way." *Hot Rod* readers responded in droves. When Henry II's desk became overrun with 20,000 ballots, he realized they had something they needed to respond to.

Dahlquist added, "It wasn't long before a Ford public relations person was calling me asking that 'I turn off the spigot. Enough already, we are going to build it.' I asked, 'Can we do it first?' and he said yeah. So one day, out my window, the Ford hauler pulls up, and they had a Cobra Jet in the back—a white one. It was a bare-bones car, and it had no miles. It was freshly built, so I had to go out and put miles on it before we tested it. [Publisher Ray] Brock said, 'Why don't you drive to

FORD'S ULTIMATE YES NO

SUPER CARS

Circle your choice in the box provided and return to: Mr. Henry Ford II, Dearborn, Michigan 48121. It may be the only way

Text and photos by Eric Dahlquist

When we got to Providence, it was a day later than anyone expected so the original scheduling went all to pot. But Tasca Ford is still impressive. There are, for example, probably more Shelby GT's here than anywhere outside Shelby's chain link fenced-in corner of the Los Angeles International Airport. Performance Manager Dean Gregson showed us through the shop area where mechanics (the likes of John Healy, who gives his undivided attention to keeping the Tasca Mystery Mustang in the 7's) hone the rolling stock to perfection; through the showrooms where a legion of salesmen make what must be the best deals in the country; through the conference room upstairs where those same salesmen man a battery of phones once a month to make sure the honeymoon isn't over with the customers, and into Bob Tasca's office which surveys a sight to gladden Dearborn's heart—a veritable sea of multi-colored Ford roofs in the lot outside.

Bestriding all of this, like the Colossus of Rhodes, was the character of the "Big Bopper" himself, Bob Tasca.

"You'll get the real story of the operation when Mr. Tasca gets back from Detroit," Dean, as well as everyone else, told us—over and over again until we began to expect some kind of superman—a Wizard of Oz who could wave his magic wand and make everything beautiful. Funny thing about it, they were right.

The original idea for going to Tasca, more or less, was to do a feature on a progressive, performance-oriented dealer. So Dean got out the scrapbooks and told us how it all began back in 1962 with a 406 Ford Tudor that had shoe polish lettering, went 13.19 and was hardly ever beaten. Then, more years of winning, with hardly a loss: an A/FX with Bill Lawton at Pomona '65, 221 wins in a row with stock-bodied cars by July of the same year—and through it all, the giant shadow of Bob Tasca.

And then, unknowingly, we began to hear the hottest scoop of the year.

"We sold a lot of 390 Mustangs last fall and into the winter, but by March they dropped off to practically nothing. That's when the snow melted off the asphalt." Soberly, Dean went on. "In fact, we found the car so non-competitive for the super-car field, in a sense we began to feel we were cheating the customer. He was paying for what he saw advertised in all the magazines as a fast car but that's not what he was getting. So we did something about it. We began to offer the customer little packages of stock pieces to make his machine like it was supposed to be."

58 HOT ROD MAGAZINE

Hot Rod's story on Tasca's KR-8 appeared in the November 1967 issue with a Yes/No checkbox and Henry Ford II's address in Dearborn. Thousands of Hot Rod readers checked Yes and flooded his desk. (©MotorTrend Group. All rights reserved.)

Fresno?' So, I took it to Fresno over a weekend. And this was the new thing, but the Hemi was out, the Buick GS 400, which was much nicer to drive, a lot plusher. So, I loaded some of the family in the car, I put on enough miles to test the car, and we ran the test at Irwindale. It ran fine, not as good as it would have run if we spent some real time with it, but we got the first story."

The story on that first Cobra Jet Mustang appeared in the March 1968 issue of *Hot Rod*. Dahlquist mused, "Everybody in Detroit is mad at us—except Ford. With the help of about 20,000 of you out there in readerland who dutifully filled out the ballot in the November issue and mailed it to Dearborn, several key executives who doubted that Ford cars lacked competitive street performance have reversed their opinions." He also said that the Cobra Jet was "probably the fastest regular production sedan ever built," a quote that Ford used in its advertising campaign.

The next morning the "Big Bopper" happened. We couldn't have imagined it; it was like standing under Niagara Falls — a ceaseless, overwhelming torrent of ideas, directions, facts, figures, percentages, analyses. We were walking alongside him, getting part of the story, grasping some of its significance. "The 390 Mustang, even the new 428, isn't competitive with the 400 Firebird, GTO, 4-4-2 Olds, Buick Special Gran Sport, Plymouth GTX, Dodge R/T, 383 Barracuda." We were getting into an egg-shell-white four-door T-Bird. "You know how many high-performance vehicles (over 300 hp) were sold in this country in 1966? 634,434. Do you know how much Ford Motor Company had of this market? 7.5 percent. That's shameful for a 'Total Performance' company."

We sat down in a coffee shop, John Healy alongside me and Bob Tasca across the table with Dean, and we were drinking something called coffee-milk.

"We can't even sell limited-slip differentials. 11.7 percent of GM units had them in '66, 10.3 percent for Chrysler and 9.5 percent for the industry. Ford? 5.2 percent. How can we? They don't work."

Now it came along — how Tasca started offering stock performance pieces to augment the 390 Mustang's and Fairlane's sluggish performance. A simple thing like a 3/8-inch gas line to replace the 5/16-inch one, a filter to match (B7T-9155A) and a better fuel pump (COAZ-9350C) for a quick 600 rpm. A more complicated thing like a 427 distributor (C5AZ-12127E), 10° plate, 2-3° of advance at 600 distributor rpm, 5-6° at 1200, 10° at 1600, 18° lead on the pulley, 32 ounces of point tension, 33° of total dwell, new spark plug cables (C5AZ-12259C), and finally, 1963½ 427 heads (C8AE-6049K 68cc) with 2.090-inch intakes (C3AZ-6057J) and 1.66-inch exhausts (C3AZ-6505E).

"Do you know what our 390 Mustang has for exhaust valves? Exactly a 1.566-inch diameter. The 396 Camaro has 1.725-inch diameter units. If it takes big valves to make a NASCAR engine go, it takes big valves to make a stocker go.

"The best cam we could find for all-around performance, especially in the mid-range, was one we already had — the '67 GTA 390 hydraulic (C60Z-6250B). By using the 1.76:1 427 adjustable rockers in place of the 1.73:1 standards, you gain .009-inch more lift (an increase in rocker arm ratio of .0003-inch) and, by tightening the adjustment down until it stops clacking, then giving it approximately three-quarters of a turn more, you have 270° duration."

The next step was inevitable after the "Big Bopper" saw the '68 Ford line-up and specifications.

"The '68 looked like more of the '67's poor performance, but worse because the cars were heavier. We had to do something about it."

That something was just an entirely new prototype Mustang using most of the parts listed previously, the main difference being a completely stock 428 short-block with 390 cam 3° advanced. The chassis was completely tuned for dragging; battery located in the right rear of the trunk, 427 Fairlane headers, 2¼-inch o.d. '66 Fairlane exhaust pipes, 2¼-inch Advance mufflers, C-6 automatic transmission (6400 rpm 1-2 shift, 6200 rpm 3-4 shift), deep-sump oil pan and a cold air package feeding a Le Mans-type Holley 4-bbl carburetor. Manifolding varied but was finally narrowed to a C6H Police Interceptor two-throttle bore configuration converted to four separate throttle bores using a Bakelite spacer that Tasca sells for 60¢. The spacer allows better direction of the intake charge, preventing some of the fuel particles from dropping out of suspension.

Even though Ford supplied much of the information and pieces for the KR-8 package (as it came to be known), Tasca realized there would be a certain amount of resistance to an outsider's bold ideas. So he did the only logical thing Bob Tasca would do — go right to the biggest bopper of them all, Henry Ford II.

"I told him I believed our cars were competitive in price, more than competitive in style and interior appointments, but hope-

(Continued on following page)

ABOVE—We don't know where it came from either, but somehow Tasca popped up with Lloyd Ruby's Le Mans engine — tunnel-ports and all. Preliminary test program on '69 KR package is already under way.

RIGHT — The "Big Bopper" himself, Bob Tasca, holding up shots of an earlier project, a restyled-the-way-they-should-have-been-in-the-first-place T-bird. Tasca continually prods honchos at Dearborn to rise above themselves and build machines that are the hot setup. He must be doing something right; he's the world's second largest Ford dealer in the nation's smallest state. TOP — KR-what? If you see some cat in a stock Mustang lift his hood and the engine compartment looks like this, put away your marbles and find a regular Ford. If factory drops out again, Tasca may become another Shelby.

NOVEMBER 1967 59

By the time Hot Rod's *Eric Dahlquist caught wind of what Tasca Ford was doing, the original Mustang KR-8 had lost its 428 PI. Nonetheless, it took Tasca to show Ford what it should have been doing, and* Hot Rod *to show "Hank the Deuce" that there were a ton of Ford fans on the street pining for something competitive. (©MotorTrend Group. All rights reserved.)*

SUPER CARS

lessly inadequate under the hood. We haven't been the hottest since the flathead V8 and that was his father's idea so I couldn't congratulate him for that."

Immediately there went out from the "glass castle" a proclamation for all the nobles from the various departmental fiefs to qualify these assertions. What Henry found out was what every kid in America already knew and that Tasca's KR-8 (which he just happened to have in the staging lane) was quick: 13.39-105.05 — with street tires and an efficient (but closed) exhaust, yet. Production 428 Mustangs, Comets and Cougars should live so long! In fact they didn't, against a GTO and Ram Air Firebird. Then the KR-8 dropped both Indians by almost a second.

The question of the moment, lo these many years, was why didn't production performance Fords live up to their advertised image. But it's not that simple. Ford is a big company and in big companies responsibility seeps into many bureau drawers. No person can give the complete, final answer. The bitter irony is that Ford has all the pieces in its inventory (a fact demonstrated by Tasca) to create the hottest volume production machine ever built. They have the talent to put it together and the racing program to fully exploit it, but the myriad of people who pull the strings, the men without whose word nothing moves, are so intoxicated by track victories like dual Le Mans (back-to-back), they cannot comprehend their street products as being counterfeit. Then too, used to the floating grandeur of an LTD or Continental, the occasional encounter with a Mustang GT must feel like a Saturn V booster. This in concert with what must be a regiment of pie-in-the-sky, silver-lined public relations people, trying their best to shout down the "yes men," must figure in a never-never-land atmosphere. Error believed in is truth in effect.

But enough water over the dam, what everyone wants to know now is what's going to happen. About the middle of August, Bob Tasca hoped the KR-8 package, or some name close to that, would be released in Mustangs and Fairlanes by January 1, 1968. Executives at Ford, when questioned a few days later, at first denied any knowledge and then, when confronted with the facts, admitted a package was under consideration. In Engineering, the boys were less than ecstatic. For one thing, if such a GTO-type car did come forth, the ad guys wanted to do something neat like put a 380 horsepower rating on it, enough to guarantee a bad class at the drags and an astronomic insurance factor. Beyond that, some of the warranty boys were yelling, and beyond that there was the strike.

It would be our utmost pleasure to report a low 13-second, 105-quarter-mile machine in street tires and exhaust, ready to pick up at your dealer for the Winternationals, but the project is still in limbo as a regular order piece. For a time, the people at Chevy, Pontiac, Olds, Chrysler and — clap your ears — American Motors held their breath, but that's mostly over. "We wondered," said one GM engineer openly, "if Ford ever will get the connection between track victories and showroom sales."

So, unless there's a big scramble, if you want a Dearborn world beater, a bunch of circumstances are going to mean you either build it yourself (from the numbers afforded you here) or buy it from Tasca. By the way, he's already working on the '69 version. Would you believe 12.50-110? Absolutely stock.

FORD "HAPPENING" CHART

Engine — Stock 428 Police Interceptor short-block (untouched out of crate)
Heads — 1963½, C8AE-6049K, 68cc per chamber
Valves — Intake 2.090-inch (C3AZ-6057J); exhaust 1.66-inch (C3AZ-6505E)
Valve springs — 427, installed at 1.82-inch
Camshaft — 1967, 390 GTA, C60Z-6250B (or SK-33222) installed with 3° advance
Intake manifold — Aluminum, Police Interceptor C6H with four-hole Bakelite spacer
Distributor — 427 dual-point, centrifugal, C5AZ-12127E, 10° advance plate, 18° lead on pulley, 33° total dwell, 32 oz. point tension
Spark plug cables — C5AZ-12259C
Spark plugs — Autolite BF-32
Transmission — C-6 automatic with heavy-duty convertor
Rear axle — 3.50:1 limited slip (28-tooth axles), alternate ratios: 3.00, 3.80, 4.10, 4.57
Fuel System — ⅜-inch gas line (replaces 5/16-inch), fuel pump C0AZ-9350C, filter B7T-9155A, 652 cfm Holley carburetor
Exhaust system — 1966, 427 Fairlane manifolds, 2¼-inch Fairlane exhaust pipes, 2¼-inch Fairlane tailpipes
Lubrication system — 427 oil pump, 6-quart, deep-sump oil pan (to be replaced with windage tray)
Chassis — Reworked to relocate 40 pounds left rear weight bias to 40 pounds right rear bias. Front: 5/16-inch spacer under left front spring pad, increase left front stabilizer link by ¾-inch, right front by ⅜-inch. Rear: Lengthen right rear spring hanger by 2 inches, left rear 1 inch. Reverse all spring leaves 180° except main leaf and clamp. Install Shelby spring snubbers same as GT-500, Autolite Superflex shock absorbers. Battery located in right rear of trunk (low voltage drop cable)

ABOVE — Tasca's hopped-up performance men, Perf. Manager Dean Gregson, left, and Asst. Parts Manager Glenn Tiberiis, discuss some of the pieces that are happily available from Ford to make their cars go. BELOW — Ford couldn't have made it look more official themselves. BOTTOM — Besides wedging suspension for more bite, all leaves on springs are reversed, save main.

60 HOT ROD MAGAZINE

Another page from the infamous Hot Rod *article on Tasca Ford's Mustang KR-8. Ford engineers initially thought the 427 was the answer, but the 428 was much easier to build—and cheaper too. (©MotorTrend Group. All rights reserved.)*

Mustang, a car and an engine that saved Ford's reputation as a Total Performance company.

Grenading the 390

In a 2010 interview with Donald Farr for *Mustang Monthly* magazine, Tasca Ford's then-president, Bob Tasca Jr., said, "I lived that story, I can tell you that much." Tasca Jr. was a teenager when he took a ride in his father's 1967 Mustang GT demonstrator with Tasca technician Billy Loomis behind the wheel—a ride that would change the course of Ford performance history.

"The Lime Gold notchback was my father's everyday driver," Tasca Jr. said. "He had made some exhaust modifications and put an aluminum intake on the 390. Billy was working on it one day, but I don't remember what he was doing. While my father was out to dinner with a Ford executive, Billy, my brother Carl, and I went for a ride [in the car] up on Route 44 in East Providence. I'll never forget—Billy turned the car around and

Eric Dahlquist's photo of Tasca Ford at night was shot during his visit to Rhode Island in the summer of 1967. At right is the used car department (with a Mercury Cyclone and Pontiac GTO). A 1967 Shelby is parked right in front of the showroom. (©MotorTrend Group. All rights reserved.)

Bob Tasca Sr. (right) with a custom 1967 Thunderbird built by the Alexander Brothers. Painted in custom Candyapple Red with matching cloth interior, the T-bird featured several mild custom touches like parking lights and side markers (inspired by the 1967 Pontiac Grand Prix), longitudinal lower body trim, and distinctive badging. (©MotorTrend Group. All rights reserved.)

floored it. He thought the shifter was in D but it was in 1. I was thinking, *When is he going to shift?* But he didn't shift it. So, it floated the valves and we blew the engine. We got it back to the dealership and my father was very upset when he found out we'd blown up his favorite car."

Tasca Ford was considered one of the premier dealerships of the early 1960s when it came to fast Fords, and Bob Tasca knew how to do his research. He was paying attention to the sales of high-performance cars and the hi-po parts options that people were ordering and began to notice a disturbing trend. As he told *Super Stock* magazine in 1968, "We did well from '63 to '65, when the car-buying market was a young one. [Then] the younger people [became] disenchanted with Ford's performance on the street and stopped buying. Consequently, we had to cut back the racing budget that year."

His numbers showed that of the 600,000-plus high-performance cars (defined at the time as those with 300 hp or more) sold in 1966, Ford's cut only accounted for 7.5 percent, and his drop in new car sales reflected that. Ford thought it had the answer for 1967 when the Mustang's engine bay was enlarged to handle the 390 FE. What seemed like a competitive idea at the time resulted in an early sales success of 390-powered Mustangs, yet it tapered off dramatically as customers began to get beaten on a regular basis by their rivals from General Motors and Chrysler.

In the 1967 *Hot Rod* magazine interview, Tasca's Dean Gregson said, "We sold a lot of 390 Mustangs last fall and into the winter, but by March they dropped off to practically nothing. We found the car so noncompetitive, we began to feel we were cheating the customer. He was paying for what he saw advertised in all the magazines as a fast car, but that's not what he was getting. So, we did something about it."

The Genesis of the 428 Cobra Jet

The chance to solve the problem of uncompetitive Mustangs came when Loomis and the younger Tasca boys grenaded the 390 in the Lime Gold car. After scolding both his sons and employees, Tasca Sr. asked assistant parts manager Glenn Tiberiis to order a 428 Police Interceptor short-block, but being the sneaky street racer that he was, he told Tiberiis to keep it a secret.

"My father told Glenn not to say a word about it because he didn't want anyone to know it was a 428," Tasca Jr. says. Digging into Tasca Ford's parts bins, Tiberiis also came up with a set of C8AE-6049-K 406 heads, a 427 distributor, a higher-flow fuel pump, 427 Fairlane headers, a Police Interceptor intake with a Holley 4-barrel carb, and a 390 GTA hydraulic camshaft.

By most accounts, this combination of parts magically transformed the GT hardtop into a real killer. It also seems obvious in hindsight that Tasca's technicians used their own hot rodding tricks, such as recurving the

The core plug of the 428 block featured these characters. No other Ford FE engine had this "Easter egg." (Photo Courtesy Steve Magnante)

Around April 1967, Tasca set up this photo to celebrate the Mustang's birthday, with Mario Andretti as special guest. The KR-8 hardtop is visible in this photo, parked right behind the Ford GT40. Bob Tasca Sr. is on the left next to Andretti. (©MotorTrend Group. All rights reserved.)

Bob Tasca Sr. is shown at his desk with a proposal for his new dealership. He was disappointed in the 390 GT engine that was available for the redesigned 1967 Mustang and voiced his displeasure to Ford. (©MotorTrend Group. All rights reserved.)

Dahlquist arrived at Tasca Ford after the KR-8's test session at Ford, so his engine shots showed the 427 Tunnel-Port with twin Holley 4-barrel carburetors that Bob Tasca Sr. obtained from the Ford Experimental Garage. (©MotorTrend Group. All rights reserved.)

Dahlquist's photo of the ram-air induction lid showing Tasca's "Ford KR8" lettering. While the 427-powered KR-8 featured dual quads, the previous iteration with the 428 PI used a 4-barrel Holley. (MotorTrend Group. All rights reserved.)

Tasca technicians not only installed the modified Police Interceptor into Tasca's 1967 Mustang hardtop but they also modified the suspension. According to Dahlquist's caption for this photo in Hot Rod, *Tasca's techs "wedged" the suspension for more bite and reversed the leaf springs except for the main spring. (©MotorTrend Group. All rights reserved.)*

Tasca Ford Performance Sales Manager Dean Gregson (left) and Assistant Parts Manager Glenn Tiberiis look over some of the KR-8 components. This photo originally ran in the November 1967 issue of Hot Rod. *(©MotorTrend Group. All rights reserved.)*

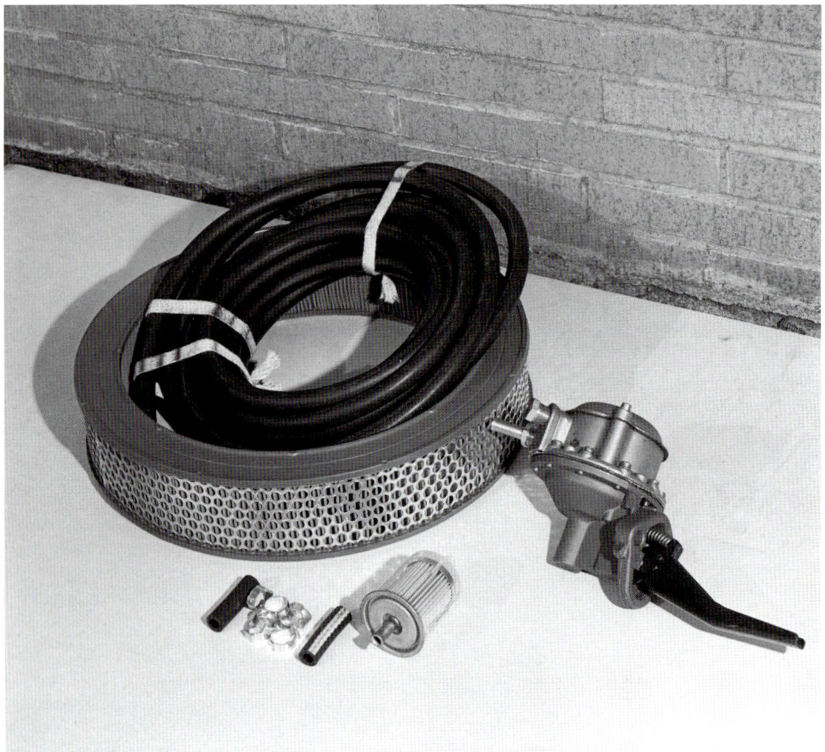

The 428 PI needed more air and fuel than its weaker 390 cousin, so better breathing was part of the KR-8 recipe. According to Dahlquist's notes from his 1967 visit, Tasca Ford offered customers a fuel upgrade consisting of a C0AZ-9350-C fuel pump, fuel filter, 25 feet of 3/8-inch neoprene fuel line, and a "non-restriction" C0AE-9601-C air cleaner. (©MotorTrend Group. All rights reserved.)

distributor, advancing the cam three degrees, and installing 427 rocker arms for more lift. They also prepped the heads for 71-cc chamber volume for more compression and installed lightweight valves with stiffer 427 valve springs. The C6 transmission and suspension were also modified to handle the increased power level and make it perform better at the drag strip. A trip to the track resulted in an ET of 13.46 at a tick over 104 mph on its first timed run. Those numbers eventually whittled down to 13.39 and 105.

With a Mustang on his hands hotter than any factory offering, Tasca and his guys let everyone know about it. Gregson has told the story about the local police asking to see what the car would do. They must have been "impressed" because "they stopped us and told us if we didn't get that car out of town in ten minutes, they'd throw us all in jail."

Tasca built a better, faster Mustang that he knew the customers would want—and used stock Ford production parts to do it—in the hopes of showing Ford how it should be done. He reportedly enjoyed the reputation of building fast Fords, but Tasca's primary motivation was money. He wanted to get Ford to build the car so he would have a car to sell better than the existing Mustang GT. Since he owned a hugely successful dealership, Tasca easily had Ford's attention, and while Ford engineers loved what he had created, the bean counters upstairs were much harder to convince.

Tasca Jr. said, "Some people from Ford came out to drive the car and they convinced my father to take it to Detroit to prove to the big shots out there that he could build a better performance car than Ford." So, in the summer of 1967, Tasca Sr. put his sons, 15-year-old Bob Jr. and 13-year-old Carl, in the back seat and technician Billy Loomis in the passenger seat and drove the KR-8 from Rhode Island to Dearborn to show Ford brass his hot rod Mustang. The Tasca boys were on summer break from school, and Bob Jr. said, "Carl and I were a lot younger then, so we fit [in the back seat]. I remember we raced Ford's 427 Mustang and other cars on the drag strip at the Dearborn Proving Grounds. We beat everything they had."

Impressed with what they saw, Ford engineers pulled the engine to see what had been done to it. Tasca Jr. commented that they criticized the short-block assembly, specifically the piston-to-wall clearance and some

1968 Big-Block Engines	390 GT	428-4V PI	428 CJ
Advertised Power (A-Curve)*	325 hp	345 hp	335 hp (411 actual)
Actual "Engine as Installed" (B-Curve) **	273 hp/360 ft-lbs	300 hp/395 ft-lbs	335–340 hp/418 ft-lbs (428 engine signoff level)

* Allowed Maximum Power Conditions for Test: Maximum compression rated, maximum clearance, no air cleaner, exhaust headers, minimum exhaust back pressure, maximum carburetor airflow (no choke plate or throttle plates), high-hour engine with no alternator, manual control of fuel and spark: optimum (LBT) fuel and spark (MBT) advance, power level corrected to 60°F at sea level standard barometer.

** "B" Power Test Conditions: Full production engine, automatic fuel and spark control, air cleaner, alternator (not charging), production exhaust manifolds, minimum exhaust back pressure, 200-mile or 15-hour break-in, power level corrected to 100°F at 29.5-inch HG.

other specs. Tasca Jr. remembers his father telling them, "I bought it from you. It's a stock 428 Police Interceptor short-block from over the counter."

The Ford engineers insisted on keeping the KR-8 powertrain for further inspection, so Tasca Sr. told them he needed something to replace it for the drive home. Tasca Jr. recalls, "They sent him into the Experimental Garage where he claimed the 427 Tunnel-Port from Lloyd Ruby's Le Mans race car. He also grabbed an experimental transmission and a special rear axle. While the Ford engineers were taking the KR-8 engine apart, we were putting the 427 in the Mustang."

Tasca Jr. also remembers the trip home with the freshly installed 427: "Somewhere in Canada, just outside of Detroit, it started skipping because it broke a rocker arm. So, we took the pushrod out and drove all the way home on seven cylinders."

Father of the Cobra Jet

Ford engineer Bill Barr once said, "Bob Tasca likes to say he was the father of the Cobra Jet, and he's right. This time he flogged the company for what he wanted. He railed for the Cobra Jet. He supplied the noise and political pressure [from *Hot Rod*'s readers] to get this thing going, and that prompted us to do something like he had done."

But there's another truth: Ford was working on a 428 Mustang before Tasca. As related by the Mustang 428 Cobra Jet Registry, "Late in the 1966 calendar year, Product Planning finally authorized the 428 GT-4V program for ASAP 1968 model year introduction . . . The program was engineered, designed, tested, validated, released, and certified between January 1967 and August 1968," according to Barr.

The rest is history, and by January 1968, Ford had built a set of 50 Wimbledon White 1968 Mustang fastbacks debuting the 429 Cobra Jet, though not with the same combination of parts that Tasca had used for the KR-8.

Barr was one of the engineers in charge of building the production version of Tasca's 428 Police Interceptor engine for the Mustang. He posted in the Mustang 428 Cobra Jet Registry's online forum in 2012, "Although many early Mustang articles suggest that the 428 Cobra Jet was designed by Mr. Tasca, there are in fact more than 30 design differences between the components used by Mr. Tasca, the 428 PI, and the released 428 CJ." The chart on page 26 shows the comparable power outputs.

Barr continued, "While most discussions comparing the engines have equivocated the 428 PI to the 428 CJ, the facts are that the 428 CJ was demonstrably more powerful than the 428-4V PI product. The 428 PI used in the early Shelby GT500s was necessarily an EPA-certified product and it used all the components—carburetors, cylinder heads, intake, and exhaust systems—of the production 1967–1968 428-4V PI, without substitution."

In other words, the production 1968 428 Cobra Jet Mustang was even faster than Tasca's legendary KR-8. Dean Gregson remembers selling 48 1968½ CJ Mustangs alone at Tasca Ford during the first month following the April 1 introduction.

"On the street, the Cobra Jet was absolutely awesome," says Barr. "Nothing I saw anywhere could touch it. For stoplight Grands Prix, the 428 Cobra Jet was the bee's knees because nothing could stay with it."

So, what happened to the original 1967 KR-8 hardtop? Bob Tasca Jr. said, "I hit a telephone pole with it in October 1967. I had just gotten my driver's license six weeks before. That was the end of that car." The 427 tunnel-port drivetrain eventually went into a 1968½ Cobra Jet fastback, known as the Tasca East Coast Exhibition car (currently owned by Oklahoma's Ben Coles).

Tasca Ford—Present Day

Tasca Ford remains in business today, although the location has moved from East Providence to Cranston, Rhode Island. The company is still noted for Ford performance—it operates one of five Shelby Mod Shops—and racing: Bob Tasca III, Bob Jr.'s son, currently campaigns a Shelby Mustang–bodied Top Fuel Funny Car in the NHRA, while Carl Tasca, who rode to Detroit in the back seat of the KR-8 Mustang in 1967, races a late-model Cobra Jet Mustang from Ford Racing.

Other members of the family are also involved with the dealership today. Bob Tasca Sr. passed away on January 8, 2010, at age 83. In the *Automotive News* obituary that day, Bob Jr. said, "He was a guy who wrote on his career paper when he was 8 or 9 years old that he wanted to be a Ford dealer. He drove them, he sold them, he built them, and he raced them. He was an icon."

Bob McClurg's book, *The Tasca Ford Legacy: Win on Sunday, Sell on Monday*, is a must-have for anyone wanting a deeper dive into the history of Tasca Ford.

Bob Tasca Sr., Bob Tasca III, Bob Tasca Jr., and Carl Tasca (from left) at the opening of their new shop in North Carolina. (Photo Courtesy Ron Lewis)

Carl Tasca racing a 2010 Cobra Jet Mustang at Orlando Speedworld, where he set a record for the CJ race cars: 7.54 at 185 mph.

Carl Tasca's record-setting Cobra Jet is powered by a supercharged 5.4L built by Chris Holbrook Racing. Output is 1,400 ponies.

Inside the KR-8 Package

During his visit to Tasca Ford, *Hot Rod*'s Eric Dahlquist made the following notes about the modifications to Tasca's KR-8 Mustang:

Heart of the KR-8

Engine: 428 Police Interceptor short-block ("absolutely stock, untouched out-of-crate")

Cylinder heads: 1963½ 427 (C8AE-6049K), 68-cc per chamber

Valves: Light, hollow-type 2.09-inch intake (C3AZ-6057I) and 1.66-inch exhaust (C3AZ-6505E) with stock 427-type valve springs (1.82-inch installed height)

Rocker arms: 1.76:1 427, adjustable

Cam: Stock 1967 390 GTA, advanced three degrees (C6OZ-6250B)

Intake manifold: Aluminum, Police Interceptor aluminum (C6H) with Bakelite spacer/divider

Carburetor: Le Mans–type Holley with four-way shooter nozzle and manual linkage curve

Transmission: C6 automatic with heavy-duty converter ("1-2 shift at 6,400 rpm; 2-3 shift at 6,200 rpm")

Fuel line: 3/8-inch from gas tank to 427-type fuel pump (C0AZ-9350C, "relieved with #13 drill bit to eliminate percolation when hot; electric fuel pump optional")

Air induction: Two 6-inch openings in grille connected to carburetor via hoses

Distributor: 427 dual-point with full centrifugal 10-degree plate and 427-hp wires (C5AZ-12127E)

Exhaust: 427 Fairlane headers modified to fit; 2¼-inch 1966 Fairlane H-pipe and tailpipes with 2¼-inch Advance mufflers

Rear end: 3.50 limited-slip (28-tooth axles)

Other: Autolite BF-32 spark plugs, Shelby GT350 power steering pulley, 427 oil pump, deep sump oil pan (6-quart capacity with filter), eliminated exhaust control valve

Suspension, front: 5/16-inch spacer under left-front lower spring pad, increase left-front stabilizer 3/4-inch link spacer, increase right-front 3/8-inch link spacer

Suspension, rear: Increase right-rear spring hangers 2 inches, increase left-rear spring hangers 1 inch, turn two leafs 180 degrees but leave main and first leafs in standard position, Shelby-type snubbers in same location as GT500, clamp rear springs similar to original equipment

Autolite SuperFlex shock absorbers.

Relocate battery to right-rear; use heavy-duty type cable.

CHAPTER THREE

DESIGNING THE 428 COBRA JET ENGINE

Once Bob Tasca proved to Ford's management and engineers that the automaker had everything at its fingertips to build a better mousetrap—and by the time *Hot Rod* readers flooded Hank the Deuce's desk with letters demanding he build the car they read about in the magazine—Ford was two months away from building the first set of 50 428 Cobra Jet Mustangs, thereby stepping up the performance of the hot-selling (but underperforming) Mustang.

A freshly restored 428 Cobra Jet engine has a million little details that Mustang Club of America judges look for in a concours restoration. (Photo Courtesy Marcus Anghel Restorations)

The Carroll Shelby Influence

Before we delve into the design differences between Tasca's KR-8 and the subsequent Cobra Jet, we should mention Carroll Shelby's influence on the package. Shelby had seen great success (at least with today's hindsight) with his little British A.C. sports car into which he swapped a Ford thin-wall 260-ci small-block and renamed it the Shelby Cobra, then followed up with a 289 Hi-Po and 427 big-block. The latter was a NASCAR-inspired engine jammed into the tiny engine compartment to create the legendary, brutally-fast-by-anyone's-standards 427 Cobra.

Of course, the 427 had found racing success in a series of lightweight Galaxies in 1963–1964, with the formula finding its way into Ford's midsize 1964 Fairlane Thunderbolt. It proved that the FE engine could be a competitor *par excellence* on the drag strip, running mid-11s in the quarter mile.

Carroll Shelby's attention then turned to helping Ford introduce the new Mustang to the racing world via the Sports Car Club of America (SCCA) series. Ford sent Shelby a truckload of brand-new K-code (289/271) Mustangs to his Venice, California, shop to transform them into the Shelby GT350, including street, race, and drag versions. Suspension and curb weight alterations, plus some minor engine modifications, made them killers on the road courses, with a GT350 taking its first win at Green Valley, Texas, on February 14, 1965, with Ken Miles behind the wheel.

As Shelby worked on the GT40 Le Mans project (in conjunction with several other builders, such as Holman-Moody), the new-for-1967 Mustang was coming off Ford production lines with an engine bay capable of handling a big-block (albeit with some shoehorning). Being a racer, Shelby was of the opinion that it's always a good idea to stuff the biggest engine you can in the lightest car (AKA 427 Cobra), so he came up with the idea for the GT500 using Ford's FE engine.

Yet the 390 wasn't holding its own on the street in the face of competition from Chevrolet, Pontiac, and Chrysler. For his big-block

The Shelby convertible was slated to be introduced midyear 1967. However, due to fitment issues with the Shelby-specific components, Ford muscled its way in to fix Shelby American's problems and the convertible was shelved until 1968. As it sits, car #67413C9A00139 was the only Shelby convertible built. (Photo Courtesy Al Rogers)

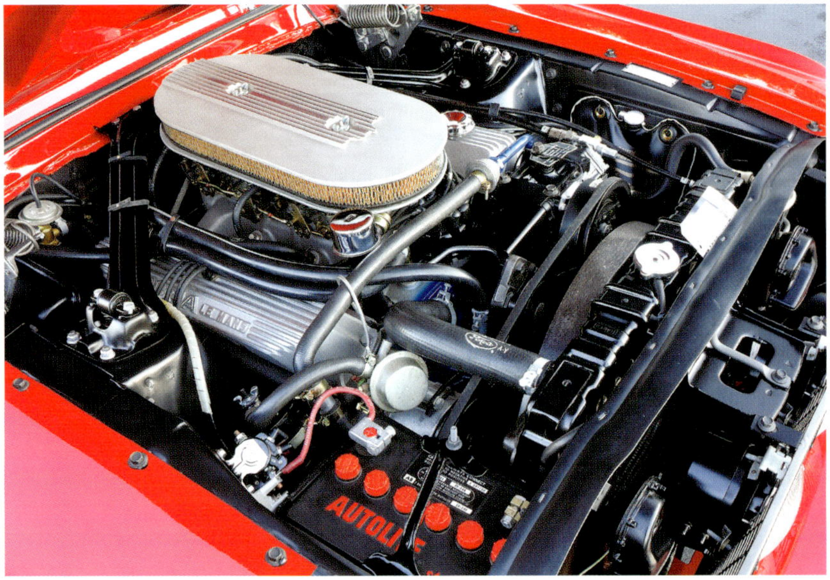

This 1967 Shelby GT500 convertible was among the first three Shelbys built with the 428. Being a 1967, it's equipped with the 428 Police Interceptor with dual-quads rated at 355 hp. (Photo Courtesy Al Rogers)

Ford produced several thousand full-size 1963½ Fords with the 427, but production limitations prevented it from being a viable option for the Mustang in 1967–1968 (although a handful were produced for the 1968 Cougar GT-E). (Photo Courtesy Al Rogers)

nameplate, Shelby earmarked the 428 Police Interceptor, the same engine that Bob Tasca would use, although Tasca had his mechanics hot rod his engine with parts sourced from other Ford engines, including 427 cylinder heads.

Alas, Ford Motor Company's relationship with Carroll Shelby had begun to sour in late 1966/early 1967 with the final straw being production problems with the fiberglass fitment on his pricey Mustangs. The truth is that Shelby American had grown a lot through 1967 and was not able to keep up with that growth. Shelby Mustang builds were subsequently contracted to A.O. Smith in Ionia, Michigan. A new entity, the Detroit-based Shelby Automotive Inc. was now responsible for running the company. The former Shelby American evolved into Shelby Racing Company and Shelby Parts Company.

Bill Barr: In His Words

The beginning of Ford's Total Performance era was 1963. At that time, Bill Barr was an engineer in the full-race Indianapolis race engine team. As he stated to the 428 Cobra Jet Registry website, "Starting in the fall of 1962, I was the Dynamometer Development/Test Engineer for the 1963 Indianapolis pushrod engine, and then one of the five engineers in the Indy Engine Group for the 1964 DOHC engine. The 1964 group included a supervisor, a principal engineer, five design engineers, and a Dynamometer Coordinator. The 1965 Indy Engine Group expanded by one engineer. After the 1965 race for which 50 'production' race engines were built and sold (Jim Clark won the 1965 Indy 500 race with one), the Indy Race Group was disbanded and personnel were dispersed to other engine engineering projects."

That's the official story, but Barr told us the behind-the-scenes reason why he was eventually moved to the passenger car world, saying, "By the end of June 1965, I was groomed out of the race group because the manager and supervisor and I didn't get along. We didn't have the same feelings about how to do things. At Indianapolis in 1965, Mario Andretti was a driver for Clint Brawner and Jimmy McGee, and his Ford engine had some problems. The supervisor gave him some really bad advice on how to clean it up, telling him to lean it out two jets on the Hilborn mechanical fuel injection and put in a hotter spark plug. He did it without consulting with the principal engineer or any of us, and we never would have recommended that, very frankly. Mario went out for his driver's test and pre-ignited a piston and hurt the engine.

"They told us [engineers] to keep our hands off the engine—the engines had been sold to the racers and we were to stay out of it. But when I walked into the garage at 7:00 that night everyone was just sitting around and doing nothing, so I said, 'What's going on? Aren't you going to fix the engine?' I couldn't stand the thought of the *Indianapolis Star* newspaper just ridiculing the shit out of us the next day when Mario showed up with an Offenhauser engine in the car, so we worked late into the night fixing it. I took it apart to see what was wrong and then took it over to Clint and Louis Meyer's place and fixed it up, rebuilt it, and put it in the car.

"Mario went out and passed his driver's test the next day. I got to be good friends with Clint and Mario after that but became persona non grata with Ford since I broke the rules to not get your hands on the engine. So, I got shifted out of there, and by the end of 1965 I had moved into the FE group. In short order, we got the Cobra Jet project going and it was very successful, and everything was level ground afterward. But I still didn't mind the bosses all the time."

Sounds like a perfect workplace attitude to have when building a hot new engine program meant to shatter the rulebook—a no-nonsense, get-it-done-by-any-means-necessary engineer who values results more than following an arbitrary rulebook. Thus, the Cobra Jet was officially born within Ford Motor Company.

Barr entered the FE program in early 1966, well after the 390 GT engine was designed. He said, "The 1967 390 GT Mustang, that boat had sailed by the time I got there. I inherited it but had no part in it in the beginning." The engine engineers who worked for him were Paul Lampela, Frank Gondoly, Bob Snider, and Matt Hecht.

What were the primary design changes between the 428 Police Interceptor and the Cobra Jet? Barr responds, "The FE engines—the 352, 390, 406, and 428—had certain issues that were hard to correct without redoing the engine completely. For one, the cylinder head was so small. Even a Boss 302 head was much larger than the 390/428 engines. The main problem was the water flow. When the head is too small, but it has to have a certain amount of iron for chamber faces and what have you, it makes for very marginal coolant passages in the cylinder head, and that was one of the things. When we made a 'Chinese copy' of the heads, we completely redid the water jacket so that it cooled the exhaust valve and spark plug seats and promoted good water flow through the head—equivalent to the water flow through the block. The block was very easy to work with since it was much bigger.

"We also fixed the ports. We designed the intake manifold and cylinder head ports so they went together [meaning no

Bill Barr: In His Words (CONTINUED)

mismatched port edges restricting flow]. So, the induction tract worked very, very well on the Cobra Jet. That was the main reason it was so responsive. We also raised the carburetor pad to get it up out of the valley because many of the FEs, they just pushed the manifold runners down in order to provide hood clearance. We raised it up so there was the opportunity for downward flow all the way from the carb to the valve. We could only put a 1/4-inch phenolic spacer under the carburetor, as opposed to the 1-inch spacer that many FEs had because of that. We fixed all those things on the intake manifold, and that's why the Cobra Jet manifold flowed so much more air than the Police Interceptor manifold. The PI engines made between 289 and 305 hp, and while the Cobra Jet was rated at 335 hp, they all made around 337, 340, 342 hp, in that range."

Induction-wise, the manifold was a cast-iron dual-plane with a 735-cfm Holley 4-barrel carburetor with center-pivot float bowls, electric choke, and vacuum secondaries. Noted FE expert Jay Brown of FEPower.com said, "The Cobra Jet manifold is an outstanding performance intake, making more mid-range torque than just about any other intake manifold ever produced for the FE. It is my opinion that the intake manifold is the reason why FEs have the undeserved reputation for being heavy. The CJ intake weighs 85 pounds! People don't realize that an FE effectively has about 25 percent of each cylinder head contained in the intake manifold; the pushrods go through the intake, and part of the valve cover rail is in the intake manifold. So, a cast-iron FE cylinder head is lighter than just about any other cast-iron head out there, but the manifolds are heavy."

Barr continued, "The ports were matched, we fixed the valves—the production FE valves weren't very nice, they weren't even a good-looking valve. An ugly duckling. We could fail engines right and left because the head of the exhaust valve would fall off. It took me about 3½ minutes of looking at the valve to realize that it was a piece-of-shit valve. Coming from the Indy engine program, I had a different perspective. The PI valve impeded airflow because it occupied a lot of space. I made the Cobra Jet valve look just like the valve in the Indy engine. The Cobra Jet valve had a real nice, large, 1/2-inch radius coming down from the stem to the backside of the head, then we swirl-polished it, put in 30-degree seats, a lot of things like that we fixed, and it made the engine much more lively and responsive."

The cylinder heads were nothing wild, but they were, in Barr's words, "One hundred percent different than the PI head." Rectangular intake ports (2.34 inches tall by 1.34 inches wide) were the same as the earlier low-riser 427 ports and the valves

This is an aluminum 428 Police Interceptor intake manifold, which looks similar to the 428 Cobra Jet manifold but is completely different. Noted FE expert Jay Brown says, "There are substantial differences between the manifolds. In my intake manifold testing, the cast-iron CJ intake always bested the PI intake at engine power levels up to 500 hp. However, swapping the PI intake with the CJ intake does have the advantage of reducing engine weight by a whopping 55 pounds." (Photo Courtesy Jay Brown)

While the 428 Police Interceptor intake was lightweight aluminum, the 428 Cobra Jet intake manifold was made of cast iron. Although very heavy at 85 pounds, the intake manifold is one of the primary reasons why the Cobra Jet flowed so much more air than other FEs. (Photo Courtesy Jay Brown)

According to Jay Brown, "The Cobra Jet cylinder heads are very similar to the 427 low-riser heads and actually have taller ports than the medium-risers, all with the same roof height. What this means is that when bolting the intake onto the engine, the roof of the intake manifold port lines up with the roof of the head port, but the floor of the intake manifold port is about 0.3 inch higher than the floor of the cylinder head port. There's a big step down for the air coming out of the manifold at the bottom of the port." (Photo Courtesy Jay Brown)

were sized 2.09/1.66 inches, intake and exhaust respectively, which was right between the bigger 427 and smaller passenger car 428 valve sizes.

It wasn't just the cylinder heads and induction tract that were changed in the 428 Cobra Jet. Ford's engineers addressed the engine's bottom-end by beefing it up with heavier main bearing caps and an improved crankshaft and rods, all without the race trickery of the 427. The block was a regular deep-skirt casting with two-bolt main caps, unlike the cross-bolted mains on the 427. Since the CJ wasn't meant for severe NASCAR use and was only designed to rev up to 5,000–6,000 rpm (instead of the 7,000-rpm limit of the 427), it didn't need the extra beef.

Ford Performance Corner literature of the day even said, "The 428 Cobra Jet is basically a street engine, but one that can be modified to run in the classes which the average performance buff can afford—the Stock and Super Stock classes—and two-bolt bearing caps provide plenty of strength for this usage."

The oil pump was upgraded to the heavy-duty type used for the 428 Police Interceptor engine and was geared for high volume. Even the crankshaft was cast steel instead of forged for cost reasons, and the pistons were castings. The connecting rods, however, were forged since FE rods had proven to be a weak spot, with caps and bolts failing given enough RPM. Ford also went with a fairly mild dual-pattern hydraulic flat tappet camshaft with 270/290 degrees of duration and 0.481/0.490-inch lift, which delivered a little more timing to the exhaust side due to the restrictive exhaust manifolds necessitated by the

Here a 428 Cobra Jet intake manifold gasket is laying on the intake manifold ports. The outline of the gasket fits the ports in the heads, so you can see the step. Why Ford designed the intake this way is anybody's guess, but dyno testing reveals that port-matching the manifold to the head doesn't result in any power increase. (Photo Courtesy Jay Brown)

There was no difference between a 428 Cobra Jet block and those equipped with the Drag Pack. The primary difference with the Super Cobra Jet was in its components. (Photo Courtesy Jay Brown)

Bill Barr: In His Words (CONTINUED)

All 428 Cobra Jet blocks came with the triple webbing around the main bearing bores, as shown here, for more bottom-end strength. (Photo Courtesy Jay Brown)

Mustang's shock towers that made the engine a tight fit in the small pony car engine bay.

Lighting the air/fuel mixture was also kept basic, with a single-point distributor and Autolite BF-32 spark plugs (later 428 Cobra Jets received a dual point).

Barr adds, "We made the engine very reliable, and production engines made easily 335 to 340 hp with SAE advertising [meaning as installed in the car]. Engines back then were always overestimated. The maximum power available was called the 'A Curve' on the dynamometer, and you took a lot of liberties to get as much power as you could so you could advertise it. But that power level was not the engine as installed in the car. For the A curve test, you cut off the choke housing, take the throttles out, plates and shaft both, put headers on the engine—it didn't have exhaust manifolds, it had headers on the damn thing on the dyno. All of those things we fixed, that's why the 428 CJ was a really great street racer.

Barr's comments are contrary to popular belief that Ford grossly underrated the 428 Cobra Jet at 335 hp to gain an advantage in NHRA's Stock class factoring, which took into account advertised factory horsepower and shipping weight data when grouping vehicles in competition classes. In a 2016 story for *Hot Rod* magazine, Steve Magnante attempted to find the truth behind how much power the CJ actually made in stock form. On an engine dyno, with stock components such as intake and

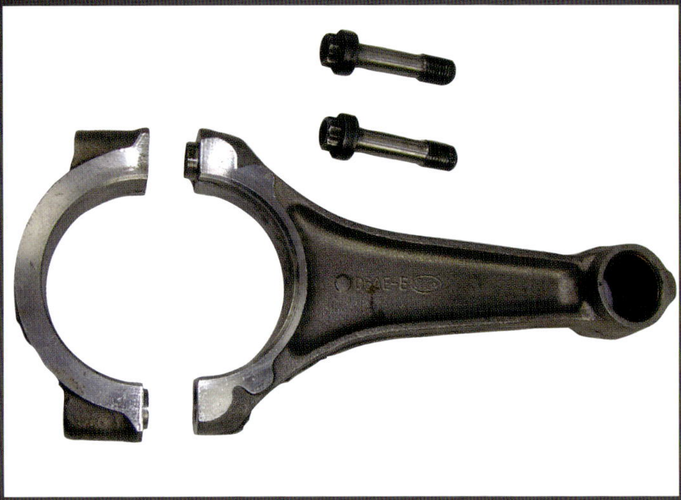

This a 428 Super Cobra Jet rod from 1969, also referred to as the Le Mans rod. The rod uses sleeves for alignment between the cap and the rod, and cap-screw bolts with a necked-down shank—they are sometimes referred to as "tri-lobe" bolts. The rods are much heavier than a standard 428 CJ rod, which uses a normal bolt and nut arrangement for the fasteners. Due to the weight of the SCJ rods, a special crankshaft sleeve with a built-in counterweight was required for SCJ engines. (Photo Courtesy Jay Brown)

The 428 Cobra Jet exhaust manifolds were far superior to the 390 GT's but are still inferior to a good set of tubular headers, which most racers used. Expert Brown says, "One thing to note is that most FE exhaust manifolds use a top and bottom bolt around the port to attach to the cylinder head. But the 428 CJ manifolds use a pair of bolts on the sides of the port, rather than top and bottom, to attach to the head on seven of the eight cylinders. The reason for this is that the shock towers in Mustangs, Fairlanes, and Torinos get in the way of the top bolts. So, 428 CJ heads are drilled with four holes around each exhaust port, not just two, so that attaching the manifold does not require use of the top bolt." (Photo Courtesy Jay Brown)

exhaust manifolds (but without accessories such as an alternator, a cooling fan, etc.), the CJ made 365.1 hp at 4,800 rpm—about 10 percent more than advertised. It also made 452.2 ft-lbs of torque at 3,700 rpm, also a little higher than Ford's claim of 445 at 3,400.

The 428 Cobra Jet was introduced to the world on January 28, 1968, when Hubert Platt raced his C/Stocker at the AHRA Winternationals; on February 4, six cars were entered in the 1968 NHRA Winternationals in Pomona, California, but, as Barr explained, the five that were entered in Super Stock classes were far from stock. "When they went out to Pomona to run Super Stock, those engines had been broadly worked over out in California. Chuck Folger and Al Joniec, they took care of preparing all those engines that went to the Winters in '68. They were *not* production engines, naturally, but that's what Super Stock is all about, as opposed to the Stock class."

Just how did the 428 Police Interceptor and Cobra Jet engines differ? Barr provides this comparison chart of the major 428 engine components to illustrate. Unless specifically noted, this comparison does not include the parts that are unique to the 428 Super Cobra Jet engine that was introduced for 1969.

Component	Tasca KR-8 (estimated)	428 Police Interceptor	428 Cobra Jet
Cylinder heads	C3AE-6049-H	C7AE-6049-D (Production 390–410–428–428 PI)	C8OE-6049-N Similar to earlier C4AE-H but with enlarged intake and exhaust ports, valve seat throat clearance cutter, and improved water jacket core print
Intake manifold	Aluminum PI	Aluminum PI	Cast iron, similar to PI with revised carburetor bore risers, relocated carburetor pad, and radiused riser to upper and lower logs to improve fuel/air distribution
Exhaust manifolds	Exhaust headers	Production 390 GT cast iron light car manifolds	Redesigned high flow, low restriction unique to the 428 CJ
Air cleaner	Unknown	Light car 390 GT	Redesigned dual inlet with hot/cold start-up system. Upgrade available to low-restriction ram air (seal to hood) and "shaker" hood with hot/cold start-up system
Thermactor secondary air system	None	Air inlet to exhaust manifolds	Air inlet to exhaust ports
Carburetor	635 or 650 CFM Holley 1.6875x1.6875-inch primary and secondary bores	Ford P&E 600-cfm 4V	Holley 735 CFM 4V (780 CFM modified with FT (Ford Truck) booster nozzles for improved atomization and emissions) 1.75x1.75-inch primary and secondary bores
Crankshaft	Production 428 PI	Production 428 PI	Production 428 PI (Note that Barr's original notes used for this page said "Special 50% nodularity for improved strength," but we can't find any evidence that suggests that the original CJ crank was anything other than the same crank used with the 428 PI)
Connecting rods	Production 428 PI	Production 428 PI	Larger bolts; SCJ had material added to outside of the big end
Crankshaft mass balance	Production 428 PI	Production 428 PI	Rebalanced special crankshaft
Crankshaft damper	Production 428 PI	Production 428 PI	Retuned damper for strengthened crankshaft
Camshaft	390 GT	390 GT	390 GT
Valve springs and valve toss speed	Production 428 PI (6,000 rpm)	Production 428 PI (6,000 rpm)	Revised valve springs for higher valve toss speed (6,700 rpm)
Intake valves	Regular production	Production 428 PI	Improved material with modified, polished backside fillet radius

Bill Barr: In His Words (CONTINUED)

Component	Tasca KR-8 (estimated)	428 Police Interceptor	428 Cobra Jet
Exhaust valves	Regular production	Production 428 PI	Improved material with modified, polished backside fillet radius
Oil filter adapter	Production 428 PI	Production 428 PI	Unique adapter with oil in and oil out provisions for external oil cooler (SCJ only)
Flywheel and clutch	Production 428 PI	Production 428 PI	Unique high (90+ percent) nodular iron with 10,000-rpm burst strength; high RPM clutch assembly
Oil pump and oil pressure	Production 428 PI	Production 428 PI	Higher relief valve pressure, unique oil filter adapter, and external oil cooling (SCJ only)
Transmission	Automatic	Automatic or 4-speed	Automatic and manual transmission available. Upgraded C6 with higher shift speed and modified clutch packs
Exhaust system	Unknown	Standard 390 GT Mustang	New 6-inch HG with minimal exhaust restriction mufflers and pipes
Rear shock absorber mounts	Production 1967 Mustang	Production 1967–1968 Mustang	Revised for staggered shock absorbers to eliminate reverse gear tramping
Power output	Unknown	295 B-Curve HP and 395 ft-lbs torque	340 B Curve HP and 420 ft-lbs torque

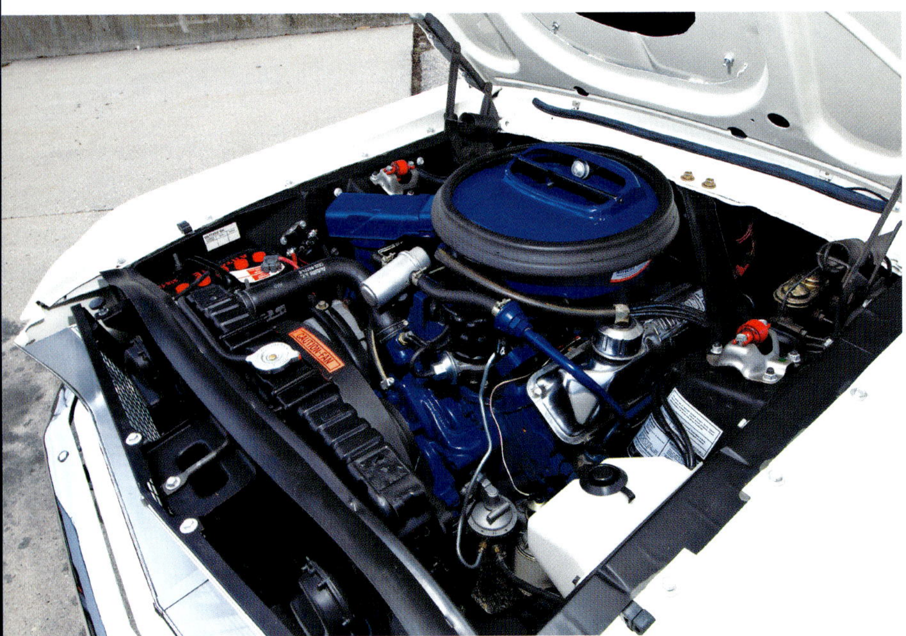

All 428 Cobra Jet Mustangs breathed through a vacuum-operated flap on top of the air cleaner that sealed to the hood with a rubber gasket. This was the first-time air induction appeared on a Mustang, and it wasn't available for lesser engines. (Photo Courtesy David Newhardt/ Mecum Auctions)

Outfitting the Car

When a Mustang buyer selected the 428 Cobra Jet engine, the GT Equipment Group was mandatory. The package could be added to any V-8 Mustang with a 302 4-barrel or better, but it was mandatory when a buyer selected the Cobra Jet. The package included grille-mounted fog lights, dual exhaust, a new bodyside C-stripe, heavy-duty suspension, 14-inch GT Styled Steel Wheels, GT gas cap, and GT emblems on the front fenders.

The 428 Cobra Jet could be ordered with either a 4-speed or a heavy-duty C6 Cruise-O-Matic 3-speed automatic transmission, and both were supported by a 9-inch rear end with gear ratio choices of 3.50, 3.91, and 4.30. Four-speed cars also received staggered rear shocks (one ahead

Except for the batch of early "135" cars (such as this one), 428 Cobra Jet–equipped 1968 Mustangs required the GT package. The only transmission available was either the "Top-Loader" 4-speed manual or C6 automatic. (Photo Courtesy David Newhardt/Mecum Auctions)

Cobra Jet Mustangs were equipped with functional ram air (ditto for Cougars, although midsize R-code FoMoCo vehicles didn't have ram air available until 1969).

The following engines and codes were available or advertised for Mustangs for the North American market:

Code	Engine
C	289-2V
F	302-2V (unofficial—three built)
J	302-4V
R	428-4V Cobra Jet
S	390-4V
T	200-1V
W	427-4V (never released)
X	390-2V

of and one behind the axle) for better wheel hop control. An Equa-Lock differential and Competition Handling Package were extra-cost options ($79 and $62, respectively).

A 1968 vehicle equipped with the 428 Cobra Jet engine featured an *R* in the fifth character of the VIN, which was coincidental since all 1968½

While we tend to envision a 428 Cobra Jet Mustang as a fastback, it in fact was also available as a coupe and convertible. The Mustang fastback was and still is considered the sportiest, and it led in popularity with 1,044 built with the CJ. Indeed, the initial 50 "135" cars were all fastbacks. Total production of 1968 Mustang Cobra Jets was 1,299.

1968 Mustang GTs ordered with the 428 Cobra Jet received Goodyear Polyglas F70-14 tires standard. There was no other available tire. The Goodyears featured raised white letters with no size indicated. (Photo Courtesy David Newhardt/Mecum Auctions)

CHAPTER FOUR

THE FIRST COBRA JETS AND THE 1968 NHRA WINTERNATIONALS

"In one fell swoop, Ford has answered all your cards and letters. Their answer is called the Mustang 'Cobra Jet.'"

So read the subhead of Eric Dahlquist's story "The Jet Set" that appeared in the March 1968 issue of *Hot Rod*, introducing readers to the car they had demanded from Henry Ford II several months earlier when the magazine profiled Tasca Ford's KR-8. Ford made good on its promise to Dahlquist to let *Hot Rod* have the first crack at publicizing the 428 Cobra Jet when the automaker delivered one in Los Angeles for a road test (a bit later than promised

This is one of the first 50 1968 428 Cobra Jet Mustangs built that was destined for racing, although some ended up in private hands. This example is a lightweight version, meaning sound deadener and sealer have been deleted. (Photo Courtesy David Newhardt/Mecum Auctions)

due to a workers' strike in the plant and the resultant time to ship it to the West Coast). Dahlquist claimed it was worth the wait, stating, "All the frustration was put out of mind the first time we let it happen—'waaah'—the secondaries came open and you realized most races would end right there, in low gear. The would-be competitor cannot believe his eyes. No Mustang outside of Tasca's 'Mystery 7' has ever moved this quickly before."

"The C.J. will be the utter delight of every Ford lover and the bane of all the rest because, quite frankly, it is probably the fastest regular production sedan ever built," wrote Dahlquist in the first paragraph of the article—an oft-quoted line that has appeared in magazines and books ever since.

Dahlquist admitted that the 428 Cobra Jet was a bit of a ringer, without the production sound deadener, bringing curb weight down to a mere 3,240 pounds and making the Mustang sound like "a 50-gallon steel echo chamber." As mentioned in chapter 3, Dahlquist put some break-in miles on the car by driving up to Fresno and back before taking it to the drag strip in Irwindale, roughly 30 minutes east of downtown Los Angeles. Out of the gate, the CJ ran 13.90 at 103.96 mph, wheel-hopping its street tires like crazy. As the story shows, clamping the leaf springs and removing the accessory belts dropped ETs to 13.56 and raised MPH to 106.64, which provoked him to say the CJ Mustang was "the fastest-running Pure Stock in the history of man. Ford did not foul up in the rating game footwork, either, slapping on an innocent 335 horsepower, and NHRA bought it lock,

Despite the stripped nature of the "135" cars, under the hood they shared the same equipment as the balance of Cobra Jet production that was built in April through the end of the model year. (Photo Courtesy David Newhardt/Mecum Auctions)

Out of the 50 "135" 428 Cobra Jet Mustangs built, 11 were sent to Tasca Ford. Of course, all of them came from the factory painted Wimbledon White with a black interior and a 4-speed. (Photo Courtesy David Newhardt/Mecum Auctions)

stock, and barrel." How could any new-car buyer with a performance bent not be turned on by those lines?

Here Comes the Cobra Jet!

April 15, 1968. That was the day Ford delivered the bacon to satisfy the appetite for Mustang performance that *Hot Rod*'s story on Tasca's KR-8 had created. This was almost four years to the day (April 17, 1964) after Ford introduced the Mustang at the World's Fair in New York.

The car that big-block Camaro and Mopar enthusiasts were dreading was coming. As Ford's press release stated, "The lively image of Ford Division's Mustang and Fairlane takes on added luster with the release of two 1968½ high-performance packages. Both cars have Ford's recently announced 428-ci Cobra Jet engine as part of a performance package that places them at the top of the 'super car' category."

But the real performance-minded enthusiasts had already seen the car in person (or in magazine pages) at three drag races months prior to the announcement—the AHRA Winter Meet at Lions; then a week later at Beeline Drag Strip in Phoenix, Arizona; and then the NHRA Winternationals in Pomona, California, where the race-prepped Cobra Jets pummeled the competition in Super Stock. But we're getting ahead of ourselves.

The "135" Mustangs

According to the Mustang 428 Cobra Jet Registry website, the first Cobra Jet Mustangs built were a limited run of 50 non-GT fastbacks (bodystyle 63A), enough to qualify for NHRA Stock class racing. They were scheduled for assembly at the Dearborn assembly plant on December 30, 1967, more than three months before regular production CJs began trickling into dealerships. The VINs were serialized consecutively starting with 8F02R135007 and ending with 8F02R135056, which is why they are known as "135" Mustangs today. All were painted Wimbledon White with black vinyl interior (code 2A), heavy-duty 4-speed manual transmission (code 5), manual drum brakes, and limited-slip 3.89 rear axle (though some door tags show code 7, meaning 3.25).

Thirty of the vehicles were assembled with seam sealer and sound deadener (noted by DSO code 844660) and 20 were built without seam sealer and sound deadener (noted by DSO code 844661). These initial 50 cars are sometimes referred to as "lightweights" but, as indicated above, only 20 were truly lightweight. There were no other weight-saving tricks, such as aluminum or fiberglass body panels or cardboard trim panels (as employed by factory drag cars earlier in the decade) to make them lighter.

The program was announced to Ford dealers in a telegram sent from Jacque Passino to regional and district sales managers on December 26, 1967.

Then and now, 1968 and 2009: Gas Ronda, Al Joniec, Hubert Platt, and Don Nicholson (L–R, with Randy Ritchie subbing for the late Nicholson in 2009). (©MotorTrend Group. All rights reserved.)

The cars were eventually distributed for sale to a small number of dealers in the United States and Canada, but the first batch went to NHRA Stock class race teams on the East and West coasts. Of the group of six Cobra Jets that showed up at the 1968 Winternationals, two of them (8F02R135050 and 8F02R135054) were true lightweight versions.

HM-S Tuned

These six Winternationals-bound cars were shipped to Holman-Moody-Stroppe in Long Beach, California, to be prepped for racing. As noted on the 428 Cobra Jet Registry website, the engines received 427-style connecting rods, a C8AX-C camshaft, stronger forged pistons (raising the compression ratio to 11.0), headers, modified 4-speeds for quicker shifting, steep 4.44:1 gears with a Detroit Locker differential, Goodyear slicks, and traction bars.

Cars prepped for Super Stock received all that plus an offset 427 aluminum intake manifold, a healthier solid lifter cam (part number C8AX-D), heavy-duty Crane valve springs, lightweight valves, a heavy-duty clutch, 4.71:1 gears on the same Detroit Locker, and bigger drag slicks. Both class mods included a dual-point distributor as part of the package. And, of course, they most likely had been tuned for the last possible fraction of a horsepower in preparation for competition.

The first car out of the gate was that of Hubert Platt, who made a "token run" (as *Hot Rod* characterized it) at the AHRA Winternationals

This was the final round of Super Stock, with Al Joniec's 428 Cobra Jet taking on Dave Wren's 1963 Max Wedge Plymouth in the Super Stock overall final. Joniec took home the win with a 12.50 at 97.93 mph run to Wren's 11.56 at 120.64. (©MotorTrend Group. All rights reserved.)

Al Joniec out ahead during eliminations at the 1968 NHRA Winternationals. (©MotorTrend Group. All rights reserved.)

To the victor go the spoils! Joniec in the winner's circle, getting it on both cheeks from Miss Hurst Linda Vaughn (left) and an unknown "trophy girl." (©MotorTrend Group. All rights reserved.)

Hubert Platt's Paul Harvey Ford 428 Cobra Jet (left) launching with Al Joniec's Rice-Holman Cobra Jet in the final round of SS/E. (©MotorTrend Group. All rights reserved.)

on January 28, 1968. Hubert's C/Stock Cobra Jet redlighted on a 12.62 run in the opening round of Top Stock. It was at Pomona on February 4, where the world understood just what Ford was unleashing on them: Hubert Platt ran C-Stock/Automatic (C/SA, 9.00–9.49 pounds per advertised horsepower); Jerry Harvey, Al Joniec, and Hubert Platt ran Super Stock E (SS/E, 8.70–9.49 pounds per advertised horsepower); and Gas Ronda and "Dyno" Don Nicholson ran Super Stock E Automatic.

The engines and cars lived up to expectations, as four made it to their respective class finals. Al Joniec was the big hero of the weekend and forever cemented himself in 428 Cobra Jet lore, defeating Hubert Platt in the final of SS/E (12.12 at 109 to Hubert's 11.59 at 113—the stock classes feature handicapped starts so a quicker ET could lose the race based on several factors) and then going on to the overall Super Stock class final, where he won the whole shebang by beating Dave Wren's 1963 Plymouth with a 12.50 at an off-the-throttle 97 mph.

Platt also entered his Cobra Jet Mustang in the Super Stock/C class and made it all the way to the final round but lost to Bill "Grumpy" Jenkins's 1967 big-block Camaro. In the Super Stock/E Automatic class, Gas Ronda went to the final round as well but lost to Dick Landy's 1968 Dodge in a nail-biter, running 12.02 at 116 mph to a winning 12.01 at 118.

Component	Production	C Stock	E Super Stock
Cylinder head	C8OZ-6049-F, Engineering number C8AE-6090-J	Same	Same
Intake manifold (aluminum)	C6AZ-9424-H, Engineering number C7AE-9425-F	Same	Offset 427, C6AZ-9424-M, Engineering number C7AE-9425-C
Intake manifold (cast iron)	C8OA-9424-A, Engineering number C8OE-9425-A	Same	N/A
Carburetor, manual (735 cfm)	C8OZ-9510-AA	Same	Same
Carburetor, automatic (735 cfm)	C8OZ-9510-AB	Same	Same
Camshaft	Hydraulic C6OZ-6250-B	Hydraulic C8AX-6250-C	Solid C8AX-6250-D
Valve spring	Not specified	427 type, C5AZ-6513-A	Crane or H-M type, spring, retainer, pushrod, and tappet
Rocker arm	Non-adjustable 1.73:1, B8AZ-6564-C, Adjustable 1.76:1, B8A-6564-B	Adjustable 1.76:1, B8A-6564-B	Adjustable 1.76:1, B8A-6564-B
Exhaust valve	C3AZ-6505-E	Same	Lightweight, sodium-filled, C8AX-6505-B
Intake valve	C3AZ-6507-AJ	Same	Lightweight, hollow stem, C8AX-6507-B
Valve lifter	Hydraulic, C3DZ-6500-B	Hydraulic, C4TZ-6500-A	Crane lightweight or 427 type C4AZ-6500-B
Piston (cast aluminum)	C6AZ-6108-AY, 10.7:1 CR	Forged, dished/eyebrows 11.0:1 CR	Forged, flat top/eyebrows 11.6:1 CR
Piston rings	C6AZ-6148-A	Moly type	Moly type
Piston rods	PI type, C6AE-6200-F; 427 type, C5AZ-6200-D	427 type, C5AZ-6200-D	427 type, C5AZ-6200-D
Crankshaft	C6AZ-6303-B1	Same	Same
Oil pan	C6OZ-6675-A	Deep sump 9-quart, C5AE-6675-N	Same
Oil pickup	C6OZ-6622-A	C5AE-6622-C	Same
Oil filter	C1AZ-6731-A	Low resistance, C8AE-6714-B	Same
Distributor	C8OZ-12127-D	Dual point, 427 type, C5AZ-12127-E	Same
Exhaust system	Not specified	Jardine or Doug's type headers	Same
Vibration damper	Not specified	Heavy-duty 427 type	Same
Clutch	Not specified	Production automatic and manual	Heavy-duty #2650 type
Transmission	2.32, 1.69, 1.29:1 ratios	Production/blocker rings cut, line lock	Same
Rear end	3.89:1, no locker	4.44:1/242L Detroit Locker	4.71:1/242L Detroit Locker
Suspension	Not specified	32-inch traction bar right side, single link bar left side	32-inch traction bar both sides
Shocks	Not specified	Heavy-duty type	Same
Tires	F70 Firestone	8.90x14, 7-inch tread	10.50x15

Shipping weight: Per the Automobile Manufacturers Association, Mustang "135" fastback: 3,267 pounds.

1968 428 Cobra Jet Drag Strip Modifications

The March 1968 edition of Ford's *Autolite Shop Tips* included a comprehensive description of the modifications made to prepare the 428 Cobra Jet engine for drag strip duty in the Stock and Super Stock classes. Here's a summary (part numbers are service part numbers unless noted as engineering part numbers):

Hubie and His Horse

"With a cloud of rubber dust and a hearty 'Everthin's gonna be awright,' Hubert Platt charges off into the 1968 season with another addition to the Ford stable. Why don't you let the 'mouth of the South' fill you in on how to build yourself a record-settin' 428 Mustang."

The April 1968 issue of *Hot Rod* (a month after Eric Dahlquist's first test of the Cobra Jet Mustang) featured coverage on the 1968 Winternationals plus what was the first profile of one of the CJ race cars—Hubert Platt's Tasca-sponsored C/SA (which was later raced as the *Georgia Shaker* for Foulger Ford). The story was called "Hubie and His Horse" by Jim McFarland and photography by Bud Lang and Eric Rickman.

Right away, McFarland brought up the drought of Ford performance that was the impetus for Dahlquist to head to Rhode Island and Tasca Ford, saying, "Despite the thrashing we took for the things we said about the lack of Ford performance pieces, we told you we'd stay close to continuing developments in the escalation of Ford drag cars. Last month, you tasted

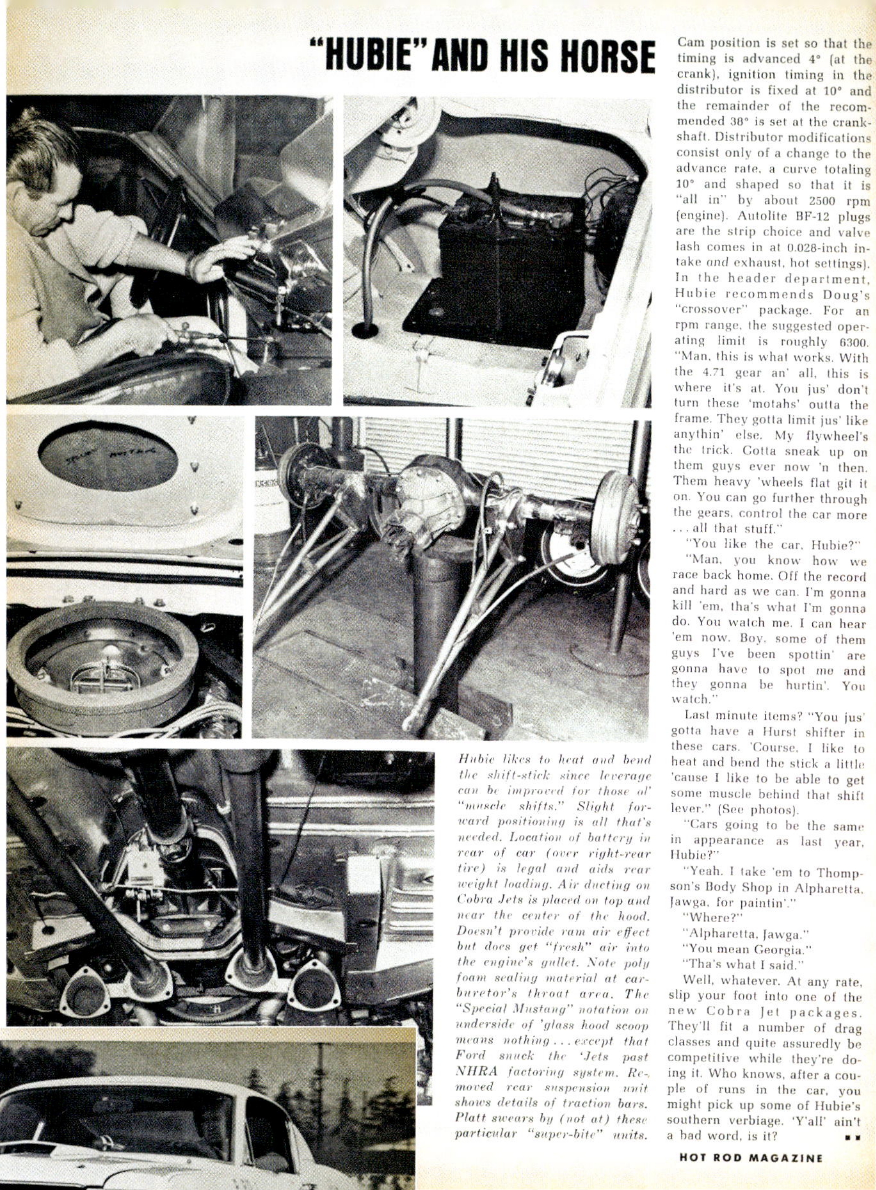
"HUBIE" AND HIS HORSE

Cam position is set so that the timing is advanced 4° (at the crank), ignition timing in the distributor is fixed at 10° and the remainder of the recommended 38° is set at the crankshaft. Distributor modifications consist only of a change to the advance rate, a curve totaling 10° and shaped so that it is "all in" by about 2500 rpm (engine). Autolite BF-12 plugs are the strip choice and valve lash comes in at 0.028-inch intake *and* exhaust, hot settings). In the header department, Hubie recommends Doug's "crossover" package. For an rpm range, the suggested operating limit is roughly 6300. "Man, this is what works. With the 4.71 gear an' all, this is where it's at. You jus' don't turn these 'motahs' outta the frame. They gotta limit jus' like anythin' else. My flywheel's the trick. Gotta sneak up on them guys ever now 'n then. Them heavy 'wheels flat git it on. You can go further through the gears, control the car more . . . all that stuff."

"You like the car, Hubie?"

"Man, you know how we race back home. Off the record and hard as we can. I'm gonna kill 'em, tha's what I'm gonna do. You watch me. I can hear 'em now. Boy, some of them guys I've been spottin' are gonna have to spot *me* and they gonna be hurtin'. You watch."

Last minute items? "You jus' gotta have a Hurst shifter in these cars. 'Course, I like to heat and bend the stick a little 'cause I like to be able to get some muscle behind that shift lever." (See photos).

"Cars going to be the same in appearance as last year, Hubie?"

"Yeah. I take 'em to Thompson's Body Shop in Alpharetta, Jawga, for paintin'."

"Where?"

"Alpharetta, Jawga."

"You mean Georgia."

"Tha's what I said."

Well, whatever. At any rate, slip your foot into one of the new Cobra Jet packages. They'll fit a number of drag classes and quite assuredly be competitive while they're doing it. Who knows, after a couple of runs in the car, you might pick up some of Hubie's southern verbiage. 'Y'all' ain't a bad word, is it?

Hubie likes to heat and bend the shift-stick since leverage can be improved for those ol' "muscle shifts." Slight forward positioning is all that's needed. Location of battery in rear of car (over right-rear tire) is legal and aids rear weight loading. Air ducting on Cobra Jets is placed on top and near the center of the hood. Doesn't provide ram air effect but does get "fresh" air into the engine's gullet. Note poly foam sealing material at carburetor's throat area. The "Special Mustang" notation on underside of 'glass hood scoop means nothing . . . except that Ford snuck the 'Jets past NHRA factoring system. Removed rear suspension unit shows details of traction bars. Platt swears by (not at) these particular "super-bite" units.

HOT ROD MAGAZINE

by Jim McFarland

"HUBIE" AND HIS HORSE

Well, here it is. Despite the thrashing we took for the things said about the lack of Ford performance pieces, we told you we'd stay close to continuing developments in the escalation of Ford drag cars. Last month, you tasted the flavor of a stock package 428 Cobra Jet, and this issue we persuaded colorful Hubert Platt to open his bag of beans and let you see what it takes to make one of these offerings strip-worthy and competition-inspired. Surprisingly enough, there are few items which require alteration, but if we were to spread out the bits and pieces, in Hubie's own vernacular, "you'd still be picking hominy grits out of your hollow tooth" when the first round of Super Stock Eliminator rolled around. So we'll request your indulgence and condense Hubie's suggestions to be compatible with the pics provided.

Suspension-wise, heavy-duty shocks are a must. Hubert leaves rear springs in an as-is condition and adds stiffer shocks to the rear only. He specifies Logghe traction bars (as shown in the photos) and sets rear gear lash at 0.003-0.005-inch, all in conjunction with stock U-joints and driveshaft. The only modification in this department is the addition of the required driveshaft loop (as per photos). Brakes are stock all around the car except for the removal of the self-adjusters on the rear units.

Race slicks are 10.50 x 15 Goodyears mounted on 6-inch rims. However, Hubert presently feels that a 7-inch wheel might be more suited to the newer types of casing design now being offered by this company. Front tires are 7.75 x 15 units carrying 40-50 psi of air. Tires of this size provide an extra margin of horizontal roll, enabling a slight edge in leave-the-line activity since more of the tire will remain in the stage lights as the car is beginning its forward movement. Short tires have less horizontal roll latitude and prevent leaving as early "on the tree."

What sort of modifications are made in the transmission? "All we do is cut the 'sincernizer' rings, de brass rings you know, and leave the detents out of the slide rails. Nuthin' else . . . and they shift slick. Them 'crash boxes' in a Ford won't work. Naturally, you gonna put a Schiefer in the car 'cause you just can't shift 'em with a stock pressure plate. They just don't want to release at high rpm. Anyway, you need some sort of a performance type clutch."

In the engine, specs are rather basic. Deck clearance is set at 0.010-inch, and stock pistons are swapped for one of the lightweight performance types. Hubert uses Venolia slugs in his engine, but the important feature is to replace the factory units with something more compatible with high rpm operation. Oil pan modifications consist of two horizontal baffles and an oil pickup that extends to the *bottom* of the pan which is altered to contain nine quarts of oil. (Actually, the sump is dropped four inches.) The pickup tube is not of the swinging variety but is an extension bent from tubing similar to the stock pipe. And even though pan capacity is increased to nine quarts, only seven are used during racing. This assures cooler oil temperatures and reduces windage on crank throws and rod ends.

Camshaft selection was the "Daytona" cam (SK-38427) which works in conjunction with Crane valve train components (springs, retainers, pushrods, etc.). Static compression ratio is near 11.4:1 with 68.5cc combustion chambers and the 0.008-0.010-inch deck height. Bottom-end clearances are basically stock and stock torque patterns and readings are incorporated.

Intake manifolding used is stock 428 (basic high-rise design) and mounts a 735 cfm Holley 4-bbl carburetor with (believe it or not) stock jetting. Rear gearing is Ford 4.71, the fresh-air hood and corresponding air cleaner is used and overall vehicle weight is 3225 (with the 32-pound rollbar).

(Continued on page 62)

With a cloud of rubber dust and a hearty "Everthin's gonna be awright," Hubert Platt charges off into the '68 season with another addition to the Ford stable. Why don't you let the "mouth of the South" fill you in on how to build yourself a record-settin' 428 Mustang

photography: Bud Lang and Eric Rickman

HOT ROD MAGAZINE

FAR LEFT—Rear portion of traction bars is critical area. Adequate fastening must be provided since torque reaction (to spring wrap) is too severe for four-leaf rear spring layout. Rear shocks can also be positioned rear of axle housings by reversing lower shock pad and providing a new mount for top of shock. ABOVE—Hubie gives you a glance at chassis attitude under a 7000 rpm "hammer" start. LEFT — Forward mounting point of the Logghe traction arms is a backing plate and hanger member as shown. Note heim joint and attending grease fitting. Backing plate is tack-welded to underside of body metal, as indicated. BELOW LEFT — Driveshaft loop is a must. Ease of installation is provided by the stock mounting holes you see here. BELOW — Dropped-sump pan is another "must" item. Sump area is capacity-increased to a total of nine quarts, even though only seven are used during actual car running. This can be accomplished by lowering sump dimensions a total of four inches. Check photo for a closer look.

In the April 1968 issue of Hot Rod, *"Hubie" all but disassembled his prepped and tested 428 Cobra Jet for readers to see what he did to make it a potential world beater in Stock class racing.*

the flavor of a stock package 428 Cobra Jet, and this issue we persuaded colorful Hubert Platt to open his bag of beans and let you see what it takes to make one of these offerings strip-worthy and competition-inspired. Surprisingly enough, there are few items which require alteration, but if we were to spread out the bits and pieces, in Hubie's own vernacular, 'You'd still be picking hominy grits out of your hollow tooth' when the first round of Super Stock Eliminator rolled around. So, we'll request your indulgence and condense Hubie's suggestions to be compatible with the pics provided."

What followed was a surprisingly candid look into the top-secret workings of a class race car, as "Hubie" admitted at least most of the things he had done to his Cobra Jet to make it as fast as possible on the drag strip. The story went on to point out that, suspension-wise, the rear leaf springs were stock, but stiffer rear shocks and Logghe traction bars were used. Hubert also set the rear gear backlash at 0.003–0.005-inch, with stock U-joints and driveshaft. The brakes were stock, but Hubert removed the self-adjusters on the rears, presumably to eliminate any chance of brake drag.

Here is the "Georgia Shaker" Hubert Platt with his 428 Cobra Jet Mustang at the Pomona Fairgrounds showing Hot Rod *and* Car Craft *some of the tools of the trade in competing in Super Stock at the 1968 Winternationals. (©MotorTrend Group. All rights reserved.)*

Hubert Platt was a racer first and foremost, so it's quite likely he had a few tricks up his sleeve and didn't reveal everything to the California publications. (©MotorTrend Group. All rights reserved.)

With the 9-inch rear end and suspension removed, we get a better look at the Logghe traction bars, which today would be considered ladder bars. The magazine article stated Hubert "swears by, not at" these particular "super-bite" units. (©MotorTrend Group. All rights reserved.)

Stock 4-speed 428 Cobra Jet Mustangs had staggered rear shocks (one each in front of and behind the axle). However, for increased axle control at the drags, Hubert moved them both behind the axle, which only required flipping one mounting plate. The little exhaust pipe under the axle housing is connected to a small straight-through "glass pack" bullet muffler (one per side), which muffled the noise for non-race situations like driving on and off the trailer. (©MotorTrend Group. All rights reserved.)

The rear slicks were 10.50x15 Goodyears mounted on 6-inch wheels, though Hubert mentioned that 7-inch wheels would work better with the new tire sidewalls of the day. The front tires were 7.75x15 with 40 to 50 psi air pressure. That was a fairly tall front tire for the era, chosen for better "rollout" from the starting line (which can help reaction time on the tree).

The Top-Loader 4-speed was "slick-shifted," meaning they cut the synchronizer rings and detents from the slide rails to make upshifts quicker, which required a performance clutch pressure plate. Hubert used a Schiefer clutch. He alluded to using a heavier flywheel (which provided more kinetic energy when he let the clutch out, making for a harder launch). And, of course, only a Hurst shifter would fill the bill.

The 428 Cobra Jet engine wasn't spared the workbench either. It was removed and blueprinted with deck clearance set at 0.010 inch, with the stock pistons swapped for lightweight Venolia pieces to handle more RPM. The oil pan's sump was increased to hold 9 quarts of oil, but the engine only held 7 quarts for less power-robbing crankshaft windage and lower oil temperatures. For the camshaft, he used a "Daytona" cam installed 4 degrees advanced, with Crane lifters, valve springs, retainers, and pushrods (with 0.028-inch valve lash). The stock 428 intake manifold and Holley 4-barrel carburetor were used, with Hubert claiming the jetting in the Holley was stock as well. It breathed through the stock CJ fresh air hood scoop with the air cleaner left in place, at least for this test. Rear gearing was 4.71:1, and vehicle weight was 3,225 pounds, 32 of which came from the roll bar.

The story pointed out that "Ignition timing in the distributor is fixed at 10 degrees and the remainder of the recommended 38 degrees is set at the crankshaft" with a curve that was "all in" by about 2,500 rpm. Auto-

As with any Stock class racer, there were modifications inside the Cobra Jet that you couldn't see but, externally, it was remarkably stock. The air cleaner lid and foam sealing element were still in place for cool air. The story read, "The 'Special Mustang' notation on underside of 'glass hood scoop means nothing . . . except that Ford snuck the Jets past NHRA factoring system." (©MotorTrend Group. All rights reserved.)

lite BF-12 plugs sparked the mix. Doug's "crossover" headers were Hubie's exhaust of choice and his rev limit was "roughly 6,300."

Hubert explained, complete with drawl, "Man, this is what works. With the 4.71 gear an' all, this is where it's at. You jus' don't turn these motahs outta the frame. They gotta limit jus' like anythin' else. My flywheel's the trick. Gotta sneak up on them guys ever now 'n' then. The heavy 'wheels flat git it on. You can go further through the gears, control the car more…all that stuff."

When asked what he thought of his new race car, Hubert nearly predicted the outcome of the Winternationals, saying, "Man, you know how we

The Top-Loader 4-speed was "slick-shifted" by modifying the synchros. This allowed near clutchless shifting during the heat of combat. (©MotorTrend Group. All rights reserved.)

Hubert always used a Hurst shifter in his race cars. For the 428 Cobra Jet, he heated it up and bent it forward a bit "for those ol' muscle shifts." (©MotorTrend Group. All rights reserved.)

As per drag racing norm, the battery was moved to the trunk, behind the passenger side tire, for better weight transfer. This was a legal NHRA move as long as there was an external master battery cut-off switch (barely seen between the taillight housing and bumper). (©MotorTrend Group. All rights reserved.)

From left to right are Hubert Platt, "Dyno" Don Nicholson, and Car Craft *staffer John Raffa. (©MotorTrend Group. All rights reserved.)*

Here Hubert launches his 428 Cobra Jet Mustang with drag slicks. Note the SS/F class designation, which was different than what he raced at the NHRA Winternationals. (©MotorTrend Group. All rights reserved.)

These two shots show the soft sidewall compound of the 10.50x15 Goodyear drag slicks and help explain what a "wrinkle wall" slick is, as the sidewall wrinkled a bit to absorb the shock of the launch. (©MotorTrend Group. All rights reserved.)

The oil pan sump was lowered 4 inches to increase capacity to 9 quarts (even though only 7 quarts were run in the 428). Excess oil can contact the spinning crankshaft, especially in a hard-launching drag car, and the friction between crank and oil robs horsepower. Also seen here are the set of Doug's Headers and a remarkably stock front suspension, drum brakes, and tall tires. (©MotorTrend Group. All rights reserved.)

Dyno Don and Dan Shields of Holman-Moody-Stroppe look over the 428 Cobra Jet in the staging lanes at Pomona. (©MotorTrend Group. All rights reserved.)

Though not spelled out in the* Hot Rod *story, Hubert Platt's 428 Cobra Jet Mustang ran mid-11s at around 113 mph. (©MotorTrend Group. All rights reserved.)

race back home. Off the record and hard as we can. I'm gonna kill 'em, tha's what I'm gonna do. You watch me. I can hear 'em now. Boy, some of them guys I've been spottin' are gonna have to spot me and they gonna be hurtin'. You watch."

Oddly enough, even though the story and photos took place on the drag strip at Pomona (assuming around the time of the Winternationals), no mention was made of the car's performance. That would be revealed during competition when Hubert ran 11.59 at 113 mph in a loss to Al Joniec.

The Six Winternationals Cars

You may know the drivers and their onslaught at the NHRA Winternationals in 1968, but you wouldn't be the only one to discover the racers weren't all "135" cars—some were converted.

8R02J117412

Sponsored by Tasca Ford and driven by Hubert Platt in C/SA, it soon became Hubert's *Georgia Shaker* with sponsorship from Foulger Ford.

8R02S117XXX

Hubert Platt's SS/E car, sponsored by Paul Harvey Ford. At Winternationals it redlighted against Al Joniec in the class final. Then, in Eliminator, it defeated Arlen Vanke in round 1 and Ronnie Sox in round 2. But for round 3, Hubert ran against Joniec again and lost in the quarter-final—again, to a red light.

Hubert eventually wrecked it, fixed it, then sold it to Randy Payne in 1969, who raced it under Foulger Ford sponsorship, then sold it to Rusty Gillis.

8R02S117414

Driven by Jerry Harvey in SS/E for Paul Harvey Ford.

8R02J117920

"Dyno Don" Nicholson drove this Mustang for Dick Brannan Ford in SS/EA. He spun a bearing in round 1 at Winternationals.

8F02R135050

Al Joniec raced in this SS/E 135 car for Rice-Holman Ford. Ford documents show that it was prepared by Holman-Moody-Stroppe in Long Beach,

Hubert Platt during SS/E eliminations dispatching an unidentified 1967 Camaro SS 396. (©MotorTrend Group. All rights reserved.)

Jerry Harvey's Paul Harvey Ford 428 Cobra Jet in Super Stock/E eliminations at the 1968 NHRA Winternationals. (©MotorTrend Group. All rights reserved.)

The Holman-Moody-Stroppe hauler is shown at the 1968 Winternationals with Dyno Don Nicholson's Dick Brannan Mustang on top and Gas Ronda's vehicle below it, plus a Torino GT. (©MotorTrend Group. All rights reserved.)

California. At Winternationals, Joniec beat Hubert Platt in the class final, then proceeded to beat Don Grotheer and Tommy Crutchfield in Eliminator rounds 1 and 2. Hubert was then defeated in the Eliminator quarterfinal, and Butch Leal lost in the Eliminator semifinal. In the Eliminator final, Joniec defeated a redlighting Dave Wren.

Gaspar "Gas" Ronda leaning on his 428 Cobra Jet in the staging lanes at Pomona in 1968. (©MotorTrend Group. All rights reserved.)

8F02R135054

Gas Ronda raced this "135" Mustang in SS/EA for Russ Davis Ford. He lost by 1/100 of a second to "Dandy" Dick Landy in the class final and again to Landy in round 1 of Eliminator.

The Other 135s

Five drivers and six cars made their assault at the NHRA Winternationals in 1968. But what about the others? Some went to racers; others went to private hands. Here are stories on several of the more prominent ones.

8F02135007

The first of the "135" cars to be built, it was originally delivered to Paul Harvey Ford in Indianapolis and raced by Bob Coble.

8F02R135031

This car was sold to racer David Lyall and sponsored by Custom Speed Enterprises of St. Claire Shores, Michigan.

8F02R135033

Bridenthal Ford in the hamlet of Greensburg, Ohio, had been campaigning Ford race cars for quite some time. Its Cobra Jet was raced by employee Fred Hertzog, seeing some duty at Dragway 42 in West Salem, among other strips. The dealership sold it in 1971.

8F02R135034

Longueuil, Quebec, Canada, was the home of Sud Automobile, which took delivery of this Cobra Jet. The dealership sold it to George Constantine for $1.00, who raced to promote the dealership. It even appeared in the 1968 NHRA Nationals.

8F02R135037

Rye Ford, located in Westchester County, New York, took delivery and raced this 428 Cobra Jet Mustang through 1969. In April of that year, the driver for the dealership bought the Mustang from the dealership, and he continues to own it today.

8F02R135038

Purchased by Tony Rainero and Frank Lundgren and sponsored by Stark Hickey Ford out of the Detroit suburb of Royal Oak, this 428 Cobra Jet Mustang was sold as a rolling chassis to the Ulrey Brothers in 1971. At some point in their possession, the Mustang was in an accident with their ramp truck and totaled.

8F02R135041

Was originally delivered to Tasca Ford, where it was used for exhibition runs by Bill Lawton. Even Mario Andretti ran it in an exhibition race in Connecticut before it was sold to Clem Smalley Ford in Muskogee, Oklahoma, in April 1969.

8F02R135042

Also delivered to Tasca Ford, it was then sent to Holman-Moody for engine preparation for the 1968 Winternationals, but it's unclear whether it raced—it may have been a backup vehicle. It often could be found racing Super Stock in the Northeast with Bill Lawton behind the wheel.

8F02R135046

This vehicle was known as *Daddy Warbucks* and was driven by Phil Bonner as a match racer. It eventually was run with a tunnel port 427.

Here is Ed Skelton and his Guy's Ford-sponsored 428 Cobra Jet Mustang paired with Ronnie Sox in the Sox & Martin Hemi Road Runner at the 1968 NHRA World Finals in Tulsa. (©MotorTrend Group. All rights reserved.)

CHAPTER FIVE

THE 1968½ COBRA JET

April 1 is April Fools' Day, a celebration of pranks and bald-faced lies meant to get people's attention in funny and/or provocative ways. So, it was an odd choice that Ford picked that day in 1968 to officially announce the 428 Cobra Jet for the Mustang and Fairlane, a month-and-change after the pony car's domination at the NHRA Winternationals in Pomona.

These two 1968 Mustang GTs with the 428 Cobra Jet reflect two of the three available bodystyles: a convertible and a 2+2 fastback.

The cars that ran at Pomona were completely race-tuned machines meant for the single purpose of covering 1,320 feet as rapidly as possible, whereas "proper" street versions of 428 Cobra Jet–quipped Mustangs and Fairlanes were a nice compromise between "fast" and "easy to live with" for the lucky few who checked the proper box on the order form.

As mentioned before, other than the 50 "135" Mustangs built at the end of December 1967, 428 Cobra Jet Mustangs required the GT package. Midsize Fords were a different animal, as the CJ was available in all models save wagons and Rancheros: Fairlane, Fairlane 500, Torino, and Torino GT. The CJ was even available on four-door models! Ford decided not to make the CJ available for the compact Falcon or full-size models such as the Galaxie, although the 340-hp 428 continued to be a regular production option for the latter.

The 428 Cobra Jet was also available for Mercury models. Unlike the Mustang, there was plenty of variation with Cougars, available on base or XR-7, with or without the GT package; the Cobra Jet also replaced the 427 that was the sole engine for the special Cougar GT-E. The Cougar also shared the ram air system with the Mustang, including a black stripe along the hood, but the cat featured a much larger hood scoop.

Similar to the midsize Fords, the Cobra Jet was available for the Mercury Comet, Montego, Montego MX, Montego MX Brougham, Cyclone, and Cyclone GT models, including four-doors. The CJ was not available for full-size Mercurys.

Ford's Answer

Ford desperately needed the Cobra Jet because it was losing the performance sweepstakes to General Motors and Chrysler. Ever since 1965, Ford's performance offerings had been somewhat lacking, appearing to operate with the presumption that the "Total Performance" onslaught on racing was enough to trickle down to the street.

What Ford was not realizing was that there a difference between *racing* and *performance*—"Win on Sunday, sell on Monday" did not work without support from all levels of the marketing channel. This was the beauty of Pontiac, as the GM brand had been successful bringing its racing success (and post-racing success, after GM reaffirmed the AMA ban early in 1963) to the street. An enthusiast inspired by a winning race car could visit a Pontiac dealership and have access to a similar performance vehicle and even obtain the off-road parts if necessary. It relied on knowledgeable salespeople to recognize what a particular enthusiast wanted and to know how to get it (made famous by Royal Pontiac in suburban Detroit).

In comparison, Ford simply wasn't "getting" it. As related in Bob McClurg's book *The Tasca Ford Legacy*, Eric Dahlquist talked about his visit to Ford headquarters to preview a proposed 427 Fairlane: "Bill Holbrook . . . explained at great length how various pieces from the Ford parts bin had been combined to create it. Most were available from the dealer. This is what Ford upper management just didn't get. By far, the greatest percentage of potential muscle car buyers were looking to buy, not build, their own cars."

And the cars available from the factory were lacking. The 1964½–1967 289 high-performance Mustang (or even a 1963½–1965 Fairlane or 1964–1965 Comet), while a fine machine, was not capable of beating up on GTOs. 427 Galaxie production fell drastically for 1965—from several thousand to an estimated 327 units.

When the Fairlane and Comet were upgraded in size (if not class) in 1966, the 390 Fairlane GT and Cyclone GT performance models simply were not competitive against Tri-Power GTOs, and the 427 Fairlane 500 built for racing made no impact on the street because only 57 were built. Production picked up in 1967, which now included the Comet (229 Fairlanes and 60 Comets with the 427), but that still was not enough to make a difference. Even the 390 for the redesigned 1967 Mustang was no help despite being lighter in weight.

Car Life, using a metaphor, stated, "Perhaps the superburger, if it is to be a superburger, needs a little more mustard." In regards to the mechanically similar 1968, *Car and Driver* wrote, "Ford's 390 engine has a reputation for being a bit of a stone."

Evidently, Ford was aware of the scenario: in a May 3, 1968, internal document titled "Lincoln-Mercury Division Performance Merchandising Plans," it was observed that "Our drag racing efforts have been worthwhile, but having suffered from the basic Company problems of creating the image with one-of-a-kind hardware but not supplying the necessary hardware to those who want to run their own performance cars."

1968½ Cobra Jet Racers

Beyond those six cars that the world saw at the 1968 Winternationals, the other 50 purpose-built 428 Cobra Jet Mustangs ended up in the hands of racers and private enthusiasts around the country, with the former experiencing varying levels of success. Thanks to the current interest in historic race cars, if not all things Cobra Jet, many of these "135" cars have been uncovered, documented, and restored.

1968½ Mustang GT: Gateway to the Cobra Jet

A prerequisite to ordering the 428 Cobra Jet for the Mustang was that the GT Equipment Group needed to be specified. This package was available with any V-8 Mustang starting with the 302 4-barrel, but it was mandatory with the CJ. This engine could also be ordered in any of the three

Phil Bonner's *Daddy Warbucks*

Phil Bonner's factory lightweight Cobra Jet Mustang (VIN 8F02R135046) was one of 20 built under DSO 844661 with deleted seam sealer and sound deadener. Known as *Daddy Warbucks*, it ran the match race circuit in Bonner's trademark blue-and-white colors. Milt Schwartz and Terry Sisson were subsequent owners of the Cobra Jet Mustang, and then it was put in storage in 1980 in Belfast, New York, where it remained until 2000.

Don Fezell subsequently bought the retired racer and commissioned Randy DeLisio to bring it back to Bonner's as-raced condition. The Cobra Jet showed a hair over 3,000 miles when it sold for $245,000 at Mecum's Kissimmee auction in 2017.

Although restored with a proper 428 Cobra Jet, Phil Bonner's Daddy Warbucks was match-raced with a tunnel-port 427 for most of its tenure before he sold it in 1969. Milt Schwartz bought it and installed a 427 Cammer. (Photo Courtesy David Newhardt/Mecum Auctions)

Phil Bonner's "135" is one of the 20 built without sound deadener or sealer. Ford sold it to him for $1, then went racing. (Photo Courtesy David Newhardt/Mecum Auctions)

Dave Lyall's Cobra Jet

VIN 8F02R135031 was originally delivered to the Highway Development for Stock Vehicles Department at Ford and then sold to racer Dave Lyall for $1 to compete in the Super Stock wars. However, confusingly, though car 8F02R135052 was earmarked for Lyall, he and others say that's not the car he received. It had received a full rotisserie restoration in street/strip configuration, complete with Cragar S/S wheels, prior to going on the block at Mecum's 2017 Kissimmee auction. Included were copies of the original window sticker, Lyall's $1 contract, a Michigan title search, internal memos on Ford's 428 Cobra Jet Lightweight Mustang program, and Marti Report. High bid was $140,000.

Dave Lyall was the driver for 8F02R135031, which was sponsored by Custom Speed Equipment of the Detroit suburb of St. Claire Shores. (Photo Courtesy David Newhardt/Mecum Auctions)

Bill Ireland's R-Code Racer

Yet another Cobra Jet Mustang racer sold at Mecum Kissimmee in 2017. This one stands out from the rest because it's not a "135" car but it was ordered as such, and in special-order 1965 Ford Poppy Red, no less. It seems that Ford Drag Council president Wild Bill Ireland was offered one of the lightweight Cobra Jets but instead chose to run a CJ Torino. He eventually learned the errors of his ways, but by that time Ford had already distributed all 50 cars. His resolution was to special-order a CJ-equipped Mustang GT fastback without sound deadener and seam sealer.

Bill Ireland of Portland, Oregon, regretted not accepting a 135 car and later ordered a similar one himself with the added novelty of a special-order color. (Photo Courtesy David Newhardt/Mecum Auctions)

Since Bill Ireland's car was ordered with a special-order color, it received a six-digit DSO. The "74" signifies the Seattle District Sales Office, and the other four digits are the special-order numbers. (Photo Courtesy David Newhardt/Mecum Auctions)

Bill Ireland's R-Code Racer
(Continued)

Ford's West Coast racing shop Stroppe & Associates prepared the Northwest Ford Dealers-sponsored Mustang for competition. After Ireland, Gordon Apgar and Gary Barnes owned the vermilion 2+2, with collector Don Fezell buying it in 2001. Randy DeLisio restored the Cobra Jet to its 1968 configuration, but he managed to retain key parts such as traction bars, the roll bar, the driveshaft loop, and stainless steel tubular headers. The new owner paid $200,000 for the honor of owning this 423-mile car.

Bill Ireland represented the Northwest as Ford's factory-sponsored racer. The Ford Drag Council president handled work for a lot of racers with his business. (Photo Courtesy David Newhardt/ Mecum Auctions)

An aftermarket Sun Super Tach graces the dashboard of Bill Ireland's Cobra Jet Mustang GT drag car. It's right in the line of sight. (Photo Courtesy David Newhardt/ Mecum Auctions)

Mustang bodystyles—fastback, hardtop, or convertible—with the majority being the fastback.

The GT package included fog lights mounted in the grille, dual exhaust, longitudinal C-stripe, heavy-duty suspension, 14-inch GT Styled Steel Wheels with Goodyear Polyglas F70x14 tires, GT gas cap, and front-fender emblems. The engine itself added $420.96 to the price of a V-8 Mustang hardtop coupe (approximately $2,700 base), which seems reasonable, but add the GT package, mandatory disc brakes, and 4-speed or Cruise-O-Matic, and the price of an R-code Mustang GT was approaching $4,000.

Hardtop

The hardtop was the bread and butter of the Mustang line, selling almost a quarter of a million units for the model year—approximately half of 1966 hardtop production, but still the market leader by miles. The hardtop may not have been the Mustang's sportiest bodystyle, but it was the bodystyle of choice for performance enthusiasts because it was the lightest Mustang at approximately 3,353 pounds (curb) with the Cobra Jet and 4-speed. Out of 4,766 GT hardtops, only 221 were built with the CJ.

While the 1968 Mustang featured no badges to suggest a Cobra Jet may be lurking underneath the hood (it made do with air induction and black hood stripe), the Shelby GT500KR featured these. (Photo Courtesy David Newhardt/ Mecum Auctions)

The Raven Black Cobra Jet fastback features a gold C-stripe complemented by a Gold Nugget interior. The addition of the GT package didn't change anything in the interior.

This 1968 428 Cobra Jet Mustang GT coupe is believed to be the first CJ coupe built. It also was a "dollar car" campaigned in SS/EA by Wayne Torkelson for Rett-White Ford in Walnut Creek, CA. Picture was taken at Vaca Valley Raceway. (Photo Courtesy Eric English)

The Mustang GT hardtop didn't look as sporty, but it was lighter than the fastback. Nonetheless, most 428 Cobra Jet buyers preferred the fastback. (Photo Courtesy Eric English)

According to research from Marti Auto Works, only 221 1968½ Mustang coupes were built with the Cobra Jet powertrain. Neil Biddlecombe owned this Highland Green CJ coupe from 1968 to 1971, then bought it again in 2008 and had it fully restored by Arild Thu. It's a factory 4.30-geared/C6 automatic car. (Photo Courtesy Eric English)

Marti Auto Works's data indicates the split between automatic and 4-speed CJ 1968½ coupes was about 54/46. If you look closely, you can see that this example was not ordered with a radio. (Photo Courtesy Eric English)

The hood scoop and stripe are subtle on John Rosengrant's 1968½ Raven Black Cobra Jet fastback. This example was originally ordered for drag racing.

With a build date on July 29, 1968, David Garton's Meadowlark Yellow car was among the last 1968½ Cobra Jet Mustangs built. It's also loaded with options like Convenience Control Panel, Interior Décor Group, Visibility Group, and console, among other items. (Photo Courtesy Dale Amy)

Fastback

When the Mustang was introduced in April 1964, the hardtop and convertible were the only bodystyles available. When the 1965 model year officially began, Ford added a stylish, contemporary fastback and christened it the 2+2. In 1966, the convertible actually outsold the 2+2, but the fastback generally was the go-to bodystyle for performance enthusiasts (and those who wanted to pretend), as evidenced by the 12,086 2+2 GTs built in 1968. For 428 Cobra Jets, 1,299 2+2s were built (including the 50 "135" cars).

According to Marti Auto Works, only 60 4-speed 1968½ Cobra Jet fastbacks were built in black.

Convertible

Catching some rays in America's favorite car was not a unique proposition as production saw both sides of 70,000 between 1965–1966. However, a 428 Cobra Jet Mustang GT convertible was an experience few had in 1968 because, out of 1,986 GT ragtops, only 34 were built with the CJ.

The optional Décor group gave the Mustang a more luxurious interior, here shown in Parchment—the perfect complement to Gulfstream Aqua.

This Gulfstream Aqua convertible is one of 34 Mustang GT ragtops built with the 428 Cobra Jet in 1968, and the only one in Gulfstream Aqua. No CJ convertibles were built without the GT package.

Shelby Mustangs

The 1967 Shelby GT500 was a unique animal in the Mustang world, being the first to receive the 428 engine and the only Mustang ever to feature multiple carburetion. The 428 Police Interceptor as used in the GT500 was rated at 355 hp with two 4-barrel Holleys atop an aluminum 427 medium-riser intake (a handful of 427 GT500s were built too).

Both the GT500 and High-Performance 289-powered GT350 featured all new styling in line with the redesigned Mustang, but the Shelby featured fiberglass bits to give it a styling edge. The nose featured a grille with two driving lights in the middle (later changed to the outer edges to comply with lighting laws in all 50 states).

The hood featured a large scoop that was lacking on the regular Mustang. Functional scoops also adorned the sides behind the door (for brake cooling) and on the C-pillar (for the interior), and out back a fiberglass trunk lid with integrated spoiler further distinguished the Shelby. Even the taillights, borrowed from the Cougar (without the chrome trim), appeared custom. All Shelbys also received an integrated, padded roll bar, racing harnesses, three-spoke wood-grain steering wheel, Stewart Warner gauges, and 140-mph speedometer with 8,000-rpm tachometer.

Despite having the biggest engine available in a pony car in 1968, the 428 Police Interceptor in the Shelby GT500 was not the fastest in the market—solid-lifter 396 Camaros and Ram Air Firebirds initially ruled the segment. (Photo Courtesy David Newhardt/Mecum Auctions)

From September 1967 to April 1968, this was the hottest Shelby. When the Cobra Jet was introduced, the GT500 was replaced by the GT500KR for the duration of the model year. (Photo Courtesy David Newhardt/Mecum Auctions)

The facelifted 1968 Shelby Mustang featured a number of changes. Perhaps the biggest was something that couldn't be seen: production was transferred from Venice, California, to Ionia, Michigan, as Ford had taken control of the builds (all from the Metuchen, New Jersey, plant) and subcontracted A.O. Smith to finish them. Otherwise, the new model year brought refinement with a redesigned hood and nose (now with rectangular fog lights) plus sequential taillights borrowed from the 1965 Thunderbird. The GT350 was downgraded to a 250-hp 302 (with a Paxton supercharger, an unusual option), while the GT500's 428 Police Interceptor was reduced to a single Holley 4-barrel yet was upgraded on paper to 360 hp.

Once the Cobra Jet was introduced in April, the GT500KR superseded the regular GT500. Horsepower was rated the same as the Mustang's, but don't let that fool you—the CJ was faster than both PIs from 1967–1968.

The distinguishing characteristics that the Cobra Jet–equipped Shelby had over other models was the "KR" designation and the "Cobra Jet 428" badges on the front fenders. (Photo Courtesy David Newhardt/Mecum Auctions)

The 1968 Shelby Mustang featured more refined styling from the 1967 redesign. Sequential 1965 Thunderbird taillights were a new feature. (Photo Courtesy David Newhardt/Mecum Auctions)

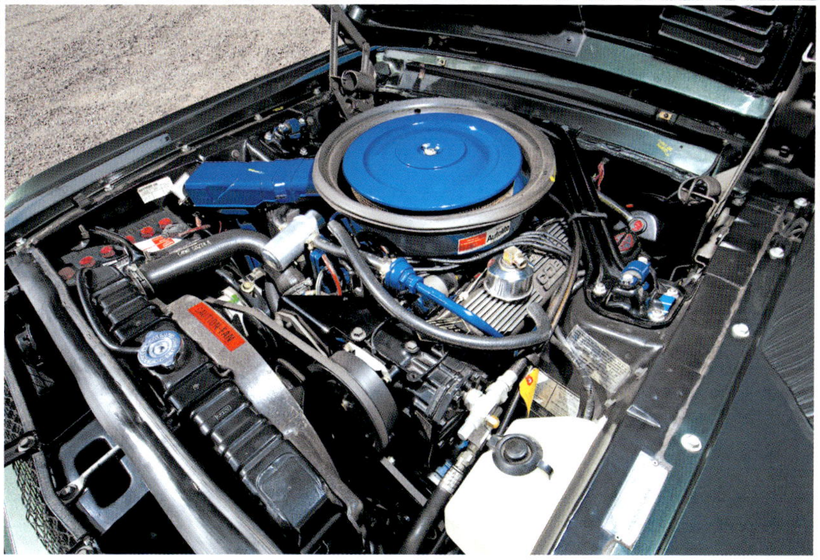

All 1968 Shelby models featured the same hood, with two scoops at the leading edge, but the GT500KR featured a functional system with Shelby-specific air cleaner and valve covers. (Photo Courtesy David Newhardt/Mecum Auctions)

Fastback

Shelby had played with experimental hardtops for 1967–1968, but none ever made production. The fastback was Shelby's core model, and with the advent of the 1968 series, it became more luxurious than before. Perhaps that rubbed purists the wrong way, but when the GT500KR was introduced, it also became the fastest Shelby ever. Interestingly, with 1,571 Shelby GT500KR fastbacks built, it was more popular than the 428 Cobra Jet Mustang.

Convertible

After an aborted attempt to produce a convertible in 1967, Shelby Automotive offered one for both the GT350 and GT500 in 1968. There was much more to the Shelby ragtop than a Mustang with fiberglass body panels—the standard roll bar featured tie-downs for surfboards. Like the fastback, when April rolled around, the GT500 convertible was replaced by the GT500KR. And in the case of rarity, 518 GT500KR ragtops were built, which was 484 more than the number of Cobra Jet Mustang GT convertibles produced.

Propelling the Cobra Jet

Except for the 50 "135" fastbacks, 1968 428 Cobra Jet pony cars came with ram air, chromed engine highlights, Competition handling suspension, F70x14 Wide Ovals, 3.50 gears (Traction-Lok was extra), and a heavy-duty 80-amp battery. Required options were the GT package (for the Mustang, not the Cougar), power front disc brakes, and 4-speed or heavy-duty Cruise-O-Matic automatic transmission. Cobra Jet–equipped Fairlane/Torino and Comet/Montego/Cyclone vehicles, on the other hand, came with similar chrome accents plus a chrome-plated air cleaner, 3.50:1 gears, a heavy-duty 80-amp battery, and 428 emblems on the front fender. They also required a Cruise-O-Matic transmission, the GT suspension (standard on the Torino GT and Cyclone GT), power front disc brakes, and F70x14 Wide Ovals.

Sitting on top of the 428 Cobra Jet for Mustangs and Cougars was a special air cleaner with a vacuum-actuated butterfly valve that funneled air directly into a 735-cfm Holley carburetor from a scoop on the hood. That scoop and its complementary black stripe was the quick way to identify a CJ on the street aside of the 50 "135" Mustangs.

Along with the 4-speed or Cruise-O-Matic 3-speed automatic transmission was a 9-inch rear end featured gear ratio choices of 3.50 (single trac-

1968 Cobra Jet Mustang Specifications

Wheelbase	Weight	Number built	Base price
108.0 inches	3,620 pounds	1,299	$3,600

Powering the Mustang

Domestic Mustang customers had a complete selection of engines to choose from in 1968:

- T = 115-hp 200-ci 6-cylinder
- C = 195-hp 289-ci 2V V-8
- F = 210-hp 302-ci 2V V-8
- J = 230-hp 302-ci 4V V-8
- X = 280-hp 390-ci 2V V-8
- S = 325-hp 390-ci 4V V-8
- R = 335-hp 428-ci Cobra Jet V-8
- W = 390-hp 427-ci V-8 (not produced)

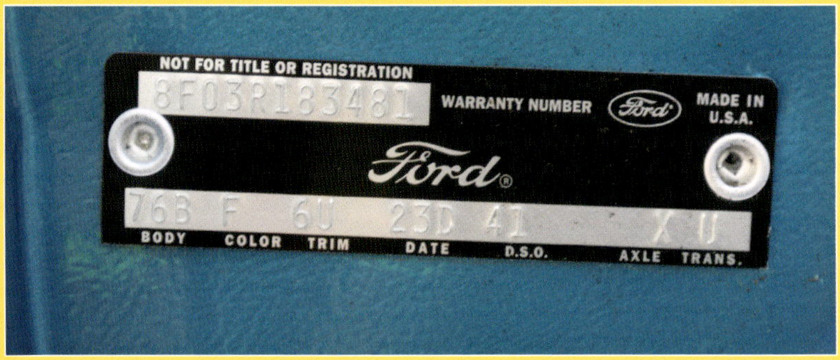

The data plate for this Mustang gives information on VIN, body code (convertible with luxury interior), color (Gulfstream Aqua), interior trim (Parchment Décor buckets), scheduled build date (April 23, 1968), District Sales Office (Chicago region), rear axle (3.91 locking), and transmission (C-6 automatic).

1968 Mustang Specifications
(Continued)

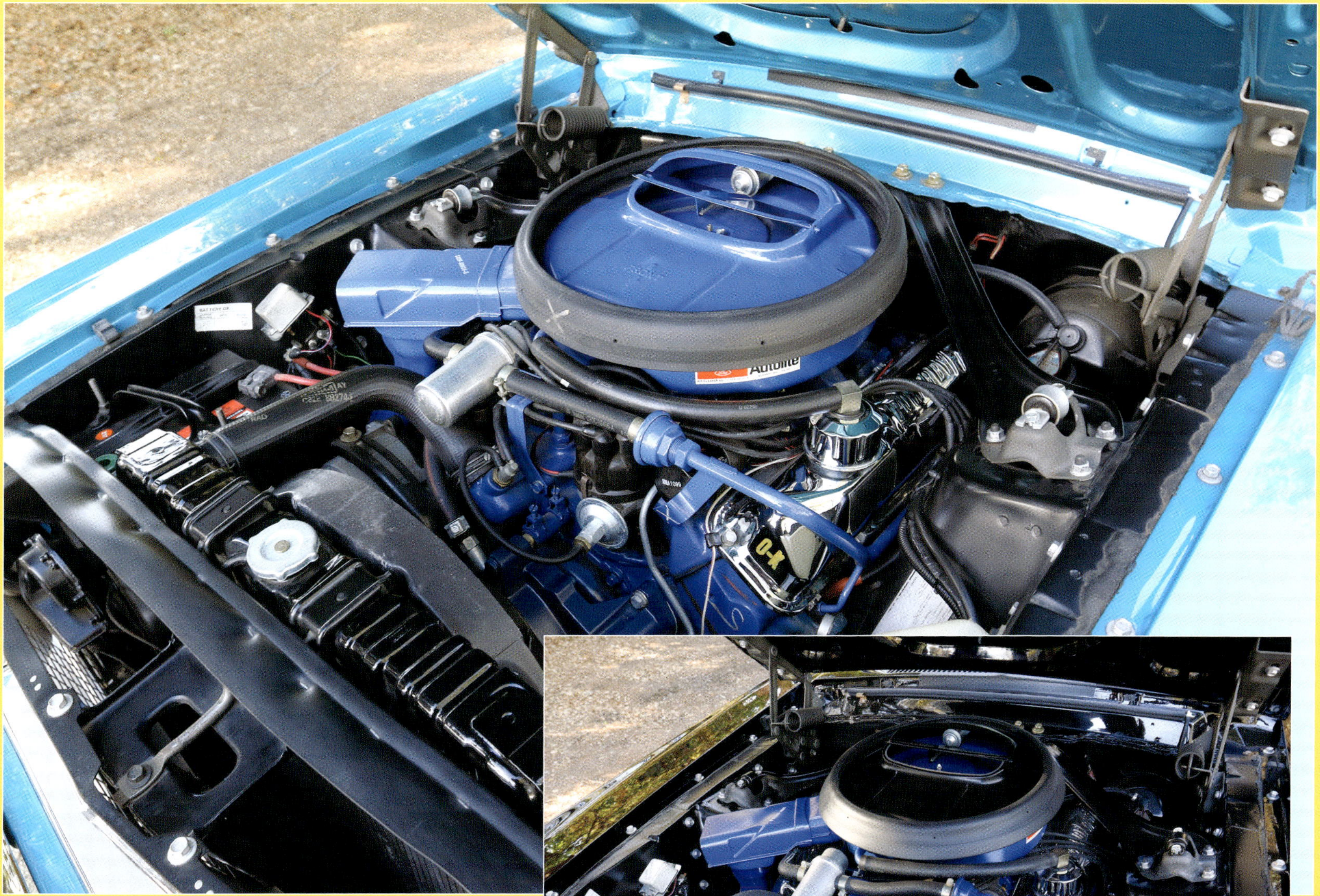

Initial Cobra Jet Mustangs and Cougars received a ram air lid painted blue. Sometime in mid-May 1968, Ford began transitioning to a black lid.

Rosengrant's Raven Black Cobra Jet has a black ram air lid. Look closely and you can see the blue air cleaner lid through the flapper valve.

Q-code Cobra Jets and 427 Mustangs?

In the Mustang world, you'll hear terms like "K-code," "R-code," and other letter-specific designations that refer to the fifth character in the VIN. In the past, some enthusiasts have erroneously believed that there were Q-code Cobra Jets in 1968, but Kevin Marti confirms that the records his company has licensed from Ford do not include any 1968 Mustangs equipped with a Q engine code—the VINs he's seen for alleged Q-code cars have all turned out to be cars that originally left the factory as C-code 289s, meaning someone modified the cars and altered the VIN. All 1968 Mustang and Cougar Cobra Jets came with ram air and featured an R in the fifth character of the VIN.

Midsize Fords and Mercurys also used the same R-code designation in 1968, although they were not available with air induction until 1969. The Q-code engine in 1968 was the 340-hp 428 available for full-size vehicles, but perhaps the crux of the confusion is that, in 1969, Q became the engine code for the 428 Cobra Jet without ram air (those with ram air were R-codes).

Which leads to another urban legend: the 427 Mustang. According to Marti Auto Works, no Mustangs were built with the 427, but the Cougar was a different story—the 427 was the centerpiece for the special-edition Cougar GT-E. The Cobra Jet replaced this engine in April 1968, and the CJ availability was expanded to all Cougars (unlike the 427, which was restricted).

What makes this Mustang unique among other Cobra Jet Mustangs from 1968 is the generous option list, including Décor interior with upper and lower consoles plus the Convenience Group, among others. (Photo Courtesy David Newhardt/Mecum Auctions)

tion was standard—Equa-Loc differential at $79 was a wise extra), 3.91, or 4.30:1. Four-speed cars also received staggered rear shocks (one ahead of and one behind the axle) for better wheel hop control.

Color Me Cobra Jet

Paint and interior options were the same as any other Mustang, so while the initial 50 Cobra Jets were all Wimbledon White with a black interior, production models ran the gamut with the full palette of Ford's 1968 colors and interiors, plus a few that were built in special-order colors per customer request.

All Cobra Jet Mustang hoods for 1968 featured a ram air scoop. After the first 50 "135" cars were built, Ford added a black scoop and stripe.

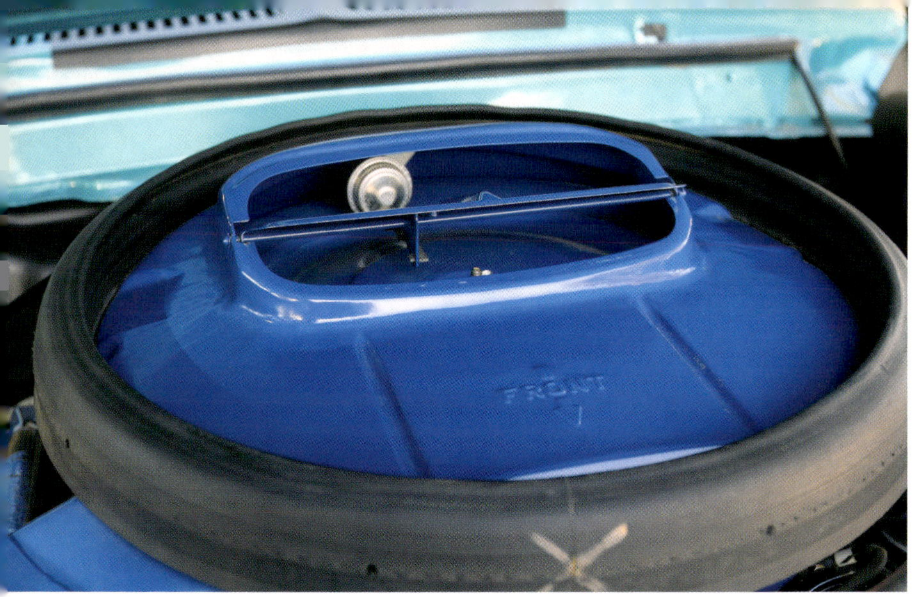

The only Mustangs to have air induction in 1968 were those equipped with the 428 Cobra Jet.

The black ram air lid was phased into production in May 1968, which included a horseshoe-shaped clip spot-welded to the underside. It mated to the air cleaner's breather tube elbow to prevent the lid from rotating due to vibration.

While the first 50 "135" cars were all plain, the rest of the Cobra Jet Mustangs were somewhat ornate due to the premium equipment included with the mandatory GT package. (Photo Courtesy Dale Amy)

Cobra Jet Plants

Mustangs were built in three plants in 1968: Metuchen, San Jose, and at "Ford Ground Zero" in Dearborn. The overwhelming majority were built in the latter, with the Shelby GT500KR only emerging from Metuchen.

Fairlane/Torino: Calling the GTO's Bluff

While the Mustang gets all the glory (with its cousin, the Cougar, barely attaining any notice), an almost identical Cobra Jet package was available for any midsize Ford save wagons and Rancheros.

The completely redesigned Fairlane/Torino was a big step for Ford. Unique among the Big Three was the fact Ford did not offer a two-door sedan—all two-doors were hardtops, while all four-doors were sedans. Styling mimicked full-size Fords, which had been facelifted from 1967. Brand new for Ford was the Torino series, somewhat replacing the Fairlane 500/XL in the Fairlane totem pole. Whereas the XL was sporty, the Torino was luxurious. The sole sporty model was now the Torino GT, replacing the Fairlane GT, with the model expanded to include a fastback in addition to a hardtop coupe and convertible.

Production Statistics

Year and Plant	Earliest VIN	Latest VIN	Total
1968 Dearborn	8F02R135007	8F02R220813	1,128
1968 San Jose	8R01R158074	8R02R172223	171
1968 Metuchen (Shelby)	8T02R199216	8T02R216332	1,571
Total 1968 Mustang:			1,299
Total 1968 (including Shelby):			2,870

(Statistics provided courtesy of Marti Auto Works and the Shelby American Automobile Club)

Like many Ford products, a 427 was advertised but never produced, leaving the 325-hp 390 as the top engine before the 428 Cobra Jet appeared in April. Air induction and 4-speed manual were not available for midsize CJs, unlike the pony cars. All told, 840 Fairlane/Torinos were built with the CJ.

Fairlane

The base Fairlane represented the value-leader of Ford's midsize product line. A two-door hardtop and four-door sedan were the available bodystyles for the model. Standard was a rubber floor mat, cloth and vinyl bench seat, heater, and not much else. Thirty-nine two-door hardtops were built with the 428 Cobra Jet.

Fairlane 500

A step up from the Fairlane, the Fairlane 500 was available as a two-door hardtop, fastback, convertible, and four-door sedan. Fancier interior trim (with the option for bucket seats) and color-keyed carpeting were the major upgrades. It is known that 22 hardtops and an unspecified number of fastbacks were built with the 428 Cobra Jet. No Fairlane 500 convertibles were built with the CJ.

Torino

The new Torino two-door hardtop and four-door sedan included a richer interior selection in vinyl and cloth, simulated woodgrain paneling on the dashboard, electric clock, matte black grille, deluxe wheel covers, and distinctive Torino moldings and medallions. An unspecified number of Torinos were built with the Cobra Jet.

Torino GT

The Torino GT was the updated replacement for the 1966–1967 Fairlane GT. Newly added to the roster was a contemporary fastback. Standard engine was a 302 2-barrel, but that was downgraded to a 289 2-barrel in the middle of the year. Included features for the Torino GT were sporty bucket seats, stripes (rocker for the hardtop and convertible, C-stripe for the fastback), and styled steel wheels with Wide Oval white sidewalls. By far the biggest recipient of the 428 Cobra Jet was the Torino GT fastback, of which 661 were built, including one with the 4-speed—apparently, it was built for a Ford executive. No information on CJ Torino GT coupes is available at this time, but 14 Torino GT convertibles were built with the CJ.

Smart racers picked the Fairlane or Fairlane 500 (pictured) for quicker ETs. Both models offered fewer frills and, hence, less weight than the upmarket Torino GT. (Photo Courtesy Keith Blasius)

Fairlane and Torino two-door hardtop coupes featured different taillights than the fastback. A 428 Cobra Jet powering an unassuming vehicle such as this 1968 Fairlane 500 was the perfect Q-ship for unassuming competitors used to eating up Fords. (Photo Courtesy Keith Blasius)

The Torino GT convertible was chosen to pace the Indianapolis 500 in 1968. Out of 709 pace cars built by Ford, only two were equipped with the 428 Cobra Jet. In total, 14 Torino GT convertibles were built with the CJ. (Photo Courtesy Indianapolis Motor Speedway)

The 1968 Torino GT fastback came equipped with racy C-stripes that distinguished it from the others in the midsize packs. Hardtop coupes and convertibles used the traditional GT stripe above the rockers. (Photo Courtesy Lennie Lawson)

Even more than the Mustang, Ford's midsize series was pining for something better than the 390. The 428 Cobra Jet seemed like a natural for the all-new Torino GT fastback. (Photo Courtesy Lennie Lawson)

This is what the 428 Cobra Jet looked like when installed in 1968 Fairlanes and Torinos. Unlike the Mustang, air induction wouldn't be available with this engine until 1969. (Photo Courtesy Lennie Lawson)

Mercury Cougar

While the Cougar and Mustang were built on the same platform, the Cougar was a different kind of cat. Sporting a wheelbase 3 inches longer and following a different marketing philosophy, the Cougar was touted as "America's first luxury sports car at a popular price" and, hence, featured a more opulent option list. The cars shared most of the same engine choices, including the 428 Cobra Jet once it was released in 1968.

There were a variety of Cougars offered when the car was introduced in 1967: the base model and XR-7, both of which came with a 302 2-barrel standard. Either model was available with the GT Performance Group, which featured a standard 6.5L 390 (rated at 320 hp) and suspension upgrades, among other items.

For 1968, there were only minor tweaks to styling and engines, but two new FE engine choices allowed the Cougar to play with the big boys. In total, Mercury built 244 Cougars with the 428 Cobra Jet in 1968.

A neat feature Cougars shared with the Thunderbird and Shelby Mustangs were sequential turn signals. Modern-day Mustangs have revived the gimmick.

Cougar

The standard Cougar, just like all other Cougars, continued to be available only as a two-door hardtop. Standard equipment included bright curb moldings, front bucket seats, 302 2-barrel with floor-shifted 3-speed, wall-to-wall carpeting, and more. The top engine was the 325-hp 390 (aside of the 427 with the GT-E package) until the 428 Cobra Jet was introduced.

John Elliot's Cougar was a base model, so in standard form it could be rather austere when superfluous options were left out. Notice the lack of radio. (Photo Courtesy Richard Truesdell)

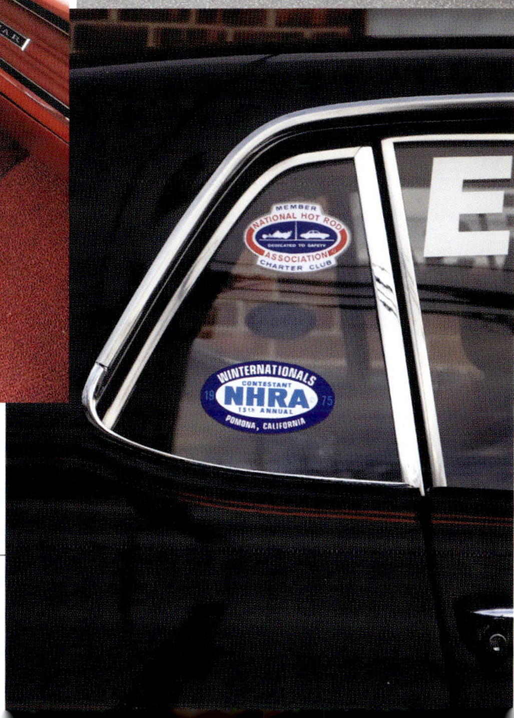

John Elliot was a driver for the Border Bandits, sponsored by Sandy Elliot Ltd. This 1968 Cougar GT with the 428 Cobra Jet was his street car that he occasionally raced in E/SA. (Photos Courtesy Richard Truesdell)

There were few changes for the Mercury Cougar in 1968. Most noticeable were the side marker lights. Note the Cobra Jet scoop seen through the windshield. (Photo Courtesy Royce Peterson)

By the end of the model year, Mercury had built 113 standard Cougars with the CJ (not including those with the GT-E package).

Cougar XR-7

The XR-7 took over from where the standard Cougar left off, somewhat playing the role of European-inspired *gran turismo*. Most notable was leather/vinyl seat trim and full instrumentation complemented with

This 1968 Cougar XR-7 with the 428 Cobra Jet was earmarked as a promotional vehicle, and rumor has it that Don Nicholson was its first owner. (Photo Courtesy Royce Peterson)

The Cougar XR-7 received a European-inspired interior, including nifty toggle switches. (Photo Courtesy Royce Peterson)

burnished walnut-toned appliqué, and overhead console. Other XR-7 equipment included insignia on the C-pillar, special wheel covers, vinyl-covered door trim panels with map pockets plus door assist straps, and more.

New for 1968 was a one-year-only sub-model called XR7-G. The *G* was a reference to American racing hero and Mercury team racer Dan Gurney. This was a special model only for 1968, as Gurney left for Plymouth the following year. The G package included a fiberglass hood scoop (shared with the 427 GT-E), road lamps, bullet-shaped racing mirror, hood pins, quad exhaust tips, radial FR70-14 tires, and more. XR-7 Cobra Jet production amounted to 94 (not including those with the GT-E package). Included in that number are 14 XR7-Gs.

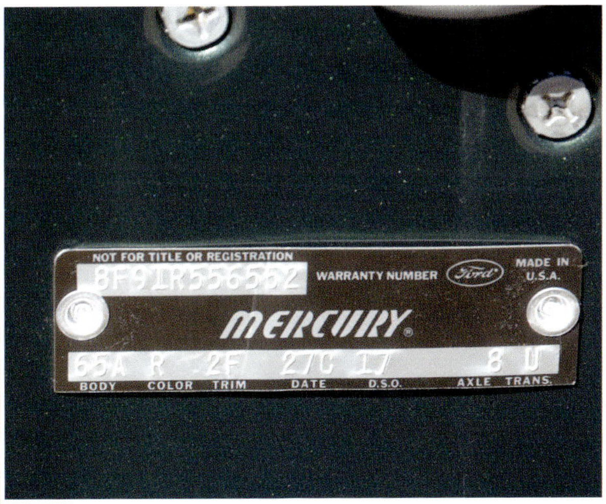

The data plate reads as follows: Standard Cougar hardtop painted Augusta Green with Saddle Décor buckets with a scheduled build of March 27, 1968, delivered to the region served by the Washington, DC, District Sales Office. It came with a 3.50 non-locking rear and C6 automatic.

The Medium Saddle Décor interior is a classic pairing with the Augusta Green paint.

Cougar GT

The GT package was available for both the standard Cougar and the XR-7. When ordered, the following items were added to the equipment list: Marauder 390 GT engine with 325 hp plus heavy-duty 3-speed manual transmission, low-restriction dual exhaust, chrome dress-up kit, low-restriction air cleaner, power front disc brakes, Firestone Wide Oval F70-14 red- or white-line tires, performance handling package, 9-inch rear, and GT identification. When the 428 Cobra Jet became available, it was also available with the GT package.

Cougar GT-E

Mercury stepped up its performance program for the Cougar with the introduction of the GT-E performance package. Equipped with a somewhat mild version of the 427 with 390 hp, paired with the Merc-O-Matic Select-Shift, the GT-E also included the performance handling package, styled steel wheels, power disc brakes, a power dome, and non-functional hood scoop; a new, functional design was implemented for the 428 Cobra Jet when it replaced the 427. CJ GT-E production amounted to 14 standard Cougars and 23 XR-7s.

Like the Mustang GT, the 1968 Cougar with the 428 Cobra Jet received a black hood scoop with stripe to the nose. The Cougar's hood scoop, however, was noticeably larger. (Photo Courtesy Richard Truesdell)

This 428 Cobra Jet-equipped 1968 Cougar, a standard model with the GT package, was the first one sold to the public. Cobra Jet Cougars were available in a number of permutations. (Photo Courtesy Richard Truesdell)

The Missing Lynx Cougar

On August 21, 1967, car 8F93W500038 was built in Dearborn. A 1968 Cougar XR-7 GT-E, it was a "Home Office Reserve" special order for "Introductory Show Car Unit" purposes. It appeared in a brochure and at least one magazine article. It also likely made appearances around the country for promotional purposes leading up to the January 1968 debut of the GT-E package.

In December 1967, car #38 went to Ford's X-garage to be reconfigured with an embryonic version of what would become the 428 Cobra Jet. Keep in mind that this was around the time when the "135" Mustangs were being built. Upon release, the rechristened GT-E was lent to both *Car Craft* and *High-Performance Cars* magazines in anticipation for the April 1968 launch of the Cobra Jet. When the need to arouse positive press was achieved, car #38 was not scrapped (as often was protocol). Instead, it was driven by a Ford employee before being sold at auction to a dealership. By the early 1990s, after 15-plus years of deterioration from sitting outside, the GT-E was saved by an enthusiast and sold to a Cougar expert who restored it over the course of nine years.

Compare this Augusta Green Cougar GT-E with the similarly hued Cougar GT that appeared previously. The GT-E featured horizontal trim on the grille and silver paint running along the lower body. (Photo Courtesy Owls Head Transportation Museum)

Early Cougar GT-Es featured a 427 exclusive to the model, but the 428 Cobra Jet replacement was shared with other Cougars. (Photo Courtesy Owls Head Transportation Museum)

Out of 37 Cougar GT-Es built with the 428 Cobra Jet, only 3 were built with the 4-speed—all of them XR-7s. (Photo Courtesy Owls Head Transportation Museum)

Interestingly, Mercury built a number of 427 GT-Es *after* the CJ was introduced—30 in April, 12 in May, and 4 in June. For the four months left in the model year, only 37 GT-Es were built with the R-code 428 GT-Es—one in April, 12 in May, 16 in June, and 8 in July, according to Marti Auto Works. Three of those were 4-speeds.

Midsize Mercurys

Like the Fairlane/Torino, the Comet/Montego/Cyclone was completely redesigned. Mercury too did not offer a two-door sedan, and convertible availability was limited as both the Cyclone and Cyclone GT convertibles were discontinued. Similar to the Torino, Mercury introduced a model name that would absorb Comet models entirely: Montego.

Mercury also advertised the 427, but it was never installed in a Cyclone or other midsize model. When the 428 Cobra Jet debuted, it was available in all midsize models save wagons, and anyone wanting ram air and/or 4-speed would have to wait for the 1969 models. Cobra Jet production was much rarer on the Mercury side, with 225 R-codes being built.

Comet

Whereas the Fairlane continued to represent part of Ford's midsize product line, all that was left for the entry-level Comet model was the Sports Coupe. "Beautifully on target for style and economy," touted Mercury in its brochure. Standard equipment included armrests front and rear, cloth and vinyl bench seat, and not much else. For the enthusiast wanting to go racing, the 428 Cobra Jet Comet was their best bet, but only 24 buyers took that opportunity.

Montego

One step up from the Comet was the all-new Montego, available as a

It was unusual for a buyer to specify the 1968 Montego with the 428 Cobra Jet, especially with the sporty Cyclone and Q-ship Comet in Mercury's arsenal. Only 11 were built. (Photo Courtesy Bob Boudreau)

two-door hardtop and four-door sedan. As to be expected, the Montego featured a little more brightwork and a fancier interior—the pleated cloth-and-vinyl variety (or all vinyl, if you preferred)—plus the color of walnut on the instrument panel, and curb moldings. Only 11 folks ordered a Montego with the 428 Cobra Jet.

Montego MX

The new Montego MX was available as a two-door hardtop, four-door sedan, and as Mercury's only midsize convertible. The MX featured upper body paint stripe, lower body side molding with simulated wood insert, bright wheel lip molding, and, for sedans, bright metal upper door frames. Inside you'd find color-keyed deep loop carpeting, simulated woodgrain on the lower dashboard and door panels, instrument panel courtesy lights, and Tremblant fabric and vinyl interior trim. Buckets were available for two-door models. It is unknown how many MXs were built with the 428 Cobra Jet.

Montego MX Brougham

At the top of the Montego series, the MX Brougham gave the Montego line a dose of Park Lane luxury in a midsized package. The two-door hardtop and four-door sedan added door assist straps, deluxe insulation package, simulated walnut deluxe steering wheel, and Camelot fabric and vinyl bench seat, among other features. No Broughams were built with the 428 Cobra Jet.

Cyclone

Close to the hearts of performance enthusiasts was the completely new 1968 Cyclone. The convertible had been discontinued, but a new fastback joined the hardtop. As before, there was both a Cyclone and a Cyclone GT, with the latter featuring standard bucket seats and a suspension upgrade, among other items. Like the Torino GT, the 390/325 was the top engine until April, when the 428 Cobra Jet gave new life to a car that was winning in NASCAR, but not so much on the streets. By far the most popular Mercury CJ was the Cyclone GT fastback with 138 built.

The 1968 Cyclone GT received upper beltline stripes as a distinguishing feature compared to the base Cyclone. A hardtop coupe was also available but much rarer. Note the 428 badge above the GT badge. (Photo Courtesy John Drilling)

Mercury dealerships in the Atlanta district created the Cyclone 500 drive-away promotion for the Atlanta 500. The Washington, DC, district joined Atlanta for the World 600 at Charlotte Motor Speedway and added a companion Cougar 500. (Photo Courtesy John Drilling)

Air induction was not available for 428 Cobra Jet–equipped Cyclones and any other midsize models in 1968. Otherwise, it was the same engine as installed in the Cougar. (Photo Courtesy John Drilling)

CHAPTER SIX

1969 AND THE DEBUT OF THE SUPER COBRA JET

Coming off the successful 1968 introduction of the 428 Cobra Jet, Ford was poised to continue the momentum and expand. And why not? The competition was stepping up its game too, and Ford didn't want a repeat of 1967, when the big-block Mustang was hunted down on a regular basis by big-blocks from other manufacturers in the stoplight grand prix.

Perhaps the quintessential 428 Cobra Jet car is the 1969 Mustang Mach I. When equipped with the R-code 428 with Shaker hood scoop, it put Ford on equal footing with the industry's best in terms of style, image, and performance.

Ford

Cobra Jet availability was expanded for 1969. Ranchero buyers could now enjoy 428 power, and the CJ wasn't restricted to Mustangs with the GT package. Perhaps the biggest news was that the CJ became standard for a new midsize model called the Cobra. It was the answer to the Plymouth Road Runner, a cheap Belvedere with standard 335-hp 383, 4-speed, and little else. The Fairlane-based Cobra and the Mustang Mach I were Ford's new image vehicles that represented FoMoCo's strength in the market. No longer would the manufacturer be an also-ran on the street.

Mustang

The king of the pony cars received a contemporary redesign to reflect the longer/lower/wider trends of the time. While the wheelbase remained 108 inches, body length increased by 3.8 inches and weight followed. Front end styling was influenced by the GT package of previous years, as now all Mustangs featured quad headlights with two surrounding both sides of the grille. A new 351 "Windsor" small-block gave Ford a much-needed step in between the 302 and the 390 (the latter making its final appearance). Engine choices remained somewhat similar to 1968 with a 250-ci 6-cylinder joining the 200 6-cylinder but the 289, 302 4-barrel, and 390 2-barrel being discontinued.

Also available for performance fans was a Trans-Am-inspired Boss 302 and a NASCAR-inspired Boss 429.

Smart racers in 1969 chose the Mustang coupe with the 428 Cobra Jet over the vain Mach I. This one has the R-code CJ, as evidenced by the Shaker. Perhaps smarter racers would choose the Q-code CJ with flat hood? (Photo Courtesy Cheryl Hazenberg)

Hardtop

Ford claimed the 1969 Mustang hardtop had all the goodies you buy a Mustang for: individually adjustable, foam-padded vinyl bucket seats; fully synchronized, floor-shifted 3-speed manual; color-keyed carpeting; dual sun visors; heater with defroster; and more. Any engine except the Bosses was available, and considering the hardtop was the lightest bodystyle in the Mustang series, smart racers took note of this. Out of 13,261 428 Cobra Jet Mustangs built, only 243 were hardtops and, of those, 52 were ordered with the Drag Pack.

Es Muy Grande!

A new addition to the 1969 Mustang hardtop coupe was the Grandé. As the Mustang's new luxury model, the Grandé featured a special soft-ride suspension, 55 pounds of extra sound insulation, a luxury cloth and vinyl seat trim, teak-toned instrument and door panels, three-spoke Rim Blow steering wheel, two-tone narrow tape stripe, and more.

The Grandé was available with any regular-production engine except the R-code Cobra Jet with ram air. Per Marti Auto Works, out of 243 Cobra Jet hardtops built in 1969, only 37 were Grandés, all built with the Q-code CJ.

Pony cars in general received upgraded trim from the cheapest models in a manufacturer's portfolio—witness standard carpet over rubber floor mat. Nonetheless, this 428 Super Cobra Jet Mustang hardtop coupe is bare bones—there is little to suggest there's more inside other than a radio. (Photo Courtesy Cheryl Hazenberg)

This unassuming Mustang coupe is a Grandé packing 428 Cobra Jet power. Not a Q-ship as much as a nose-heavy luxury grand tourer. (Photo Courtesy Nelson Cardadeiro)

The Q-code 428 Cobra Jet came with chrome dress-up items regardless of Mustang model. The engine was a snug fit. (Photo Courtesy Nelson Cardadeiro)

A peek at the upscale Grandé interior. Wood highlights, plush cloth seats, and sporty three-spoke rim blow steering wheel were some of the standard features. (Photo Courtesy Nelson Cardadeiro)

A common misconception about the Mustang Grandé is that they all came with a vinyl top—it was an option. Note the Grandé-specific stripe. (Photo Courtesy Nelson Cardadeiro)

Jim Woods's Grandé

Jim Woods from North Carolina displayed his Raven Black 1969 Grandé Cobra Jet at the 50th Anniversary Cobra Jet Reunion in Norwalk, Ohio, in July 2018. The 4-speed Top-Loader transmission makes Jim's Grandé one of nine, and the only one of those painted black.

Interestingly, the car was ordered as Stock, meaning that it was ordered by Bob Reed Ford in Denver for the sales lot. Why a dealer would order such a car is a mystery, since its market appeal was limited compared to a CJ Mach I. The Grandé was built on October 25, 1968, but didn't sell until October 16, 1969, to Mary Ann Valentine.

Ms. Valentine kept the car until around 1980, at which point it went through "a bunch of flippers," according to Jim. Denver restorer Kris Kanack restored the Grandé in 1992, and it was later bought by California collector Kenn Funk. Years later, Jim found it at a consignment dealer.

More of a driver than a show car, Jim's Grandé shows 98,000 miles. "I like to show up at big events because of its unusual scarcity. I love it when people walk away from the car muttering, 'It can't be a real car, they didn't make any of those.' The power steering and power disc brakes make it a very pleasant driver. It doesn't require a lot of work and goes down the road really nice."

A substantial 150,637 Mustang hardtops were built in 1969. According to Marti Auto Works, 105 of those were built with the Q-code 428 Cobra Jet without ram air, and 37 of those were Grandés. Of those, nine had 4-speeds but only one was Raven Black.

Jim Woods's Grandé
(Continued)

The Mustang Grandé was a way to increase the Mustang's appeal to those who desired a bit more luxury. It worked for the Mercury Cougar XR-7, right?

When the 428 Cobra Jet was ordered, the Mustang Grandé was restricted to the Q-code CJ, so you will not find one with a Shaker.

The Grandé outfitted the hardtop with an upscale interior among other items. This 428 Cobra Jet also is equipped with a 4-speed, which was unusual for this model.

Jim Woods's 428 Cobra Jet Grandé does pretty decent burnouts! Believe it or not, it was ordered for dealer stock—this was not a customer-ordered vehicle.

Convertible

The Mustang convertible was America's favorite ragtop when it first hit the streets, but convertible sales began a decline that eventually led to their disappearance in the 1970s. Nonetheless, the Mustang convertible managed to carry the series in style for 1969. In addition to the features included in the hardtop, the convertible featured a manual top with vinyl backlight, color-keyed boot, and fastening latches—pretty basic stuff. But a Mustang convertible didn't have to be basic, as the series had an arm's length of options available for the penny-pincher or the high roller. Like all the other Mustang bodystyles, the 428 Cobra Jet was available for the convertible. Out of 14,744 ragtops, only 122 were built with the CJ. According to Marti Auto Works, 14 of those were built with the Drag Pack.

2+2 = SportsRoof

The signature fastback was now referred to as "SportsRoof" for 1969. The SportsRoof featured all the hardtop's equipment plus included an integrated Kamm-like spoiler, ventless side glass, swing-out rear quarter windows, and tinted rear glass in addition to what was standard for the hardtop. The SportsRoof consisted of the bulk of 428 Cobra Jet production with 12,896 built, most of them Mach Is.

Ford produced 122 1969 Mustang convertibles with the 428 Cobra Jet, which was half of the number of Shelby GT500 ragtops built. Of the 122, 50 were Q-code CJs. (Photo Courtesy Jerry Heasley)

Ferguson Four-Wheel Drive

Ferguson Research Ltd. was a British company founded by Harry Ferguson to develop four-wheel-drive systems for automobiles. As part-owner of Massey-Ferguson tractors, Ferguson didn't live to see the success of his system beyond the development of the Coventry Climax Formula 1 racer in 1960, but his company's tenure through the end of the decade included the production Jensen FF (Ferguson Formula) in 1966 and numerous experimental vehicles in a bid to interest manufacturers.

One of those was a 1969 Mustang imported to a European division of Ford Motor Company. It was a Q-code 428 Cobra Jet SportsRoof with Cruise-O-Matic, Traction-Lok differential, Competition suspension, power steering with tilt, and air-conditioning. According to the January 2000 issue of *Classic Cars*, upon arrival to the United Kingdom, it was fitted with an oil cooler and Koni shocks, plus the 428 was blueprinted by John Brabham. Ferguson Research subsequently converted it four-wheel drive assisted by a Dunlop Maxaret anti-skid braking system. All told, production was not viable due to the modifications making the Mustang twice the price of a contemporary Aston Martin DB6.

Of course, four-wheel drive would find its place several decades later.

This 1969 Mustang SportsRoof with a 428 Cobra Jet suffered a 300-pound penalty with Ferguson Formula All-Wheel-Control and other supporting modifications. (Photo Courtesy James Anderson)

Despite the weight penalty of the Ferguson Formula system, performance was an improvement over a factory stock 428 Cobra Jet–powered 1969 Mustang: 0–60 in 5.5 seconds. (Photo Courtesy James Anderson)

Mach I

The final year of the 1960s also saw the debut of the sporty new Mach I, the Mustang's new image model. Based on the SportsRoof, the Mach I shared the sporty look of the regular fastback but took it up several notches with new styling and performance features: reflective striping on the body sides, a pop-open gas cap, dual exhaust, matte black hood with simulated hood scoop, color-keyed dual racing-type mirrors, hood pins and lanyards, reflective stripes sides and rear, and styled steel wheels with Goodyear E70 Wide Oval Polyglas tires. The Mach I also featured a deluxe interior with high-backed bucket seats, simulated wood trim, extra sound deadening, remote sports mirrors, and other comforts. All Mach Is also came with dual exhausts and heftier shocks, springs, and stabilizer bar.

But it was what was under the hood that really gave the Mach I distinction. Like other sporty vehicles from Ford, the Mach I's base engine—a 351 2-barrel—was nothing to brag about, but a 290-hp 351 4-barrel,

This Black Jade 1969 Mach I is one of 2,766 SportsRoofs built with the Q-code non-ram air 428 Cobra Jet. Of those, 1,485 were backed with a 4-speed. It also has the Drag Pack with 4.30 Traction-Lok axle. (Photo Courtesy David Newhardt/ Mecum Auctions)

All Mach Is received a non-functional hood scoop like this. Ordering the Shaker hood scoop (which was included in the R-code 428 Cobra Jet) would give you a functional air induction system. (Photo Courtesy David Newhardt/Mecum Auctions)

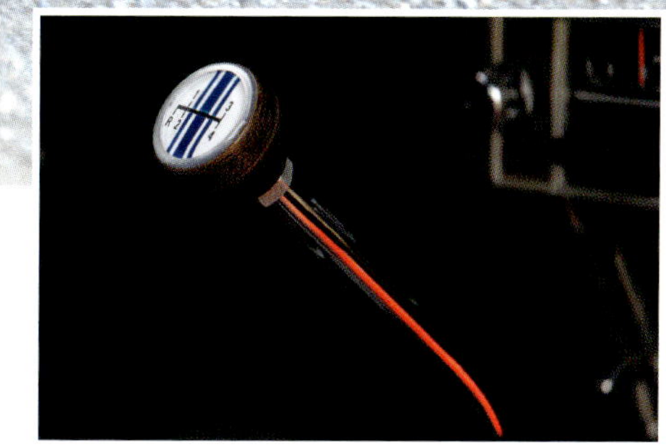

Standard with the 428 Cobra Jet was a close-ratio 4-speed manual transmission. (Photo Courtesy David Newhardt/Mecum Auctions)

320-hp 390, and the 428 Cobra Jet were available. Neat options for the Mach I included a rear wing, chin spoiler, and rear-window louvers. For those who wanted a true air induction system, Ford offered a new-fangled "Shaker" scoop that was attached to the air cleaner, rather than the hood, and would shake with the engine's vibrations; it was available with any Mach I engine.

The Mach I was a very popular model, with 72,458 cars built out of 299,824 Mustangs for the model year. And despite having a low-performance engine standard, a large percentage of the 12,896 Cobra Jet SportsRoofs built were Mach Is. Included in those numbers were 3,115 SportsRoofs built with the Drag Pack, with 2,869 being Mach Is, according to Marti Auto Works.

The 53rd Detroit Auto Show, held at Cobo Hall in November 1968, showcased this 1969 Mach I 428 CJ. Preproduction Mach Is lacked the "Mach I" script on the rear tail panel. (Photo Courtesy Mike Bradford)

For some reason, Ford offered two 428 Cobra Jets—one with ram air, the other without—but the Shaker itself was available optionally for 351- and 390-equipped Mustangs. (Photo Courtesy David Newhardt/ Mecum Auctions)

This Foulger Ford–sponsored Super Stock I Automatic (SS/IA) racer was painted in a style to create the impression the dealership was campaigning more than one Mustang. (Photo Courtesy David Newhardt/Mecum Auctions)

Mustang GT

The GT Equipment Group had represented the sportier side of Mustang since 1965 but, by 1969, thanks the introduction of the wildly successful Mach I, the GT started to play second fiddle. Basic equipment was similar for both the GT and Mach I, including engines, with the GT visually relying on Ford's traditional racing stripe just above the rocker panels. When the model year was over, 6,694 Mustangs were equipped with the GT package, and then it met its demise.

Out of the 50 Q-code 428 Cobra Jet Mustang convertibles built in 1969, 30 had the GT package. Note the simulated hood scoop that was part of the GT package. (Photo Courtesy Nelson Cardadeiro)

The Q-code 428 Cobra Jet as it appeared in the 1969 Mustang. More people ordered theirs with the R-code Shaker air induction system. (Photo Courtesy Nelson Cardadeiro)

The 1969 Mustang SportsRoof with the GT package. Rearview shot shows the beefier stature of the redesigned Mustang. (Photo Courtesy Glenn A. Benza)

What About Shelbys?

When the 428 Cobra Jet was introduced in April 1968, the GT500KR replaced the GT500. While the CJ was carried over into 1969, Shelby reverted back to the GT500. Just like the Mustang, when 3.91 or 4.30 gears were desired for the GT500, the Drag Pack was the way to go, triggering certain heavy-duty equipment. Out of 1,402 GT500s built for 1969, 192 were equipped with the Drag Pack.

All that was wrapped in a new svelte body that distinctly stood out from the Mustang more than before. The fiberglass front fenders and hood formed a wide-mouth grille with dual headlights situated inside. Driving lights were now mounted below the bumper, which were surrounded on both ends by rectangular parking lights. And in an era of air scoops, the Shelby had them in spades—three NASA-style scoops on the hood were complemented by two rectangular exit vents, plus there were scoops on both the front and rear fenders (the latter in different positions depending whether it was a SportsRoof or convertible). The trunk continued to feature an integral spoiler, with 1965 Thunderbird taillights just below. For the first time since 1965, Shelbys had a different stripe, this one being a thick mid-body reflective stripe surrounded by two thin stripes on both sides.

But the Mach I proved too popular . . . and much more affordable. Ron Brinkhoff, general manager of Courtesy Ford in Denver, was quoted by Ford as saying, "The Mustang Mach I Cobra Jet has been such a popular seller here, it's taken some of our Shelby business." That was the nail in the

The 1967–1968 Shelby GT500 Mustang used the 428 Police Interceptor. Midway through 1968, the GT500KR replacement included the 428 Cobra Jet. In 1969, the GT500 returned, now with standard CJ power. Only 245 GT500 convertibles were built that year. (Photo Courtesy David Newhardt/Mecum Auctions)

The 1969 Shelby GT500 featured a NASA air induction system, so the plumbing underneath the hood was different than Shaker-equipped Mustangs. (Photo Courtesy David Newhardt/Mecum Auctions)

This 428 Cobra Jet badge on the 1969 Shelby GT500 is unique among all CJ-equipped vehicles from Ford Motor Company. (Photo Courtesy David Newhardt/Mecum Auctions)

Cobra Jet + Drag Pack = Super Cobra Jet

The 1969 428 Cobra Jet engine was basically identical to the 1968 version, although improvements included larger intake ports, larger runners in the intake manifold, diecast rocker covers, and nodular iron flywheel for manual transmission cars. A more significant upgrade for 1969 was a complementary package for Mustang buyers who selected either of the optional V- or W-code 3.91:1 or 4.30:1 gears. It triggered a host of upgrades that turned the engine into a 428 Super Cobra Jet (SCJ): more durable pistons, wrist pins, crankshaft, cap screw "Le Mans" connecting rods (with shorter bolt heads), flywheel, flexplate, harmonic balancer, plus an external oil cooler mounted in front of the radiator (relocating the driver's side air horn to the passenger's side of the radiator core support) and a timing pointer with slightly more length to clear the harmonic balancer.

Starting in February 1969, Ford branded the upgrades as a package called the "Drag Pack." The Drag Pack was available for the Cobra Jet regardless of whether or not it was equipped with ram air.

CJ & SCJ Interchanging Components

According to the 428 Cobra Jet Registry, a common misconception is that all SCJs were equipped with forged pistons (while CJs had weaker cast pistons), but a page from Ford's *Muscle Parts Description and Interchange* book (a supplement to the original Muscle Parts catalog) from July 1970 clearly states that "all 428 engines use dished cast aluminum pistons with two sets of eyebrows cast so they can be used in right or left bank."

Apparently, Ford went through at least three piston designs during the 428 CJ and SCJ production run to address durability problems. The later piston, which first appeared around December 1968, is marked "428" and "SUPER" and differs from the earlier pistons by having additional metal in the pin boss area. The Registry indicates, "The 'SUPER' mark does NOT mean that the pistons were used only in SCJs! Though different part numbers were used for standard-sized CJ and SCJ pistons (perhaps to provide slightly different installation tolerances), most folks that I've talked to believe that the pistons were in fact identical."

The reciprocating assemblies between the Cobra Jet and Super Cobra Jet do not interchange with each other—mixing the two can cause severe balance problems. However, all other components of the engines interchange with each other, such as the block, heads, manifolds, etc., as they are identical. A CJ block stamped "SUPER" on the front generally gave instruction to factory engine assemblers to use SCJ internals when building the engine. Despite the heavy-duty upgrades, factory horsepower and torque ratings remained the same for the SCJ.

The easiest way to tell a Super Cobra Jet from a base 428 Cobra Jet is that SCJs had an engine oil cooler mounted in front of the radiator on the driver's side, with both horns moved to the passenger's side, as seen on this 1969 Cobra Jet W-code Drag Pack convertible.

coffin for Shelby, although the high-performance market in general also had experienced a downturn from which it would never recover.

Fairlane/Torino/Ranchero

As in 1968, the 428 Cobra Jet engine was not limited to just the Mustang series. For 1969, CJ availability now included the Ranchero series. The addition of air induction for the midsize models also was new for 1969. Otherwise, all but wagons were available with the 428 Cobra Jet plus the Drag Pack.

Fairlane, Fairlane 500, and the all-new Cobra featured a gray horizontal grille with two chrome longitudinal bars, with the Cobra featuring the same but blacked out. Torino and Torino GT grilles were a different design, which was a mesh affair with a horizontal chrome/red bar bisecting it.

When it came time for Ford to answer the Dodge Charger 500 for NASCAR homologation, Ford took 750 Q-code Cobra automatics and converted them into Torino Talladegas, complete with modified front end.

Fairlane

The base midsize Ford continued to be the Fairlane, although 1969 would be its final year. Buyers could choose a two-door hardtop (without the B-pillar)—unusual in the segment—or a four-door sedan. While a six was standard, engines did not become interesting until the new 351 Windsor with 290 hp. The 390 4-barrel offered 320 hp, and the 428 Cobra Jet was the top dog. While ram air was available, a smart enthusiast could spec out a Fairlane hardtop with the Q-code CJ and the Drag Pack (with 4.30:1 gears, no less) and appear as an unassuming 302 Fairlane. Per Marti Auto Works, it is known that 26 Fairlane two-door hardtops were built with the R-code Cobra Jet, plus an unknown number of Q-codes.

Fairlane 500

Up a rung in trim level, the Fairlane 500 model was available as a two-door hardtop but also offered a convertible, SportsRoof fastback, and four-door sedan. Compared to the standard Fairlane, the Fairlane 500 added lower-body chrome trim, roof drip rail and rear window reveal moldings, and carpeting instead of a rubber floor mat. While the authors don't know how many Fairlane 500s were built with the 428 Cobra Jet, it is known from Marti Auto Works that 21 Fairlane 500 two-door hardtops were built with the Drag Pack.

The 1969 Torino GT was the logical model to order the 428 Cobra Jet, but some folks preferred the more pedestrian Fairlane 500. Only three convertibles were ordered with the R-code CJ and 4-speed. (Photo Courtesy Donald M. Vories)

This Black Jade 1969 Fairlane is one of 17 two-door hardtops built with the R-code 428 Cobra Jet and 4-speed. As the bottom-of-the-line vehicle in the series, this Fairlane was originally purchased by the service manager of Bud Miller Ford in Conneaut Lake, Pennsylvania, in October 1968 for the specific purpose of drag racing. (Photo Courtesy Dan Mendice)

Cobra

Ford added a companion model to the Torino GT in 1969 and called it the Cobra. While the GT was available as a convertible and came standard with a tepid 302, the Cobra was only available as a SportsRoof fastback or hardtop coupe and included the 428 Cobra Jet standard. As the Cobra was Ford's new intermediate performance darling and answer to the extremely successful Plymouth Road Runner, it eschewed the Torino GT's upscale interior for something that was more utilitarian, à la Fairlane. The standard Q-code CJ received a flat hood, while the optional R-code CJ with ram air received a vacuum-operated system similar to the Mustang's from the year before; of course, the Drag Pack was available for either CJ. As Ford's midsize "image" car, the Cobra was featured in a prodigious media and advertising effort.

The Cobra was the basis of the Talladega homologation special. All were Q-code automatic SportsRoofs that received extended front fenders with special bracing, special flush-mounted grille, modified front bumper, rolled rocker panels, staggered rear shocks (the only automatic 428 Cobra Jet vehicle to use this setup), oil cooler, and blacked-out hood, among other modifications. The Talladega was only available in Presidential Blue, Wimbledon White, and Royal Maroon. A robust 750 were built, eclipsing the 500-unit homologation requirements.

The final tally at the end of the year was 3,786 Cobra coupes

Compare this Raven Black 1969 Cobra SportsRoof with the Torino GT that appears later in this chapter—this Cobra was built with the 428 Cobra Jet with ram air, C6 Cruise-O-Matic transmission, and a 3.00:1-geared Traction-Lok rear end. According to Marti Auto Works, 3,543 Cobra fastbacks were built with the R-code CJ/auto combination. (Photo Courtesy Richard Truesdell)

The only optional engine for the 1969 Cobra was the 428 Cobra Jet with ram air. Ordering the R-code engine added a hood scoop, as the standard Cobra had a flat hood. (Photo Courtesy Richard Truesdell)

In September 1968, Ford issued a bulletin: "Cobra decal emblem has been changed to a 3-dimensional metal emblem." (Photo Courtesy Richard Truesdell)

The 1969 Cobra was also available as a coupe. Note the flat hood and engine badges on the front fenders of this Q-code SCJ Cobra coupe. Only 705 Cobra coupes had the Drag Pack. (Photo Courtesy Larry Slevin)

Compare this red Cobra coupe with the R-code 428 Cobra Jet to the black car on the previous page. Notice the hood scoop and the placement of the badges. (Photo Courtesy Vern Eide Motorcars Specialty and Classics)

Bunkie's Talladega

Ford's Total Performance program brought trophies to Dearborn in just about every major race around the world, but NASCAR was the most popular for many Americans, and Ford was a perennial winner in that circuit. When engineers determined that aerodynamics was another way to add speed to the top end, they began testing modifications such as spoilers. Dodge upped the ante in 1969 with the Charger 500, which didn't include a spoiler (unlike previous Hemi Chargers) but featured several aerodynamic body modifications to the stock Charger R/T: a flush nose, covered A-pillars, and a backlight faired to the flying buttresses. Ford, in turn, returned the serve with the Torino Talladega (with assistance from Holman-Moody).

Unlike other aero homologation specials, the Talladega's modifications were handled on the assembly line: extended front fenders (15.5 inches added up front, plus special bracing), sectioned rear bumper reconfigured for the front, and tucked rocker panels.

Interestingly, the Talladega's cross-town cousin, the Mercury Cyclone Spoiler II, shared only the bumpers, grille, and parking lights—no sheet metal modifications were shared between the two.

There were 14 preproduction and pilot Torino Talladegas built along with another 736 production units. Of the former, one was built by Kar-Kraft for Ford President Bunkie Knudsen. Several features distinguish it from production Talladegas, including yellow paint, a white bucket seat interior, and console. (Photo Courtesy Jerry Heasley)

(including 705 with the Drag Pack) and 11,099 Cobra SportsRoofs and Talladegas (with 1,387 Cobras having the Drag Pack).

Torino

Introduced the year before, the Torino was the crown jewel of Ford's midsize series, destined to wipe out the old-fashioned Fairlane nameplate from the series. Unto itself, the Torino was the most luxurious car in the series, but it too could be ordered with either of the 428 Cobra Jets plus Drag Pack. Standard equipment on top of the Fairlane 500 included bright trim, full wheel covers, accent stripes, fancier grille, foam-padded cloth seats, loop-pile carpeting, and "padding where it counts." Torino CJ production is unknown, but it is known that eight Q-code 4-speed hardtops were built.

Torino GT

The GT continued to play the role of Ford's traditional midsize sporty model. Debuting in 1966 as the Fairlane GT, it came with a 390 4-barrel

A 1969 Torino GT SportsRoof ordered in a special-order color. As Richard Petty was with Ford that year, the Charlotte, North Carolina, district ordered a host of Petty Blue Torinos for promotion. (Photo Courtesy Mecum Auctions)

standard, then the 1967 edition was downgraded to a standard 289. Ford continued to play that game with the renamed 1968 Torino GT, as standard motivation was a pedestrian 302.

Ford's bag was that you could make the Torino GT anything you wanted it to be, so the 290-hp 351 4-barrel was the smallest engine that would likely get enthusiasts' blood flowing; from there, one could opt for the 320-hp 390 4-barrel or either of the Cobra Jets, plus the Drag Pack.

Torino GTs featured more brightwork and a fancier grille (shared with the regular Torino), plus standard C-stripes (redesigned from 1968's model) for the SportsRoof or classic GT stripes for hardtops and convertibles. Also included with the model were "wide-oval belted tires on competition-styled steel wheels," GT suspension (upgraded to competition handling suspension when the CJ was ordered), and fancier bench seat. GTs were the only model in the series that came standard with a hood scoop, but it only was functional with the R-code CJ. Cobra Jet GT SportsRoof amounted to 1,986 (with 170 of those having the Drag Pack); for the hardtop

The 1969 Torino GT SportsRoof wasn't in the spotlight like the Cobra, but this black example with a red C-stripe and interior is one of 1,285 built with the R-code 428 Cobra Jet with ram air. (Photo Courtesy Eric English)

Unlike the Mustang, the Torino GT (and other midsize Fords) did not use the Shaker air induction system. (Photo Courtesy Eric English)

The Torino GT received a standard hood scoop, but it was only functional when ordered with the R-code 428 Cobra Jet. (Photo Courtesy Eric English)

coupe, 314 CJs were built (45 with the Drag Pack); and for the Torino GT convertible, 11 automatic (and an unspecified number of 4-speed) Q-codes and another 54 R-codes were built, including 16 with the Drag Pack per Marti Auto Works.

Ranchero

Ford decided to make the Cobra Jet available for the Ranchero for 1969. Available as Ranchero, Ranchero 500, and Ranchero GT, the latter was analogous to the Torino GT in equipment, so engine choices ranged from a 302 to the 428 Cobra Jet, including ram air and/or the Drag Pack if a buyer so chose. For the base Ranchero, the authors cannot determine how many were built with the CJ; for the Ranchero 500, 77 were built with the 428, including 18 with the Drag Pack. Only 255 Ranchero GTs were built for the 1969 model year with the Cobra Jet, including 34 with the Drag Pack.

Mercury

Ford's upscale sister division also got its performance game on for 1969. Its performance roster was advertised as part of the Streep Scene, which was a hybrid strategy catering to the enthusiast who drove his/her performance car regularly yet enjoyed competing at the drags on weekends: "A car that combines the guts and go needed for drag strip competition with the comfort and handling ease that people want for cars for street use." Drag racing associations had developed their own respective stock classes, and Mercury's newly christened Streep Scene was the division's way of showing enthusiasts what they could buy from the factory and how they could take advantage of these classes with tuning tips and modifications. If a Mercury owner wanted to move into something more radical, such as Super Stock, the Streep Scene program also had him/her covered.

New on the scene was the Cyclone CJ, the sister car to the Ford Cobra. It joined the regular Cyclone as Mercury's midsize performance car. Midyear, another image car joined the scene: the Cougar Eliminator. While it didn't have a standard 428 Cobra Jet like the Cyclone CJ, it demonstrated strength in a market that was at its strongest.

Ford only built 1,658 Ranchero GTs in 1969. Only 80 were built with the R-code 4-speed. (Photo Courtesy Barrett-Jackson)

The 1969 Ranchero GT came with the C-stripe that was part of the Torino GT. Like the latter, the Ranchero GT included the hood scoop, but it was only functional with the R-code 428 Cobra Jet. (Photo Courtesy Barrett-Jackson)

New Cat with Winning Ways

Think about Mercury-Lincoln dealers in the mid-1960s, at the height of the muscle and pony car wars. Their lots were full of Comets, Montereys, and a Lincoln Continental here and there; meanwhile, Ford dealers across town were garnering all the attention with the hot-selling Mustang. Two years after the Mustang debuted, Mercury answered the call with the 1967 Cougar, the division's upscale version of the Ford pony car. After great success for 1967–1968, how did Mercury follow up?

For 1969, the redesigned Cougar family grew to include convertibles in both standard and XR-7 trim. With a new horizontal grille, ventless side windows, sculpted body lines, rallye-styled parking lamps, and new dashboard design finished in simulated rosewood, the Cougar was more contemporary yet remained completely Cougar. Additionally, the wheelbase was stretched 3 inches.

Unlike the Mustang, the Cougar started out strong, with the new 351 2-barrel instead of a six or 302. The similarities with the Mustang converged from there, with a 351 4-barrel, 390 4-barrel, and two versions of the 428 Cobra Jet. While the Mustang's ram air system was the Shaker, Mercury used a similar vacuum system from 1968. Like the Fords, the Q-code was the basic CJ while the R-code was the CJ with ram air. Both were available with the Drag Pak (note Mercury's spelling).

Cougar

"Completely restyled with new power. The big cat's got a deeper V-8 growl . . . 351 cubic inches now standard, and all the sporty ideas Cougar

A base 1969 Cougar convertible looks unassuming, but under the hood is a Q-code 428 Cobra Jet. Only three were built with a 4-speed per Marti Auto Works. (Photo Courtesy Mecum Auctions)

Note the Mercury Q-code air cleaner lid and compare it with the Mustangs that appeared earlier in the chapter. (Photo Courtesy Mecum Auctions)

made famous," said the TV commercial. The base Cougar didn't lack for amenities, as it featured foam-padded bucket seats, wall-to-wall carpeting, courtesy lights, and full door panels. A Decor Group for hardtops included full wheel covers, bright curb moldings, more luxurious bucket seats, fully padded front/rear armrests plus windshield pillars and roof rails, and wood-toned rim-blow three-spoke steering wheel. Additionally, base Cougar convertibles featured a standard power-operated top. The 428 Cobra Jet production numbers totaled 353 hardtops (not including Eliminators) and 36 convertibles.

Cougar Eliminator

Initially a show car appearing toward the end of 1968, the production Cougar Eliminator was introduced at the 1969 Chicago Auto Show in March. Only available for the standard Cougar hardtop, the Eliminator package included a matte black grille, hood scoop (only functional with

Conspicuous on the Cougar Eliminator was a rear spoiler, while a front air dam was more subtle. Other features included with the package were a blacked-out grille, side stripes, 12-slot wheels, non-functional hood scoop, driver's side remote racing-style mirror, and XR-7-style rocker moldings. (Photo Courtesy Mecum Auctions)

Resplendent in Competition Orange, the 1969 Cougar Eliminator with the 428 Cobra Jet was the perfect example of a "streeper," a car capable of laying plenty of rubber all day at the track yet ready to take your date to the movies. The owner added the wheel moldings. (Photo Courtesy Joe Biglione)

the R-code Cobra Jet), racing-style remote driver's mirror, matte black fiberglass front air dam, rear spoiler, "Eliminator" side graphics, argent slotted wheels with F70 14 belted BSW traction tires, rocker panels, performance axle ratio and handling package, high-back bucket seats, rim blow steering wheel, and a few other interior components. Standard was the 351 4-barrel with options up to the 428 Cobra Jet, plus the Boss 302—the only Mercury to offer this engine.

Colors were restricted to Competition Orange, Bright Blue, Bright Yellow, and White. Among the 2,250 Eliminators built, 302 were equipped with the Cobra Jet.

Florida's Brian Styles owns these two XR-7 Cougar convertibles with the 428 Cobra Jet. The 1969 is an R-code but the 1970 is a Q-code with ram air—an interesting quirk between Ford and Mercury that year. (Photo Courtesy Brian Styles)

The 1969 Cougar XR-7 with the 428 Cobra Jet was a stout-looking muscle car when not equipped with the vinyl top. This and the new-for-1969 Mustang Grandé would spawn competition in 1970 with the Dodge Challenger SE and Plymouth Barracuda Gran Coupe. (Photo Courtesy Mecum Auctions)

For 1969, the redesigned Cougar featured a full-width concave taillight panel. Note the optional styled steel wheels. (Photo Courtesy Mecum Auctions)

Cobra Jet Cougar Special Features

Here are some tidbits that made 428 Cobra Jet Cougars special.

- 4-speed or C6 automatic only—no 3-speeds
- C6 transmission was a special unit with additional clutch plates, cast-iron tail shaft, and R servo
- Wraparound shock towers—actually, all 1969–1970 Cougars had wraparound towers, but Mustangs only had the wraparound towers with FE-based engines
- All had some performance handling package, including larger front sway bar; 1970s included a rear sway bar
- 4-speed cars received the staggered shocks to eliminate wheel hop
- Power steering–equipped cars featured a power steering cooler
- All had 31-spline rear axles
- All had 24-inch heavy-duty radiators
- All had 730-cfm Holley carbs (no Autolite carbs)
- All had a smog system from the factory (required due to the Holley carb)
- Drag Pak V-code 3.91 and W-code 4.30 rear axles turned the 428 Cobra Jet into a Super Cobra Jet
- Ram air was optional for both years; 1969s had an R in VIN
- Hood scoop was available only on ram air cars and Eliminators, but only functional with the R-code Cobra Jet
- All 428 CJs had dual exhaust
- All had heavy-duty battery (Group 27F)
- All rear end ratios were available, from 2.75 open to 4.30:1 (with Detroit Locker available for 1970)
- All bodystyles could have the 428 CJ, from standard Cougars to XR-7, hardtops to convertibles
- All paint and interior choices were available

A 1969 Cougar XR-7. Hints pointing that it's equipped with the 428 Cobra Jet include the hood scoop and stripes. Rear spoiler is an owner-added Eliminator accessory. (Photo Courtesy Richard Truesdell)

Although the 428 Cobra Jet was the hot choice for the Cougar, four CJ Cougars were converted into Boss 429 cars, with Eddie Schartman and Don Nicholson each receiving one, and the additional cars used for prototyping and magazine features. (Photo Courtesy Richard Truesdell)

The 428 Cobra Jet Cougars ordered with ram air received hood stripes that were either black or silver, depending on the paint color. (Photo Courtesy Richard Truesdell)

Cougar XR-7: A Higher Breed of Cougar

Mercury considered the Cougar XR-7 the "ultimate personal sports car" with European style and flair. Included with this trim level were distinctive XR-7 medallions, left-side color-keyed remote-control racing mirror, bright belt and curb moldings, unique wheel covers, glove-soft leather and vinyl bucket seats, deluxe seat belts and shoulder harnesses (the latter for hardtops only), "super-puff" door panels with assist traps, door-mounted courtesy lights, map pockets on the back of each front seat, simulated burled-walnut inserts, rocker-type switches for map light and other accessories, and clock and tachometer, among other niceties. Engine choices were the same as the standard Cougar, aside from the Boss 302, which was an Eliminator exclusive. For the Cougar XR-7, 676 hardtops and 173 convertibles were built with the 428 Cobra Jet.

Quicksilver: The Midsize Cobra Jet Mercs

The Montego series (including Comet and Cyclone) had been redesigned for 1968, so there were only detail changes for 1969. New three-piece Continental-inspired grille, luxury interiors, and engines arguably made 1969 an improvement over the previous year. While the 302 4-barrel was discontinued, a new 351 made up for it, plus the 390 made its final appearance. But of course the hot topic was the 428 Cobra Jet, which continued to be available for midsize Mercurys other than wagons; additionally, the new Drag Pak added heavy-duty components to cars equipped with digger gears. The Cyclone and all-new Cyclone CJ were the performance models of the bunch, but pedestrian Montego two-door hardtops (no Montego MX convertibles or four-doors) could be equipped with the CJ, albeit only without air induction.

Comet

The base midsize model was the Comet, formerly the name for the whole series but again left with only a two-door hardtop representing the model. Interestingly, Mercury tried to arouse creativity in the brochure, stating, "One Comet, or a dozen? Who's to know for sure unless you get your imagination working? We'll get you started by pointing out there are *sporty* Comets (with options like the gutsy new 290-hp 351-4V engine, 4-speed manual transmission, and deluxe wheel covers with spinner) . . . *luxury* Comets (with optional special appearance equipment group, 4-way power bench seat, and rim blow) . . . and *high-performance* Comets (with optional CJ 428 engine, power front disc brakes, and Traction-Lok differential)." Very few took the latter route, but those who did were restricted to the Q-code CJ.

Montego

Since 1968, the Montego had taken primary control of the former Comet series. The base Montego, available as a two-door hardtop and four-door sedan, featured dual paint stripes to "emphasize Montego's big 206-inch overall length." Standard interior was cloth and vinyl bench.

The 1969 Mercury Montego MX could be ordered with the 428 Cobra Jet, but only the Q-code without air induction. While appearing less sporty than the Cyclone, it still imparted a muscular look. Cobra badges, Cyclone ram air scoop, and mag wheels are owner-added. (Photo Courtesy Kimberly Nelson)

Nothing fancy yet not austere, the Montego two-door hardtop nonetheless was the only base Montego available with the 428 Cobra Jet, with 32 buyers taking that opportunity.

Montego MX

A step up from the base Montego, the MX featured more elaborate chrome moldings, pleated bench seat and interior panels (the latter with wood-tone applique), and generous teakwood-grain use on the dashboard. The MX was available as a two-door hardtop and four-door sedan but also featured the only midsize convertible in the series. Like the previously mentioned models, only a handful Montego MX hardtops were built with the Q-code 428 Cobra Jet.

Montego MX Brougham

As "the most luxurious car in the intermediate field," the Montego MX Brougham's richness really shone in the interior: stain-resistant cloth and vinyl bench seat, plush wood-toned padded doors with leather-like door pulls and carpeted lower door panels, color-keyed deep-loop carpeting, and Deluxe wood-toned three-spoke rim blow steering wheel were among the fine-car touches. And a 428 Cobra Jet available for the two-door Brougham hardtop? A car where one can have his or her cake and eat it too.

Cyclone

The Cyclone received minor tweaks, most noticeably the grille, but the biggest changes were that the hardtop model was discontinued (leaving only the fastback), and that the GT was relegated to an appearance package.

The base Cyclone continued as before, with a 302 2-barrel as the standard engine; optional was the new 351 (with the 4-barrel offering 290 hp), the 320-hp 390, and the 428 Cobra Jet. Like its Ford sister, the 428 was available with ram air (which included a hood scoop) and/or the Drag Pak. Optional side stripes, running along the beltline, were a nice evolution from what was standard on the 1968 Cyclone GT.

Painted in Competition Orange, this 1969 Mercury Cyclone CJ is equipped with the R-code 428 Cobra Jet with ram air, side tape stripes, and styled steel wheels. Cyclone CJs received a black grille, unlike the base Cyclone. (Photo Courtesy American Muscle Car Museum)

The Cyclone GT was no longer a model for 1969. Rather, the "GT appearance group" included Comfortweave vinyl bucket seats, rim blow steering wheel, remote-control racing mirror, turbine wheel covers and wide-tread fiberglass-belted white sidewall tires, and GT decal on the trunk lid.

Cyclone Spoiler

Midyear, Mercury introduced the Cyclone Spoiler, a NASCAR-inspired homage to Cale Yarborough (white/red) and Dan Gurney (white/blue). Standard was the 351 4-barrel with options up to the Cobra Jet. The Spoiler was the basis of Mercury's version of the Torino Talladega, which was called the Cyclone Spoiler Sports Special or "Spoiler II." While the cars—especially the nose—looked identical to the Talladega, there were several subtle differences. Car for car, the biggest difference was that the Spoiler II's only available engine was the 351 4-barrel backed by an automatic. The number of 428 Cobra Jet Cyclones built, including Spoilers, was 393.

Cyclone CJ

The big news for 1969, however, was the new Cyclone CJ model. Sister to the Ford Cobra, the Cyclone CJ came standard with (surprise!) the 428 Cobra Jet paired to a 4-speed. The biggest difference between the Cyclone CJ and the regular Cyclone was that the former was positioned at a lower trim level (more like the Montego than Montego MX) as it competed with the Plymouth Road Runner. From the outside, the CJ featured a black-out grille and hood stripes in black or silver; when ram air was ordered, the CJ received a hood scoop painted in the same color as the stripes. A total of 2,175 Cyclone CJs were built in 1969, with 357 of those having the Drag Pak.

Just like the 1969 Ford Cobra, the Cyclone CJ came standard with the Q-code 428 Cobra Jet, but those wanting air induction had to order the R-code 428 CJ. (Photo Courtesy American Muscle Car Museum)

The 1969 Mercury Cyclone CJ was created to do battle with the Plymouth Road Runner but, like the Mopar, that didn't mean the standard interior couldn't be upgraded to something more comfortable and driver oriented. (Photo Courtesy American Muscle Car Museum)

Performance: It's the Going Thing

After several years of missing the boat, Ford got on board with the 428 Cobra Jet in 1968. For an encore the following year, Ford integrated a number of marketing elements to make 1969 among Ford's best years during the muscle car era.

Published in a binder for dealer staff *Performance: It's the Going Thing* was akin to an integrated marketing guide/training manual that covered the performance market, including supporting material like product information, merchandising information, competitive information, biographies of dealerships' experiences in the performance market, and the how/what/why of motorsports.

What follows are several other complementary marketing programs that helped make Ford a contender beyond the Cobra Jet.

Here is Hubert Platt racing his SS/IA Mustang SportsRoof with the 428 Cobra Jet. He won his class in the 1969 NHRA Winternationals. (Photo Courtesy Allen Platt)

An integral part of the Ford Drag Team of the 1960s, Hubert "the Georgia Shaker" Platt's exploits on and off the track—including conducting performance seminars at Ford dealers as part of the Drag Team's marketing/promotion efforts—really solidified the 428 Cobra Jet as one of the top engine packages available from any manufacturer. (Photo Courtesy Allen Platt)

This "Going Thing" 428 Cobra Jet fastback was among a group of Mustangs and Fairlanes built for a "drive and buy" promotion at the All-Ford Performance Day event at Thompson Drag Raceway in Ohio. (Photo Courtesy Tammy Jefferson)

Created by Ford's Cleveland zone, the "Going Thing" promotion vehicles resembled Ford Drag Team race cars, including the C-stripe (similar to that of the Boss 302). Many were special ordered in Petty Blue. (Photo Courtesy Tammy Jefferson)

Performance: It's the Going Thing *(Continued)*

1969 Performance Digest

This was an eight-page, full-color insert included in magazines and available at dealerships that presented Ford's performance roster and pointed prospects to the Performance Corner (more on that to come) to add parts to their car's muscle and maneuverability. Vehicles getting top billing were the Cobra, Mustang Mach I, and the full-size XL GT, with the Torino GT and Mustang GT playing second fiddle in the image wars.

Performance Corner

A dealer could elect to build traffic by setting a Performance Corner in its showroom, relying on the Cobra, the Mustang Mach I, and the 428 Cobra Jet as Ford's calling card in the performance car field. C.A.R. Corporation of Livonia, Michigan, produced the Performance Activities Kit (also known as The Pit Kit) to assist dealerships in exploiting the hottest segment in the market and build more traffic and profits. Included were outdoor and indoor display items and ideas to promote Ford performance vehicles. "With an imaginative Performance Corner, you'll attract the performance crowd from the handling enthusiasts to the appearance buyers, to the influential muscle car buffs," encouraged Ford.

Ford suggested designating a performance sales specialist to preside over this area of the showroom and supporting it locally with advertising, supplementing Ford's advertising campaigns on TV, radio, national magazines, and leading buff magazines. Also included were suggestions on how to organize and profit from conducting a performance program at the local drag strip, a performance night in the showroom, building a Performance Corner in the used car lot, and more.

One didn't need to be a hardcore enthusiast to be supporting Ford's efforts in the high-performance piece of the pie—Ford offered performance training materials to help dealership staff establish, maintain, and exploit the position as a performance dealer. The Ford Marketing Institute had a special portion of its sales training course exclusively devoted to performance selling. "A complete half day of the regular 6-day Basic Retail Selling Course for new salesmen will zero in on all the techniques used by successful performance salesmen. There also will be a 3-day course for experienced salesmen on how to become a performance sales specialist." C.A.R. Corporation also produced the monthly *Performance Corner Newsletter* to offer sales staff all sorts of information to more effectively sell performance.

Ford Muscle Power Parts

Ford always had a vibrant parts portfolio, but dealer parts managers felt the way it was managed put them at a disadvantage compared to speed shops. Ford/Autolite's Muscle Parts program sought to create a more integrated marketing effort by recruiting Bonneville veteran Danny Eames and NHRA cofounder Ak Miller. The program and its accompanying catalog sought to streamline the following: (1) information on parts interchangeability for different engine series, (2) competitive pricing, and (3) the best parts for a particular combination.

"Nobody tells you that you can invest a ton and only get a pound of performance if you buy the wrong pieces. So, Ford got the idea to do it," a Ford Muscle Power Parts catalog said. Ford also developed several kits in stages, depending on how far an enthusiast wanted to go.

Ford Total Performance Show

Ford believed that every 1969 motorsport event was an opportunity for the Total Performance Show. "Ford puts you in the performance business. And, it is planned to take this show into Ford Districts at the dealer level to give added impetus to performance car and parts sales throughout model year '69. This Show generates traffic and sales-excitement at the dealer, district, and national levels," a Total Performance Show flyer said. With more than 50 million motorsports spectators, the Total Performance Show's purpose was to promote Ford's high-performance automotive portfolio, Muscle Parts, and Ford Performance Parts to these enthusiasts because "performance people buy performance cars and parts."

There were two traveling units that made appearances at NHRA, NASCAR, and other events. Each was a magnificent 40-foot trailer with four huge canopy wings extending from it—80 feet long and 48 feet wide for a total of 4,000 square feet. They contained record-holding race cars, a 200-mph Mustang Funny Car, a Grand National stocker, high-performance parts and accessories display, and *The Sound of Speed* film.

Ford Drag Team/Drag Team Seminars

The Ford Drag Team, another C.A.R. Corporation production for Ford's Marketing Division, was introduced for the 1969 model year to bank on Ford's newfound strength in the horsepower wars and, in turn, to build traffic at dealerships. Both coasts were represented by their own respective team: the

Eastern Drag Team was headed by the "Georgia Shaker" Hubert Platt, and Ed Terry was captain of the Western Drag Team. Platt piloted a SS/IA 428 Cobra Jet Mustang SportsRoof, with teammate Randy Payne handling a Cobra SportsRoof, both equipped with C6 automatics. Ed Terry's sidekick was Dick Wood, both of whose respective Mustang and Cobra CJs were 4-speeds. Holman-Moody-Stroppe blueprinted the 428s and equipped them with ladder bar suspension and many other modifications. The Eastern team used a blue with white theme while the Western team used the inverse combination. All four vehicles rode on chrome-plated Cragars.

Each team also campaigned 1969 Mustang SportsRoof match racers with the 427 SOHC. Those rode on American Racing Torq Thrust wheels.

The teams would visit participating dealerships during the week to host Drag Team Seminars for those interested in promoting tech and product advice; when the weekend arrived, they were competing at a nearby drag strip.

When a dealership scheduled a Drag Team Seminar, a team coordinator would visit the dealership before the event to assist in making all the necessary press releases to the local news media and supply free material to qualified club members. Stipulations included promoting racing at supervised strips, taking an interest in member activities (including hosting meetings), conducting service clinics, and carrying out advertising and publicity activities.

Ford Drag Club

Drag racing was attracting 20 million enthusiasts between the ages of 16 and 60, with 800,000 participating in the sport. It was only natural to encourage Drag Team Seminar participants to sign up for a respective dealer's Ford Drag Club, which helped the dealership maintain a relationship with local performance enthusiasts "to tie you in with the Drag crowd, gain publicity and goodwill, promote salesroom traffic and increase Parts sales," touted Ford.

John Brantmeier, who was the National Coordinator and Eastern Drag Team Coordinator for the Ford Drag Clubs, told journalist Jerry Heasley, "We would bring two of the cars, typically the Super Stock Mustang and Fairlane Cobra. Then, Hubert and Randy Payne would put on a seminar, including a film about Ford's racing efforts, muscle parts on display boards, and a question and answer session to get a chance to talk [about] what would make a Ford run fast. Ford also built colorful trucks and haulers to move the cars around the country. They handed out fliers and brochures and jackets. They even published a newsletter."

Hubert Platt gives the skinny on Ford Muscle Power Parts. Part of his contract with Ford was to play the role of salesman and (to use a contemporary word) influencer. (Photo Courtesy Allen Platt)

To introduce the 428 Cobra Jet alone did not solve Ford's problems on the street, and Ford Drag Team members such as Hubert Platt helped spread the word that yes, Virginia, Ford had the suds from the parts department AND from the factory to take all comers. (Photo Courtesy Allen Platt)

CHAPTER SEVEN

1970 AND THE DEBUT OF THE 429 COBRA JET

Ah, the 1970s! Generally regarded as the high point of the muscle car era, 1970 was a moment that would be fleeting—real performance wouldn't reappear until decades later. This was the year of the Kent State University tragedy, continued civil rights battles, and the gradual invasion of small, fuel-efficient cars from Japan. The latter, combined with increasing insurance premiums and a looming oil crisis, would go on to change the American automotive landscape forever.

Regional specials such as the 1968 California Special and 1966–1968 High Country Special Mustangs have national awareness on the collector market. The 1970 Twister Special Mustang is another regional variant that has gained national prominence over the years. (Photo Courtesy David Newhardt/Mecum Auctions)

Aside from this identifying decal and a black longitudinal stripe, Twister Special Mustangs were simply Grabber Orange Mustang Mach Is. Ninety-six were built for Kansas City–area dealerships featuring either the 351 4V or 428 Super Cobra Jet. (Photo Courtesy David Newhardt/Mecum Auctions)

In 1970, Chevrolet released its killer LS6 454/450 in the Chevelle, Chrysler continued to pump out Hemis and introduced it in its completely redesigned Barracuda, and even American Motors had a new red-white-blue Rebel Machine to join 390 Javelins and AMXs. Ford kept the 428 Cobra Jet as a top-tier performance workhorse and introduced a dramatically different—and more powerful—companion engine: the 429 Cobra Jet.

The 428 Cobra Jet (and the Drag Pack upgrade) for 1970 was identical to the 1969 version, including the 335-hp rating that it was born with. As with the previous year, checking the Drag Pack on the order sheet gave you a Super Cobra Jet engine with either 3.91 or 4.30 gears, an oil cooler, and all the other upgrades. The final year for the FE-based 428 CJ was 1970, as Ford was phasing out the engine (and series) and phasing in the 429-ci 385 engine that had been introduced in the 1968 Thunderbird and expanded for full-size vehicles and the Mustang (in Boss form) in 1969. Hence, while the redesigned midsize series received the new 429, the carryover Mustang and Cougar were the only vehicles available with the 428 CJ in 1970.

Ford

It was a big year for everyone. While the performance market was already in decline, 1970 would be marked as the year when competition peaked. Ford was heavily armed, carrying over the 428 Cobra Jet for the facelifted Mustang and maintaining its strong form against the onslaught from Chrysler with its new E-Bodies. And General Motors? The F-Bodies (Camaros/Firebirds) were delayed until the middle of the 1970 model year, giving the Mustang an opportunity to avoid what could have been heavy competition.

The midsize Torino series—the bread and butter of the performance market—was all-new with several debuting engines but maintaining the unit-body construction of the previous several years. The innovative Shaker hood scoop that was introduced in 1969 for the Mustang was now also a part of the Torino series. With a solid new 429 engine series powering the most powerful Torinos, Ford was loaded for bear among the 7.5L engines from General Motors and expanded Six Pack availability from Chrysler.

Mustang

The 1970 Mustangs themselves were facelifted with a few cosmetic changes, including two headlights instead of the four (with simulated intakes in place of the former outboard headlights), inset taillights, and the removal of the simulated air intake on the top of each rear quarter panel (which was previewed by the 1969 Boss 302). Cobra Jet models also received a rear sway bar. New "Grabber" colors helped highlight the Mustang's sporty character with the youth set. The GT package was gone for 1970, but the Boss 429 and Boss 302 continued for a second and final year, with the latter becoming much more popular—likely a function of the phenomenal popularity of the Camaro Z28.

A large segment of enthusiasts feel that the 1969–1970 generation is the most attractive Mustang. Also, while it was slightly bigger than earlier Mustangs, the 1969–1970 series was a better-driving, better-handling car in many respects.

This 1970 Mach I was a special promotional Mustang used at Michigan International Speedway as part of the American Raceway Incorporated (ARI) Pace Car program. All pace cars from the five racetracks received distinctive stripes and identifying decals, plus "428 CID" painted on the hood. There were five Mach Is and five convertibles (plus a number of 351 Mach Is for Texas International Raceway). ARI went bankrupt before finishing all five tracks. (Photo Courtesy Peter Linney)

This 428 Cobra Jet Mustang came with the Drag Pack, as identified by the engine oil cooler mounted in front of the radiator (on the right) and relocated horns on the left. (Photo Courtesy Peter Linney)

A 1970 Mustang racing at Milan Dragway near Detroit. Based on the longitudinal stripe, could this be an ARI Mach I originally built for Michigan International Speedway? (Photo Courtesy Steve Magee)

This Dark Ivy Green metallic 1970 Mustang SportsRoof was built with the R-code 428 Cobra Jet with Shaker and 3.00 Traction-Lok gears. Only 496 SportsRoofs were built with this engine, 39 of those with C6 Cruise-O-Matic. (Photo Courtesy Jerry Heasley)

Hardtop

The bread and butter of the Mustang line, there were few changes, notably high-back bucket seats and a Hurst shifter for the 4-speed (which was available with the 302 and larger engines). As before, the hot route for racers was to order a coupe with the 428 Cobra Jet plus the Drag Pack. The Q-code CJ did not include ram air, while R-codes received the Shaker hood scoop, which could be complemented by a hood stripe like what was standard on the Mach I. According to Marti Auto Works, 56 hardtop coupes (not including the Grandé) were built with the CJ, of which 15 had the Drag Pack.

Grandé

The fanciest of Mustangs continued its luxury ways after a successful 1969 introduction. In fact, Plymouth and Dodge responded in kind with the Barracuda Gran Coupe and Challenger SE, respectively. Luxury cloth and vinyl seat trim, special sound insulation package, wood tone appliqués, dual body side paint stripes, dual color-keyed racing mirrors with driver's side remote, and rocker panel moldings. New was a Landau-style vinyl roof black panel appliqué on the rear. Only 14 Grandés were built with the Cobra Jet.

SportsRoof

The sporty style of the fastback returned for 1970, featuring all the goodness that made 1969 a successful redesign. As before, the 428 Cobra

These pictures may invoke images of a Mach I, but this Mustang SportsRoof features the R-code 428 Cobra Jet with optional black stripe. (Photos Courtesy Jerry Heasley)

The most obvious design change for the 1970 Mustang was its nose, with two headlights inside the grille surrounded by simulated intakes in place of the outboard headlights that were on the 1969s. The Cobra Jet and Drag Pack were mostly the same for 1969–1970. (Photos Courtesy David Newhardt/Mecum Auctions)

Jet was available with or without the Shaker. It was possible to order a wide stripe across the hood, like what was standard on the Mach I. For the base SportsRoof, 567 were built with the 428 Cobra Jet, of which 198 had the Drag Pack.

Mach I

Back again after spearheading the Mustang's new performance image, the Mach I featured many changes beyond what was done for the basic Mustang's facelift. Most noticeable were the two "sports lamps" in the grille. The hood featured a huge stripe from front to back in either black or white (complete with 351 or 428 engine callouts), which was paired with a wide stripe on the decklid. Below, on the back panel, was a black honeycomb appliqué. Along the sides, the Mach I eschewed the side stripe used in 1969

In 1968, air-conditioning was not available with the 428 Cobra Jet. But it was for 1969–1970, even with the Shaker hood scoop. Its appearance here implies this vehicle does not have the Drag Pack.

and instead used dark argent extruded aluminum rocker panel moldings.

Other features included color-keyed dual racing mirrors, rim blow deluxe three-spoke steering wheel, hood lock pins, console with wood-tone appliqué, NVH sound package, and more. The 351 2-barrel was standard, but the new 300-hp 351 4-barrel "Cleveland" was the high-output answer the Windsor may not have been. The 390 was gone, so all that was left was the 428 Cobra Jet, plus the Drag Pack. Mach I CJ production was 3,185, with 857 having the Drag Pack.

Since the 1970 Shelby GT500 was basically reserialized 1969s, differences were minor. The most noticeable update was the black painted stripes on the hood. (Photo Courtesy David Newhardt/Mecum Auctions)

Convertible

Convertible sales continued their downward trend, but how could you have a Mustang without a convertible? It featured the same standard items as the hardtop but with the addition of a power-operated top with a glass backlight and courtesy lights under the dashboard. The 428 Cobra Jet was available, as was the Drag Pack, with 47 Q- and R-codes built. Of those, 9 were SCJs.

Shelby

Both the Shelby GT350 and GT500 SportsRoof and convertible were carryovers from 1969. No, it's not that they didn't receive any changes, but rather they were reserialized leftover 1969s because Ford decided it did not want to continue Shelby production. To distinguish the 1970s from 1969s, Ford

From this profile, the 1970 Shelby GT500 looks like it may have influenced the styling of the redesigned 1971 Mustang. (Photo Courtesy David Newhardt/Mecum Auctions)

The R-code 428 Cobra Jet, as equipped in the 1969–1970 Shelby GT500, was identical to the Mustang's, aside from the air induction system. (Photo Courtesy David Newhardt/Mecum Auctions)

painted two black stripes on the hood and added a chin spoiler. In total, Shelby sold 380 GT500 SportsRoofs (104 of those were equipped with the Drag Pack) and 90 convertibles (with 21 having the Drag Pack).

Midsize Fords

Ford was moving away from the rounded body lines that had characterized the 1968–1969 Fairlane/Torino series, instead moving toward a more angular, swoopier design for 1970. Penned by Bill Shenk, the inspiration was from the supersonic airplanes with narrow middles and pronounced front and rear "fuselages" designed for the rigors of supersonic speeds.

The 1970 Fairlane/Torino featured more aggressive long-hood/short-deck styling (a hallmark of sports and pony cars) and was longer/lower/wider than the previous year's model. With a longer 117-inch wheelbase, 5 inches added to its length, and a wider 60.5-inch front track (60 inches in the rear), the series was now 100 pounds heavier. The good news with the increase in size was that the space between the shock towers in the engine compartment was widened, allowing for the new 429 to fit comfortably. However, the suspension was a carryover from 1969. The windshield rake was increased, which lowered the roofline, and the fastback SportsRoof models (Torino Cobra, Torino GT, and come midyear, Torino) had a very flat roofline for a contemporary, racy look. These changes made the Torino appear far more aerodynamic than before, although wind tunnel tests proved otherwise.

Engine choices began to get interesting with the 4-barrel 351 Cleveland with 300 hp, then a trio of 429s next on the option list: the first was the 429 Thunder Jet (in Ford literature, it was "429 4v") with 360 hp, which was the standard engine for the Torino Cobra. Next was the 370-hp 429 Cobra Jet ("429 Cobra" in Ford literature) with a two-bolt main block, hydraulic lifters, 715-cfm Rochester Quadrajet carburetor.

The top option was the 429 Cobra Jet with ram air (Ford called it "429 Cobra Jet Ram Air"). Both of the latter two Cobra Jets were available with the Drag Pack, which brought horsepower up to an advertised 375. As before, the Drag Pack included either the 3.91 or the 4.30:1 axle ratio plus four-bolt main engine block, forged pistons, 780-cfm Holley carburetor, external engine oil cooler, and a solid lifter cam.

The Detroit Locker rear differential was available midyear for 4.30:1-geared vehicles; otherwise, both axles came with Traction-Lock limited-slip differential. A 3-speed transmission was standard on all models except for the Cobra, which came with a 4-speed. The Cruise-O-Matic (FMX or C6, depending on the size of the engine) was optional for all engines, while the 4-speed transmission was available on all engines starting with the 351 2-barrel.

Air induction was optional for the 351 2-barrel and 4-barrel and standard with the 429 Cobra Jet with ram air, but it did not change the advertised power ratings. The Shaker system that resulted in many "me too!" responses was now the way to better breathing for the Torino series, using a scoop attached to the top of the air cleaner and protruding through a hole in the hood.

The model year started off with 13 different models in the series but closed the year with 17. The Fairlane was discontinued, leaving the Fairlane 500 as the base model until midyear, when Ford introduced the 1970½ Falcon, a model placed below the Fairlane 500; for the two-door, it was the only midsize Ford coupe with a B-pillar. At top was the new Torino Brougham, which came standard with hidden headlights.

It was a pretty successful year for the Torino, named the *MotorTrend* Car of the Year for 1970, with the magazine saying that the Torino was "Not really a car line in the old sense, but a system of specialty cars, each for a different use . . . from luxury to performance." Ford produced 230,411 Torinos for 1970, along with 110,029 Fairlane 500s and 67,053 Falcons, for a total series production of 407,493 units. And yes, all of them were available with the 429 Cobra Jet engine, though most of them had the 302 or 351 2-barrel.

Falcon

Ford announced the 1970½ Falcon as "Ford's all-new edition of America's all-time economy champ." For only one-half of a model year, Ford

Midyear in 1970, Ford reintroduced the Falcon name as an entry-level intermediate. Compared to a performance-oriented Torino Cobra, the Falcon's lack of amenities made it lighter, making the Falcon a favorite of wise drag racers not conscious about image. This Grabber Green C-code Falcon features an owner-added GT hood. (Photo Courtesy Barrett-Jackson)

offered a cut-rate midsizer something it had lacked since 1967: a two-door sedan with a B-pillar. There was a mild recession in 1970, and several manufacturers introduced value-added alternatives to their portfolio. Hence, the 1970½ Falcon was introduced to put "economy ahead of all but comfort and good looks."

The series included several bodystyles (including a four-door sedan and a wagon), but racers gravitated to the two-door. Included with the Falcon was a vinyl-coated, color-keyed floor covering, two-spoke steering wheel, and an all-vinyl bench seat in black or blue. Best of all, the 429 Cobra Jet was available, as was the Drag Pack. When the model year was over, 165 Falcon two-door sedans were built with the Cobra Jet, with 135 having the Drag Pack.

Fairlane 500

With the base Fairlane now gone, the Fairlane 500 was the base model for the Torino series at the beginning of the 1970 model year (until the debut of the Falcon). Touted as "modest, but not timid," the Fairlane 500 came with cloth and vinyl bench seats, concealed windshield wipers, wheel lip moldings, and bright trip moldings as some of the standard features. As before, Ford used two grilles to separate lower and higher trim levels, so the Fairlane 500 used a distinct design (shared with the Falcon and Torino Cobra) that was not available with hidden headlights. No stats are available on how many two-door hardtops were built with the Cobra Jet, but 20 had the Drag Pack.

Torino

Only two years before, this model was introduced to eventually usurp the Fairlane, and its job was almost done. Atop the Fairlane 500 model, the Torino added nylon-rayon color-keyed carpeting, improved interior trim like textured cloth and vinyl seats, bright window frames, hood and fender moldings, body side moldings, and a black decklid appliqué. All Torinos featured a deep eggcrate grille, with the option of hidden headlights. Midyear, Ford added a Torino SportsRoof bodystyle, giving consumers a bit of sportiness at a pedestrian price. According to Marti Auto Works, 40 J-code Torino two-door hardtops were built, but C-code hardtop and CJ SportsRoof production is unknown.

Only 69 1970½ Falcon two-doors were built with the C-code 429 Cobra Jet. There were more J-code ram air cars built. (Photo Courtesy Barrett-Jackson)

The Torino N/W was a regional promotion for the Northwestern United States. There were 395 built, with only 1 featuring the J-code 429 Cobra Jet. To boot, it has the Drag Pack. (Photo Courtesy Mark Andersen)

Torino GT

Maybe the Torino Cobra was getting all the press, but the Torino GT was the looker. As "Cobra's luxury-loving cousin," the Torino GT came standard with a 302 2-barrel, so enthusiasts needed to order at least the 351 4-barrel to obtain performance that matched the GT's looks. Like the Cobra, the Torino GT lost the hardtop coupe, but the GT model also featured the only convertible of the series. Distinguishing equipment included a simulated hood scoop (replaced by the Shaker when air induction was ordered) and hash marks with GT badges just behind the doors. Other standard equipment included full-width honeycomb taillight inlay with black decklid appliqués, rocker panel and wheel lip moldings, and dual color-keyed racing mirrors, among other items. Optional visual candy included hidden headlights, and Laser stripes that transition from one color to another end-to-end. Production of 429 Cobra Jet SportsRoofs totaled 1,293, with 241 of those equipped with the Drag Pack. For the convertible, 94 were built with the CJ, 19 of which had the Drag Pack.

This 1970 Torino GT features optional hidden headlights and J-code 429 Cobra Jet with ram air. The Shaker was attached to the engine, not the hood, hence the name. (Photo Courtesy Eric English)

The 1970 Torino GT came standard with a hood featuring a simulated hood scoop. When ordered with ram air (for 351s) or the 429 Cobra Jet with ram air, a Shaker air induction system was utilized. (Photo Courtesy Eric English)

Note the engine oil cooler, an easy way to identify the Drag Pack option on a 429 Cobra Jet. That meant this car is powered by a Super Cobra Jet. (Photo Courtesy Eric English)

The redesigned 1970 Torino GT convertible was the only midsize droptop available. Note the standard grille with exposed headlights, side GT identification, and optional Laser stripes. Only 64 were built with the J-code 429 Cobra Jet with ram air. (Photo Courtesy American Muscle Car Museum)

Only the Torino GT received full-width taillights with a honeycomb taillight inlay. The GT convertible in particular also had its own trunk lid, so it didn't feature the built-in spoiler or black highlights of its SportsRoof counterpart. (Photo Courtesy American Muscle Car Museum)

The standard 1970 Torino GT hood included a non-functional wide-mouth scoop. When ram air or the J-code 429 Cobra Jet was ordered, the Shaker mechanism was used. (Photo Courtesy American Muscle Car Museum)

Torino Cobra

The Cobra was the Torino's image model for the performance set. It was now part of the Torino line but continued to be trimmed out like a Fairlane 500 in its role as capturing enthusiasts shopping for the Plymouth Road Runner. The Torino Cobra now was only available as a SportsRoof and came standard with a Hurst-shifted 4-speed, Competition suspension, flat black hood (with twist-style hood latches), blackened Fairlane 500 grille, and F70-14 tires. *MotorTrend* tested a Cobra with the 429 Cobra Jet, an automatic, and 3.50:1 gears and it ran 0–60 in 6.0 seconds and the quarter mile in 14.5 seconds at 100 mph flat. Not earth-shattering but impressive for a car carrying that weight and size.

MotorTrend editors said, "The weight obviously helped traction, as it was fairly easy to accelerate away from a standing start with only a modicum of wheelspin." The magazine also tested a 429 SCJ with a 4-speed and 3.91:1 gears that ran 0–60 in 5.8 seconds and a 13.99 ET at 101 mph. *Super Stock and Drag Illustrated* bettered that in its SCJ Cobra with C6 automatic and 3.91:1 gears with 13.63 at 105 mph, but that was with some carburetor tuning. With drag slicks, the time dipped to 13.39 at 106. Out of 7,675 Torino Cobras, 4,462 featured the Cobra Jet. Of those, 1,475 were ordered with the Drag Pack.

The 1970 Torino Cobra was only available as a SportsRoof fastback. Standard equipment included a 429/360, Hurst-shifted 4-speed, Competition suspension, a flat black hood with twist-style hood latches, black grille, and F70-14 tires. The Shaker scoop means it has the J-code 429 Cobra Jet. (Photo Courtesy Eric English)

The 1970 Torino Cobra could have the Shaker air induction system only when the 429 Cobra Jet ram air engine was ordered. However, for the Torino GT and other models of the series, the Shaker was also available for both 351s. (Photo Courtesy Eric English)

All 1970 Torino Cobras came with 429 engines, with 4,462 of 7,675 being powered by the Cobra Jet. (Photo Courtesy Eric English)

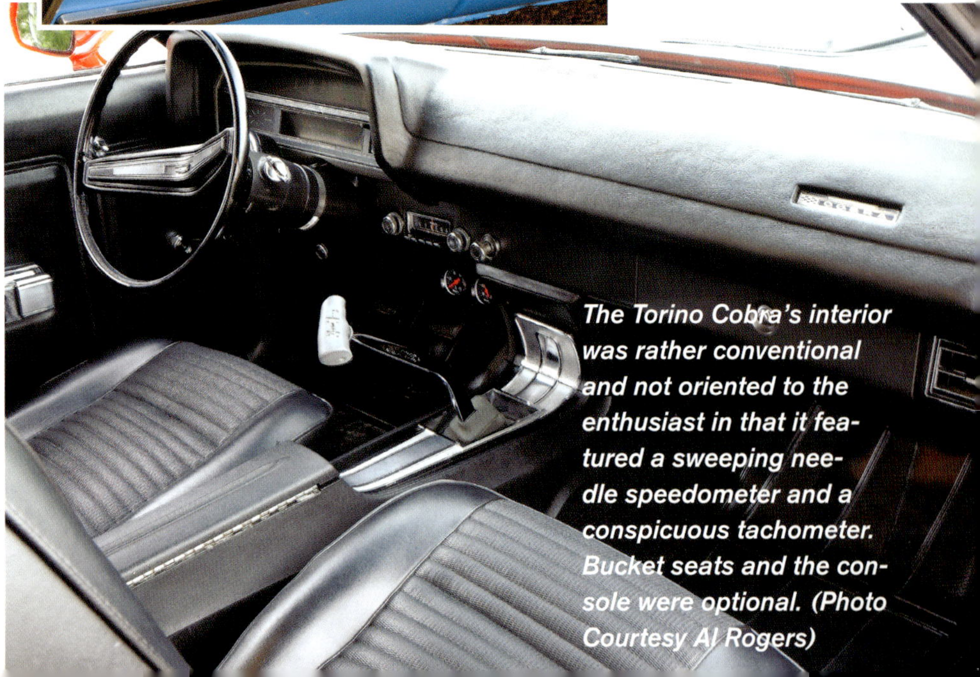

The Torino Cobra's interior was rather conventional and not oriented to the enthusiast in that it featured a sweeping needle speedometer and a conspicuous tachometer. Bucket seats and the console were optional. (Photo Courtesy Al Rogers)

King of the Torino Cobras

Designed as an answer to Mopar's "winged warriors," the Ford Torino King Cobra never made it to production, the result of unfinished aerodynamic development, organizational cuts (both executive and budget), and perhaps a reflection of the changing market as well. Two are known to exist, with this yellow one possibly saved from the crusher by Ford racing legend Bud Moore.

Ford had done well with its long-nose 1969 Torino Talladega (and its Cyclone Spoiler II counterpart) as an answer to Dodge's Charger 500 thanks to drivers David Pearson, Richard Petty, Cale Yarborough, and LeeRoy Yarbrough. Despite Dodge upping the ante with the Charger Daytona, Ford still managed to capture the 1969 Championship.

With a Superbird variant of the 1970 Road Runner being planned, Ford Racing director Jacque Passino instructed Ford's Special Design Center director Larry Shinoda to create aerodynamic improvements for the all-new Torino SportsRoof, which had several stylistic features that were counterproductive for slippery top-end runs. It is said Passino was inspired by the Le Mans–winning GT40, so Shinoda and Special Vehicles Engineering designers Chuck Mountain and Ed Hall drafted up a sloped front clip that could be transplanted to the front of a stock Torino. The new nose extended the Torino's length by more than half a foot; like the Talladega (and Spoiler II), the rocker panels were rolled to assist in lowering the vehicle profile.

Alas, real-world testing uncovered a fatal flaw. While the nose managed to add 200 pounds of downforce, the SportsRoof's backlight created a lot of turbulence and, hence, lift. Before the problem could be corrected, Ford president Semon "Bunkie" Knudsen was fired. And the racing budget was trimmed. Considering NASCAR began mandating one car per dealership to homologate a vehicle, Ford would need to sell more than 3,000 King Cobras. It simply was not in the cards.

In town to pick up Mustangs for the 1971 Trans-Am racing season, race car builder Bud Moore was taken by the King Cobra that was in a Ford garage and asked that it be included in the set. Basically, a C-code Cobra with a prototype fiberglass nose cone (NASCAR regulations required steel pieces), the King Cobra remained in Moore's possession for several decades, acquiring several hundred miles on the odometer before being sold. Today, it sits with fewer than a thousand miles.

Along with the revamped front clip (which added 6 inches to the length), the King Cobra also was planned to have rolled rockers à la the 1969 Torino Talladega. (Photo Courtesy David Newhardt/Mecum Auctions)

This King Cobra started off as a C-code Torino Cobra that was subsequently fitted with a prototype GT40-inspired nose that, along with the hood, was made out of fiberglass. Production pieces would have been steel per NASCAR requirements. (Photo Courtesy David Newhardt/Mecum Auctions)

The rear of the King Cobra is stock Torino Cobra. Evidently, the concave backlight created turbulence that rendered the vehicle unstable at high speed. (Photo Courtesy David Newhardt/Mecum Auctions)

Torino Brougham

As the new top-line model, the Brougham was somewhat a mid-size LTD in attitude. Hidden headlights were standard, as was a more luxurious interior, special soundproof package, and full wheel covers. While performance fans didn't naturally gravitate to the Torino Brougham, 25 ordered a two-door Brougham with the 429 Cobra Jet, with 2 of those having the Drag Pack.

The 1970 Torino series' top trim level was the Torino Brougham, which usually wasn't ordered with performance options. This one, however, is one of three built with the J-code 429 Cobra Jet with ram air and 4-speed. (Photo Courtesy Eric English)

The 429 Cobra Jet in the 1970 Torino was identical to that most often found in the Torino Cobra and Torino GT. Even the Drag Pack was available. (Photo Courtesy Eric English)

Ranchero

Like its copycat competitor, the Chevrolet El Camino, the Ranchero featured a pickup-style bed behind the front seats. And like the Torino series, the Ranchero featured a similar hierarchy of trim levels, from Ranchero, Ranchero 500, Ranchero GT, and Ranchero Squire (complete with simulated wood paneling). The drivetrain options were similar, with the GT starting off with a 302 2-barrel and all models being available with the 429 Cobra Jet plus the Drag Pack.

There were 201 Ranchero GTs built with the 429 Cobra Jet, including 60 with the Drag Pack. The writers don't have complete CJ statistics for other Ranchero models, but, according to Marti Auto Works, 7 Rancheros and 9 Ranchero 500s were built with the Drag Pack.

The 429 Cobra Jet, as installed in the Ranchero, was most popular on the Ranchero GT. As installed in a lesser Ranchero like the Ranchero 500, it makes for a very interesting collectible, especially with the Shaker. (Photo Courtesy David Newhardt/Mecum Auctions)

Interestingly, the 1970 Ranchero 500 was built with the Fairlane grille through December 29, 1969. Afterwards it utilized the Torino grille. This early example is one of nine built with the Drag Pack. (Photo Courtesy Aaron Somerville)

Mercury

Like its sister division, Mercury featured a little old and a little new, but nothing stale in the least. With 1970 being a carryover year for the Cougar, it was only refreshed with new styling (harkening back to 1967–1968) and a more outrageous Eliminator. The 428 Cobra Jet was the largest engine available, again with or without air induction. The Boss 429 was advertised but not built.

The Montego series was all-new for 1970, with the Comet finally disappearing (although the name would be revived in 1971 for Mercury's version of the compact Maverick). The Cyclone models also were reconfigured to target specific segments of the performance market. The marketing strategy possibly may have been sound, but 1970 was not a good year for high-performance car sales, with the Cyclone being among the weakest despite wide availability of the new 429 Cobra Jet.

Cats Prowling

The 1970 Cougar was very similar to the 1969 model, but the front end returned to the "electric shaver" look from 1967–1968, now with a big center hood extension that wrapped in between the grilles. High-backed bucket seats, like those used in the 1969 Eliminator, became standard on all Cougars. Other changes included a new taillight bezel pattern, new front bumper and fender extensions, and larger side markers. In 1970, 71,343 Cougars were built, which was a sales drop of 25 percent from 1969, but the pony car market as a whole was down.

Engine-wise, the base offerings were the 351 2-barrel and, new for 1970, the 351 4-barrel Cleveland with 300 hp. The 390 was officially gone, but you could get a Boss 302 for the Eliminator and, of course, the 428 Cobra Jet. As before, the Drag Pak was available; when equipped with 4.30:1 gears, it became the Super Drag Pak, with the Detroit Locker becoming available midyear.

The 1970 Cougar Eliminator was the only Cougar that featured a stripe on the hood. Note the blacked-out grilles. (Photo Courtesy David Newhardt/Mecum Auctions)

Ford Versus Mercury Cobra Jets

As you've read in previous chapters, the 1968 428 Cobra Jet was signified by an R in the fifth character of the VIN, whether a Ford or Mercury, whether ram air (pony cars) or not (midsizers). In 1969, with an expanded Cobra Jet program, both pony cars and midsize vehicles generally had a choice of two Cobra Jets: non–ram air cars featured a Q in the VIN, while ram air cars received an R (why FoMoCo used a different character for air induction is anyone's guess).

But in 1970, Mercury did things in a different manner than Ford. While the Mustang maintained the Q- and R-code system, the Cougar only used the Q for Cobra Jets. Want ram air? Then it would be ordered as a separate option—it would not trigger a different engine code.

The 429 Cobra Jet was similar. For the Fairlane, Torinos, and midyear Falcon, it was either C or J, but Montegos and Cyclone only used a C, with the choice of ram air a separate option.

For 1971, both Ford and Mercury were back to using the same characters for the 429 CJ.

Cougar

Thanks to a lengthened hood to complement the new front end, plus the wraparound front bumper, 2.3 inches were added to the Cougar's length. Otherwise, what was new was a Rosewood appliqué for the instrument panel, high-back buckets (previously only available for the Eliminator), and Hurst shifter for the 4-speed. A Décor Group added a dose of luxury to the Cougar: full wheel covers, bright curb moldings, Comfort-Weave knitted vinyl buckets, courtesy lights, three-spoke rim blow steering wheel with Rosewood appliqué, and rear seat armrests; this package was standard on the Cougar convertible. When the 428 Cobra Jet was ordered, there were no identifying marks other than a hood scoop when ram air was specified. There were 84 non-Eliminator hardtops with the CJ, plus an additional 7 convertibles.

This 1970 Cougar convertible is one of seven built with the 428 Cobra Jet engine. Motor Wheel Spyders are an owner add-on. (Photo Courtesy John Griffin)

Eliminator

The Eliminator performance package was much more in-your-face for 1970. Only available for the standard Cougar hardtop, it featured a new standard engine in the 4-barrel 351 Cleveland. Optional were the Boss 302 and the 428 Cobra Jet. The Drag Pak was optional for the latter, and the Super Drag Pak was optional for both.

Unique to the Eliminator were a black-out grille and taillight panel, new black beltline stripes and identifying decals by the rear side markers, fiberglass rear spoiler with Eliminator callout and stripes, hood with black stripe and black hood scoop (only functional when ram air was ordered with the 428 Cobra Jet), black front spoiler, and fuel filler door. New hues included a host of "Competition" colors plus Pastel Blue. Out of 2,267 Eliminators built, 374 had the CJ.

The Eliminator package for the Cougar hardtop featured three categories of components: exterior appearance items, performance equipment, and interior treatments. This 1970 Competition Orange Eliminator struts the stripes and the front and rear spoilers that were part of the package. (Photo Courtesy David Newhardt/Mecum Auctions)

Only 374 1970 Cougar Eliminators were built with the 428 Cobra Jet. The ram air option did not use the Shaker scoop like on Fords but, rather, a vacuum-operated butterfly on top of the air cleaner that rammed fresh air directly from the hood's plenum. (Photo Courtesy David Newhardt/Mecum Auctions)

A houndstooth cloth interior was available in two colors for the 1970 Cougar. Out of 1,772 standard Cougar hardtops built with the black/white houndstooth interior, only 92 (including Eliminators) were built with the combination of this interior and Competition Orange paint. (Photo Courtesy David Newhardt/Mecum Auctions)

The 1970 Cougar Eliminator came standard with a hood scoop, but only the 428 Cobra Jet had ram air as an option. (Photo Courtesy David Newhardt/Mecum Auctions)

A unique aspect of the 1970 Cougar Eliminator, which distinguished it from the 1969 version, was the stripe on the spoiler. Stripes were only available in black. (Photo Courtesy David Newhardt/Mecum Auctions)

Cougar XR-7

Once again, the XR-7 played the role of the luxurious Cougar. A grille with chrome and black highlights distinguished it from the standard Cougar; the center section also featured an XR-7 emblem. Other distinguishing features included color-keyed remote racing mirror, unique wheel covers, belt moldings, interior with leather trim, simulated burled walnut trim (including on the standard three-spoke rim blow steering wheel), map pockets behind the front seats, gauges for alternator, temperature, and oil pressure, and visual check panel for low fuel and door ajar, among other items. Like the standard Cougar, there was no visual identification for the 428 Cobra Jet aside from the hood scoop for cars equipped with ram air. XR-7 production with the CJ was 309 hardtops and 66 convertibles.

No, this is not an Eliminator—it's a Competition Yellow 1970 Cougar XR-7 ordered with the 428 Cobra Jet and ram air. Few cars in the market offered this mix of luxury and performance. (Photo Courtesy Eric English)

All 1970 Cougars equipped with the 428 Cobra Jet were Q-codes, unlike in 1969 when there was an R-code that included ram air. If you wanted an air induction system for a 1970 Cougar, one simply ordered ram air as a separate option for the CJ. (Photo Courtesy Eric English)

Only 309 Cougar XR-7 hardtops were built with the 428 Cobra Jet in 1970. Of those, 163 were equipped with ram air. (Photo Courtesy Eric English)

The Cougar XR-7 convertible was the luxurious Cougar, surrounding passengers in leather and vinyl. Add the 428 Cobra Jet and luxury would be surrounded by tire smoke. (Photos Courtesy Mecum Auctions)

Out of the 66 Cougar XR-7 convertibles built with the 428 Cobra Jet, 37 were equipped with ram air. (Photos Courtesy Mecum Auctions)

428 + 1

The 429 used by midsize Ford and Mercury products was a completely different engine from the 428, despite the similarity in size. The block, cylinder heads, and pretty much everything else were completely different. The Drag Pack (or Drag Pak, for Mercury) was also offered for the 429 Cobra Jet to create the 429 Super Cobra Jet.

The 429 CJ's life span was pretty short, lasting only through 1971, thanks to a combination of a changing market, emissions regulations, and Ford deciding not to offer a low-compression version in 1972. And despite it only having a 1-cubic-inch advantage over the 428 CJ, the 429 CJ was rated 35 horsepower more, at 370 hp at 5,400 rpm and 450 ft-lbs of torque at 3,400—add the Drag Pack for another 5 horses. Those are only slightly higher than the base 429 "Thunder Jet" numbers (at 360 hp). However, knowing how manufacturers routinely sandbagged on power output, and looking at the parts differences between the two engines (larger carburetor, larger valves, and a compression ratio of 11.3:1 compared to 10.5:1 for the standard 429), it would not be unreasonable to think the 429 CJ put out at least as much as the 428 CJ.

Midsize Mercurys

Like the Fairlane/Torino, the Mercury Montego was completely redesigned for 1970, with a protruding hood and grille being the most noticeable feature. The Comet model was finally dropped, leaving only the Montego, Montego MX, Montego MX Brougham, and a trio of Cyclones: Cyclone, Cyclone GT, and Cyclone Spoiler. The 429 Cobra Jet was only available on the Cyclones, so the top engine for the Montego models was the 429 4V "Thunder Jet."

Visually, the obvious difference with the Cyclone was the gunsight center surrounded by rectangular running lights. All 429 Cobra Jets were C-codes regardless of air induction or not, and Drag Pak continued to be available for all Cyclones.

Cyclone

The standard Cyclone was the replacement for the Cyclone CJ, so it matched the Torino Cobra for standard engine equipment: 429/360. Also included was a 4-speed transmission, Competition handling package, G70x14 whitewalls, and all-vinyl interior with bench. Standard Cyclones received two pod taillights per side. Also, the standard Cyclone was the only model of the trio to feature a flat hood, with the scooped hood installed when the 429 Cobra Jet with ram air was ordered. All told, 240 Cyclones were built with the CJ, with 89 having the Drag Pak.

Cyclone GT

The Cyclone GT returned as a full-fledged model for the first time since 1968, cousin to Ford's Torino GT except for the standard 351 2-barrel with 3-speed manual. The major distinguishing features were standard hidden headlights, three taillights on each side surrounding a back panel in black or silver, and lower-body trim with, for most colors, contrasting tone-on-tone combinations (contrasting in black, green, or blue, depending on color, or could be deleted).

Other standard features include an integral hood scoop (only functional with the 429 Cobra Jet with ram air), left-hand color-keyed racing mirror with matching right-hand manual mirror, hub caps with trim rings, bright belt and trunk lid moldings, high-back bucket seats, and three-spoke rim blow steering wheel, among others. Engine options included the 351 4-barrel, 429/360, and the 429 Cobra Jet plus the Drag Pak. Only 394 GTs were built with the CJ, of which 73 had the Drag Pak.

Cyclone Spoiler

The Cyclone Spoiler returned for 1970 as a full-fledged model equipped with everything you'd ever want in a performance car: wild colors, stripes, spoilers front and rear, air induction, 4-speed, 3.50 gears with Traction-Lok, G70x14 white-letter tires, bucket seats, full instrumentation, and Competition suspension. Did we mention it came with the 429 Cobra Jet standard as well? Hidden headlights were optional for the Spoiler. All told, 1,631 spoilers were built, with 341 of those equipped with the Drag Pak.

The 1970 Cyclone Spoiler came standard with the 429 Cobra Jet with ram air. No other FoMoCo product came with that engine standard. (Photo Courtesy American Muscle Car Museum)

The Cyclone GT was the style leader of the 1970 Cyclone series. Despite being the most popular Cyclone, the GT with the 429 Cobra Jet was much rarer than the Cyclone Spoiler with the same engine. (Photo Courtesy of Richard Truesdell)

The stripes of the 1970 Cyclone Spoiler were somewhat understated compared to the Cougar Eliminator's, but the bright colors and spoiler spoiled the subtlety. (Photo Courtesy American Muscle Car Museum)

All 1,631 Cyclone Spoilers were built with the 429 Cobra Jet. There was no other way to equip a 1970 Spoiler. (Photo Courtesy American Muscle Car Museum)

CHAPTER EIGHT

1971: THE BEST OF TIMES; THE WORST OF TIMES

While 1971 is often considered the swan song of the muscle car era, the truth is that sales had already started its a downward trend after 1968. Even with strong Mustang Mach I sales for its 1969 debut (72,458), production fell to 40,970 in 1970. The 428 Cobra Jet production for the Mustang fell from 13,261 to 3,489 between the same years.

Out of 42 Mustang convertibles built with the 429 Cobra Jet, only 8 had the Drag Pack. This car's owner added the Mach I grille. (Photo Courtesy Eric English)

And it would get much worse for 1971. But Ford toughed it out, producing high-compression horsepower almost as if there was no end in sight. In comparison, General Motors lowered the compression of its engines in 1971 in anticipation of the new regulations for 1972. The 351 Cleveland and 429 Cobra Jet continued to persevere, while the 428 Cobra Jet was finally discontinued as Ford completely depended on the more modern 385-series 429 for the performance crown.

The 429 Thunder Jet, which had been standard for the 1970 Ford Torino Cobra and base Mercury Cyclone, was discontinued for midsize applications but continued to be available for full-size cars. For the Mustang, the new Boss 351 took over where the Boss 302 left off and, come midyear, a low-compression 351 Cobra Jet would give a preview for what was coming for 1972.

The midsize models were mildly facelifted after being redesigned the previous year, but the Mustang and Cougar were all-new. Larger and heavier, they reflected divergent markets that would be even more distinct two years later.

1971 429 Cobra Jet

While the basic Cobra Jet was identical to the 1970 version, there were several improvements for 1971. Most notably, 1970 Cobra Jet came with two-bolt main bearing caps (at the numbers two, three, and four journals), while the Super Cobra Jet came from the factory with four-bolt mains; for 1971, all 429 Cobra Jets featured four-bolt mains.

1970 and 1971 429 CJs	1970 429 Cobra Jet	+ Drag Pack	1971 429 Cobra Jet	+ Drag Pack (Mustang-only)
Carburetor (cfm)	Rochester 700	Holley 780	Rochester 700	Holley 780
Compression ratio (:1)	11.3	11.3	11.3	11.3
Horsepower	370	375	370	375
Torque	450	450	450	450
Block type	Two-bolt mains	Four-bolt mains	Four-bolt mains	Four-bolt mains
Piston type	Cast aluminum alloy	Forged aluminum alloy	Cast aluminum alloy with steel struts	Forged aluminum alloy
Connection rods	Forged steel	Forged steel	Forged steel	Forged steel
Crankshaft type	Nodular cast-iron alloy	Nodular cast-iron alloy	Nodular cast-iron alloy	Nodular cast-iron alloy
Cylinder head casting number	D0OE-R	D0OE-R	D0OE-R	D0OE-R
Combustion chamber type	Closed	Closed	Closed	Closed
Combustion chamber size (cc)	–	–	69.7–72.7	69.7–72.7
Valve sizes (Intake/Exhaust, inches)	2.248/1.728	2.248/1.728	2.248/1.728	2.248/1.728
Valvetrain type	Hydraulic	Mechanical	Hydraulic	Mechanical
Valve lift (inches)	0.500/0.500	0.515/0.515	0.500/0.500	0.515/0.515
Camshaft duration (degrees)	282/296	300/300	282/296	300/300
Overlap (degrees)	58	72	58	72

1971 351 Cobra Jet

The May 1971 introduction of this engine was somewhat curious since it was so close to the end of the model year, and all it offered was a low-compression route to high performance. As part of the Cleveland series, the 351 Cobra Jet included open-chamber heads, special intake manifold, special long-duration camshaft, special valve springs and dampers, 750-cfm Motorcraft carburetor, dual-point distributor and, interestingly, four-bolt mains. Horsepower was 280 with 350 ft-lbs of torque. Compression was 9.0.

Not many people (or dealerships) were clear on the midyear 1971 introduction of the 351 Cobra Jet. Only 145 were built, including 32 hardtops. (Photo Courtesy Catherine Krupinski)

A preview of what was to come for 1972, the 1971 351 Cobra Jet nonetheless featured a reasonable 9.0 compression that would be cut to 8.6 for 1972. (Photo Courtesy Catherine Krupinski)

1970 351C and 1971 351C and CJ	1970 351 4V	1971 351 4V	1971 351 CJ	1972 351 CJ
Carburetor (cfm)	Autolite 630	Autolite 630	Autolite 750	Motorcraft 750
Compression ratio (:1)	11.0	10.7	9.0	8.6
Horsepower	300	285	280	248/262/266 net
Torque	380	370	345	301 net
Block type	Two-bolt mains	Two-bolt mains	Four-bolt mains	Four-bolt mains
Piston type	Cast aluminum alloy	Cast aluminum alloy	Cast aluminum alloy	Cast aluminum alloy
Connection rods	Forged steel	Forged steel	Forged steel	Forged steel
Crankshaft type	Nodular cast-iron alloy	Nodular cast-iron alloy	Nodular cast-iron alloy	Nodular cast-iron alloy
Cylinder head casting number	D0AE	D1AE	D1ZE	D1ZE
Combustion chamber type	Closed	Closed	Open	Open
Combustion chamber size (cc)	61.3–64.3	64.6–67.6	73.9–76.9	74.3–77.3
Valve sizes (Intake/Exhaust, inches)	2.195/1.715	2.190/1.71	2.190/1.71	2.190/1.71
Valvetrain type	Hydraulic	Hydraulic	Hydraulic	Hydraulic
Valve lift (inches)	0.430/0.450	0.430/0.450	0.480/0.488	0.480/0.488
Camshaft duration (degrees)	268/280	268/280	270/290	270/290
Overlap (degrees)	37	37	46	46

Ford

Ford was last among the Big Three to introduce a redesigned pony car (although AMC did introduce a redesigned 1971 Javelin based on the old platform), but timing wasn't the greatest because the model year was on the cusp for severe engineering changes both under the hood and up front. As such, the 1971 Mustang offered features that would never be seen again, including high-compression engines and a new Boss Mustang

The pedestrian engines were more or less reruns from 1970, but the high-performance engines were a mix of old and new. The 351 4-barrel lost 5 hp to 285 thanks to a slight compression cut to 10.7:1. The next step up was exclusive to the Boss 351 package: a 351 4-barrel with 11.7:1 compression for 330 hp that arguably was the fastest small-block during the muscle car era. Based on the SportsRoof, the Boss 351 was the successor to the Boss 302 (which had been planned but was axed at the last minute). Also included in the package were the 351 HO, ram air, full hood in black or argent, longitudinal racing stripes, 4-speed manual (the only transmission offered), 3.91 Traction-Lok differential, front spoiler, Competition suspension with staggered rear shocks, front disc brakes, F60-15 tires, dual racing mirrors, and more.

The Torino weathered the uncertainty alright, continuing to offer much of the good stuff from 1970, but there were many downgrades to appeal to those less willing to weather the tangled web of insurance rates and emissions. Those who still wished to go full throttle in a 429 Cobra Jet could still satisfy that need.

The Drag Pack continued to be available, but only for the Mustang. Enthusiasts had the choice of either 3.91 or 4.11:1 gears, the latter with the Detroit Locker. The SCJ received a 5-hp bump from the regular CJ, but its true value was in its heavy-duty components. The 1971 Mustang was the only FoMoCo product to have the Drag Pack as an option for 1971, even though it may have been advertised in literature and the press.

Mustang

The completely redesigned Mustang bore little resemblance to earlier Mustangs, but the front end appeared to be influenced by the 1969 Shelby GT. Ford touted the new Mustang as "America's challenge to the great European road cars," with its new size and stance making for a better handling vehicle, according to Ford. At the top was the 429 Cobra Jet still rated at 370 hp. Like the engine available for the 1970 Torino, it featured 11.7:1 compression and was available without ram air (C-code) or with (J-code): the C-code included the Competition suspension, non-functional NASA hood, and 3.25 non-locking rear, while the J-code received a functional air induction system, hood paint in argent or black, twist-type hood lock pins, and 3.50 non-locking rear.

When the 429 Cobra Jet was ordered for a non–Mach I Mustang, it received a NASA scooped hood. However, only J-code CJs came with hood paint and pins. (Photo Courtesy David Newhardt/Mecum Auctions)

An all-new Mustang demanded an all-new interior. The standard seats and door panels rose up a notch or two in style. Note the Instrumentation Group and the three-spoke rim blow steering wheel. (Photo Courtesy David Newhardt/Mecum Auctions)

The new engine series for the 1971 Mustang was paired with a new air induction system, which received callouts like any self-respecting performance car of the era would. (Photo Courtesy David Newhardt/Mecum Auctions)

Midyear, the Q-code 351 Cobra Jet was introduced as a companion to the 351 4-barrel. The main difference between the two was that the CJ offered lower compression and could run on regular fuel.

The ram air system was completely revamped for 1971. After two years of the gee-whiz Shaker system, the Mustang went with NASA ducts that could be made functional with the 351 2-barrel and 4-barrel; it was standard with the Boss 351 and when the J-code 429 with ram air was ordered.

Otherwise, the magic that was the Mustang continued as before, with long hood/short deck proportions that defined the pony car market.

Hardtop

The new hardtop featured flying buttresses and an inset backlight as the C-pillar blended into the trunk lid. Included were fully synchronized 3-speed manual on the floor, DirectAire ventilation, armrests, courtesy lights, concealed windshield wipers, mini console, recessed door handles, and lower back panel appliqué with bright molding. All-vinyl high-back buckets were of a new design (with knitted vinyl or cloth/vinyl when the Décor Group was ordered), and color-keyed loop-pile nylon carpeting kept things pretty and

A 429 Cobra Jet Mustang hardtop was possibly the greatest Q-ship available in 1971. (Photo Courtesy David Newhardt/Mecum Auctions)

The Mustang's interior was also redesigned for 1971. Despite the austere exterior of this Pastel Blue coupe, it is equipped with rare power windows. (Photo Courtesy David Newhardt/Mecum Auctions)

prestigious, considering the Mustang was rather austere in standard form.

The 429 Cobra Jet was available for the lowly hardtop, which added the NASA hood. In total, 48 standard hardtops were built with the 429 Cobra Jet, including 16 with the Drag Pack.

For the 351 Cobra Jet, only 32 hardtops (including Grandés) were built.

Grandé

The Grandé was in its third year of giving Mustang buyers a softer, quieter pony car experience. In addition to the features of the hardtop, the Grandé came with Lambeth luxury cloth and vinyl seat trim, special door panels with integral handles and armrests, courtesy lights, deluxe two-spoke steering wheel, black instrument panel appliqués, electric clock, bright pedal trim, dual color-keyed racing mirrors with left-hand remote control, wheel covers, rocker trim, wheel lip moldings, dual body side stripe, vinyl top, and more.

There were 38 Grandés built with the 429 Cobra Jet, including 5 with the Drag Pack. For the 351 Cobra Jet, 32 were built (including standard hardtops).

SportsRoof

The fastback continued to be marketed as a SportsRoof, the only vehicle of this style in the segment. The redesign created a profile with "a roofline that's nothing but zoomy" since the backlight was practically horizontal (thankfully, it was tinted). Otherwise, everything that was standard on the hardtop was standard on the SportsRoof.

Only 86 SportsRoofs were ordered with the 429 Cobra Jet and, of those, 53 had the Drag Pack. Another 29 were built with the 351 Cobra Jet.

The C-code 429 Cobra Jet without air induction was rated at 370 hp. Ordering the CJ triggered the NASA hood, even though it was non-functional. (Photo Courtesy David Newhardt/Mecum Auctions)

The hood paint and pins suggest this 1971 SportsRoof was ordered with ram air. In this case, it's the J-code 429 Cobra Jet. (Photo Courtesy David Newhardt/Mecum Auctions)

The striping included on the hood carried over to the rear panel for J-code Mustangs save the Mach I, which used a honeycomb insert. (Photo Courtesy David Newhardt/Mecum Auctions)

Mach I

The Mach I gave the Mustang a contemporary race car look, completely shedding its 1960s origins. The main distinguishing feature over other Mustangs was the honeycomb grille with "sport driving lamps" and color-keyed front bumper. Other standard equipment included the 302 2-barrel (a downgrade from the 351 2-barrel of previous years), flat hood (upgraded to NASA hood with optional engines), E70-14 whitewall tires, wheel trim rings, Competition suspension, dual color-keyed racing mirrors with left-hand remote control, dual exhausts, rear honeycomb appliqué, pop-open gas cap, black or argent lower body paint (including front and rear valences), and rear tape stripe with Mach I decal plus two more on front fenders. Optional engines included the 351 2-barrel, 351 4-barrel, midyear 351 Cobra Jet, and a pair of 429 Cobra Jets along with the Drag Pack.

The 1971 Mustang Mach I came standard with body-colored bumpers and special grille hosting the parking lights. When the J-code 429 Cobra Jet or ram air was ordered, the hood was painted in black or argent depending on the body color. (Photo Courtesy Keith Devers)

The Mach I came standard with rear deck stripe and lower body paint. This one features the optional rear spoiler and side stripe. (Photo Courtesy Keith Devers)

The Shaker air induction system was discontinued for Mustangs in 1971. The new NASA-scooped system used vacuum-operated air control valves. (Photo Courtesy Keith Devers)

Only 1,651 429 Cobra Jet Mach Is were built, of which 531 had the Drag Pack. An additional 79 were built with the 351 Cobra Jet.

Convertible

The convertible continued to play the role of the stylish Mustang. Additional features beyond what was standard for the hardtop included a power-operated vinyl top with glass backlight, color-keyed boot, easy-action top fastening latches, courtesy lights underneath the instrument panel, and bright upper back panel molding. In previous years, a big-block CJ convertible was a rather rare specimen, and 1971 was no exception: only 42 429 Cobra Jet ragtops were built, including 8 with the Drag Pack. Five 351 Cobra Jet convertibles also were built.

The Mustang convertible did not have a performance variant, unlike Plymouth's 'Cuda. The optional side stripe shows what it would look like if Ford had one. (Photo Courtesy Eric English)

Torino: Free of the Fairlane

Indeed, the Fairlane 500 had finally been put to rest (as had the Falcon) for 1971, with the series totem pole now being Torino, Torino Cobra, Torino 500, Torino GT, and Torino Brougham. There were only marginal changes for 1971, with one needing a sharp eye to notice some of the tweaks, such as amber parking light lenses. For the Torino 500 on up, the grille was completely different for 1971; when the optional hidden headlights were ordered, the grille was the same as 1970's, aside from the center medallion.

Engine choices remained almost the same, although there were several slight compression ratio adjustments. For the ones that counted for performance enthusiasts, the 351 4-barrel was now rated at 285 hp, and the 429/360 was discontinued, leaving the 429 Cobra Jet (as usual, with and without ram air) as the only other engine for performance enthusiasts. Interestingly, no Torinos received the Drag Pack in 1971; it was only offered for the Mustang for some reason.

Perhaps a reflection of the times, an interesting option appeared for non-performance models: the Laser stripe. While only available for the Torino GT in 1970, its availability was expanded in 1971 to include the Torino Cobra and the Torino 500 SportsRoof. In respect to the latter, performance was dying, and many manufacturers had resorted to dolling up cars with high-performance regalia on more pedestrian mechanical equipment. While it was possible to order a Torino 500 with the 429 Cobra Jet with a Shaker poking through the hood, there was a segment of the population who was more interested in looking sporty rather than paying huge insurance surcharges for something as innocuous as a 4-speed transmission. According to Marti Auto Works, 2,529 Torino 500 SportsRoofs were ordered with the body side tape stripe.

Torino

The standard Torino replaced the Fairlane 500. As such, it featured an argent grille with divider similar to what was used for the 1970 Fairlane 500 (as well as the Falcon and Torino Cobra). A two-door hardtop and four-door sedan were the only bodystyles available. Standard equipment included DirectAire ventilation (for the hardtop), color-keyed vinyl-covered floor mat, and not much else beyond the usual 3-speed manual transmission and heater/defroster blower. The 429 Cobra Jet was available for the standard Torino, but only 10 C-code two-door hardtops were built, plus an unspecified number of J-codes.

Torino Cobra

As the image leader of the Torino series, the Cobra SportsRoof was the victim of changing times. As the previously standard 429/360 had been deep-sixed from the Torino series, and since high-performance cars were in a downward spiral, Ford saw fit to include the 351/285 as the standard engine for the Torino Cobra. Other equipment included was a wide-ratio 4-speed with Hurst shifter, dual exhausts, F70-14 wide-oval whitewalls, heavy-duty load suspension, pleated all-vinyl interior, carpeting, wheel lip moldings, tinted backlight, and a blackened version of the Torino grille.

Visually, there were some tweaks with the Torino Cobra: a blackened rear tail panel and decklid, the hood blackout with a split down the middle, a new Cobra medallion on the grille, and redesigned identifying decals (along with cartoonish nameplate) on the rear fenders. Optional was the 429 Cobra Jet, with or without ram air. Out of 3,054 Torino Cobras built, 968 were powered by a 429 CJ.

This picture shows several of the 1971 Torino Cobra's changes: Cobra medallion in center of grille, split in hood blackout, and available Laser stripes. (Photo Courtesy David Newhardt/Mecum Auctions)

The most noticeable changes made to the 1971 Torino Cobra were the blackout for the rear and the decals and Cobra script on the rear fenders. Magnum 500 chrome wheels were optional. (Photo Courtesy David Newhardt/Mecum Auctions)

The Torino Cobra was rather basic in standard form, but it was possible to dress it up with bucket seats and even power windows. The 4-speed (without console) was standard. (Photo Courtesy David Newhardt/Mecum Auctions)

Torino 500

The Torino 500 was a new model in the series, sitting in the position where the 1970 Torino formerly resided. Most noticeable from the standard Torino was the argent eggcrate grille divided by a crest, which not only defined higher trim levels but also distinguished 1971s from 1970s.

Available as a two-door hardtop, SportsRoof, four-door sedan, and four-door hardtop, the Torino 500 came with full wheel lip moldings, carpeting, cloth and vinyl trim, bright rocker panel moldings, bright drip and full belt moldings (for the SportsRoof), and trunk lock cover. Yes, the 429 Cobra Jet was available for this model, but all we know at the time of printing is that 14 C-code 4-speed hardtop coupes were built.

Torino GT

The sportiest of Torinos continued to offer the only convertible in the series, in addition to the SportsRoof. GT identification changed, moving from the rear fenders (and eliminating the simulated louvers) to the rockers with accompanying dark argent rocker panel molding. The simulated hood scoop, honeycomb taillight inlay, and black inserts in the trunk lid remained.

The 302 2-barrel was still standard, with a duo of both 351s and 429 Cobra Jets available as options. Other standard features included pleated all-vinyl interior, dual color-keyed racing mirrors and left-hand remote, bright drip, full belt moldings, and tinted backlight (for the SportsRoof), and power convertible top and instrument panel courtesy lights (for the convertible). The optional Laser stripe now extended to the rear wheel arches. As before, hidden headlights were an option.

Out of 31,641 Torino GT SportsRoofs, 489 were built with the 429 Cobra Jet. Of the 1,919 Torino GT convertibles, 30 were C-codes, with an unknown number of J-codes built.

Torino Brougham

Amid the series shuffling, the Torino Brougham remained the top-of-the-line Torino. Available as a two-door hardtop and four-door

A 1971 Torino GT convertible is shown with the standard hood. The Laser stripes and hidden headlights were optional. (Photo Courtesy Lee Lundberg)

The 429 Cobra Jet was even available on the high-zoot Torino Brougham. Not only were two built with the J-code CJ but they were both 4-speeds sold within 15 miles of each other. (Photo Courtesy Bill Kulenkamp)

The Mustang introduced the Shaker air induction system in 1969, but only the Torino series offered it in 1971. It was available with both 351s and included when the J-code 429 Cobra Jet with ram air was ordered. (Photo Courtesy Bill Kulenkamp)

hardtop, it was the only Torino model aside of the GT that came standard with a V-8. Other equipment included full wheel covers, Brougham ornamentation, hood and fender moldings, bright lower body side moldings with black fill and quarter panel extensions, wheel lip moldings, an appliqué between the taillights, cloth interior trim, and a soundproofing package. Unlike in 1970, hidden headlights were now optional. Only two J-code two-door hardtops were built; no information is available on C-codes.

Ranchero

So, the Torino series might have moved around a bit for 1971, but the Ranchero series stayed static: Ranchero, Ranchero 500, Ranchero GT, and Ranchero Squire. The biggest change was with the Ranchero GT—while Laser stripes were standard in 1970 (unlike the Torino GT), for 1971 they were optional. Interestingly, the Ranchero GT had an optional hood blackout, which wasn't available for the Torino GT.

There also was a promotional package called the Special, available for the Ranchero, Ranchero 500, and Ranchero GT. All came in one of eight "chromatic" exterior colors with unique longitudinal body stripes plus "Carousel"

The Ranchero GT featured an option list different than the Torino GT, although they initially appeared similar in content. For example, the flat black hood paint was available for the Ranchero GT but not for the Torino GT. (Photo Courtesy Colin Comer)

For some reason, Ford did not offer the Drag Pack for 1971 Torinos and Rancheros. However, the 429 Cobra Jet was updated to four-bolt mains, which was shared with Drag Pack–equipped 1970s. (Photo Courtesy Colin Comer)

The 1971 Ranchero Squire may not have been the sportiest Ranchero model, but it performed that way when equipped with the 429 Cobra Jet. Only two were ordered with the J-code 4-speed. (Photo Courtesy Rod Kotiga)

or "Spectrum" stripe interior trim, blackened hood, black vinyl roof, special black accented box, twin body-color racing mirrors, and bright hubcaps and trim rings.

When the dust settled, 254 Ranchero GTs were built with the 429 Cobra Jet. Another 76 Squires were built with the same engine. No information is available at this time for the Ranchero and Ranchero 500.

Mercury

The all-new Cougar featured the 429 Cobra Jet for the first time, replacing the FE-based 428, but it was no giant-killer, especially since the Drag Pak was not offered. Clearly the Cougar was moving more toward the personal-luxury realm, yet it still had the suds for enthusiasts to appreciate, including the optional 351 4-barrel and the return of the GT package (which added handling components for an American-style *gran turismo*). A 351 Cobra Jet also appeared midyear.

Changes to the Montego series were minimal, but both the base Cyclone and Cyclone Spoiler experienced engine downgrades that made them weaker in standard form than what was offered in 1970. However, the 429 Cobra Jet was available, equaling what was offered in 1970 aside from the Drag Pak being gone from the options list.

The Cat Gets New Claws

If the Mustang was redesigned, it could only mean the Cougar followed suit. However, Mercury took a divergent path as the Cougar was evolving from a more luxurious pony car into something akin to a mini Thunderbird.

The redesigned 1971 Cougar now featured fixed headlights divided by an upright grille. Hood scoop suggests either GT package and/or J-code 429 Cobra Jet—in this case, the latter. (Photo Courtesy American Muscle Car Museum)

Perhaps a "personal sports car," as Mercury called it, would be appropriate?

As was the trend for most cars from the era, the 1971 Cougar became longer, lower, and wider. A longer hood helped exaggerate the pony car proportions. Like the Mustang hardtop, the C-pillar featured a flying buttress backlight, although on the Cougar it appeared more pronounced. The most noticeable change was the elimination of the hidden headlights, with the prow that previously divided the grille in 1970 evolving into a proper diecast vertical grille. Out back, the taillights lost their full-width design that previously mimicked front-end styling, but they still retained the trademark sequential blinkers.

The wheelbase was lengthened 1 inch with the front tread widened by 3 inches and rear tread by 2.5. Nonetheless, length from front to back was

The flying buttresses appeared more pronounced on the 1971 Cougar compared to the Mustang. Taillights were no longer full-width but still featured sequential lights. (Photo Courtesy American Muscle Car Museum)

The 429 Cobra Jet was new for the Mercury pony car, replacing the 428 Cobra Jet that had set the streets afire since April 1968. The vacuum air induction system was similar to what was used before. (Photo Courtesy American Muscle Car Museum)

up less than 1 inch, with width increasing an even inch. These subtle changes were not much, but the redesign made the Cougar appear much larger.

The small-blocks remained relatively static aside from a mild compression cut. The standard 351 2-barrel now featured 240 hp, while the 4-barrel had 285. All new was the replacement for the 428 Cobra Jet, now 1 cubic inch bigger with the 429 CJs. The 429 CJ's available air induction system was similar to previous years. Like the Mustang, the 351 Cobra Jet became available midyear.

The Eliminator was eliminated, leaving no Cougar performance package. However, a GT package left hope for those wanting a sportier cat.

Cougar

"Dramatically new from bumper to bumper" was no lie but, feature-wise, the Cougar remained rather consistent. The base Cougar came standard with a 351 2-barrel backed by a consolette-mounted 3-speed manual, but it was far from austere, especially since it was set off by triple lower body paint stripes. Nonetheless, those wishing for a bit more luxury could opt for the Décor Group (available on the hardtop, standard on the convertible), which included lower-body rocker panel moldings, deluxe wheel covers, deluxe two-spoke steering wheel, door pull strap, Comfortweave vinyl seats, unique door and quarter trim panels, and bright pedal trim. The black camera finish instrument panel, which continued to feature four round gauges, was more cockpit-oriented than before.

The 429 Cobra Jet did not include a hood scoop unless the J-code 429 Cobra Jet was ordered. For the standard Cougar, 26 hardtops (not including GTs) and 20 convertibles were built with both the C-code and J-code 429.

The Cougar GT reappeared for 1971, this time only for the standard Cougar. The hood scoop was included with the package even though the 351 2-barrel was standard. This example is 1 of 15 GTs built with the C-code 429 Cobra Jet—four being 4-speeds. (Photo Courtesy Jeff Koch/Hemmings Motor News)

The taillights bore no resemblance to those from the Cougar's four previous model years. Mercury did a fine job distinguishing the 1971 Cougar from the Mustang coupe. (Photo Courtesy Jeff Koch/Hemmings Motor News)

The C-code 429 Cobra Jet looks like what you'd find in the Mustang, but the Cougar did not have the benefit of having the Drag Pack available. (Photo Courtesy Jeff Koch/Hemmings Motor News)

The Upbeat Stripe Cloth and Vinyl trim option was available for hardtops in four colors, including black, medium blue, medium ginger, and medium green. Matching floor mats were included if the Appearance Protection Group was ordered. (Photo Courtesy Jeff Koch/Hemmings Motor News)

Cougar GT

The Cougar GT returned for the first time since 1968. The package was only available for the standard Cougar hardtop and included the base 351 2-barrel with 3-speed, hood scoop (only functional with the J-code 429 Cobra Jet), E78-14 whitewall tires on hub caps with trim rings, GT badges on the front fender, dual racing mirrors with driver-side remote, black instrument panel, three-spoke rim blow steering wheel covered in black camera case vinyl, tachometer, variable ratio power steering, Competition Handling Package (with rear stabilizer for 4-barrel engines), and Performance Cooling Package. Of the 787 Cougar GT hardtops built, 46 were equipped with the 429 Cobra Jet.

Cougar XR-7

XR-7 returned to play the role of sophisticate, full of upgrades worthy of sporty European luxury vehicles. Leather and vinyl upholstery remained a standard feature of the XR-7, as did full instrumentation that included a tachometer and oil and alternator gauges plus toggle switches. A unique vinyl roof was standard, a 3/4-roof design from the windshield to the front edge of the C-pillar (a conventional vinyl roof was still optional). Other XR-7 upgrades included cherry woodgrain instrument panel, molded door panels with door assist strap, door and quarter belt moldings, driver-side remote racing mirror, three-spoke rim-blow steering wheel, slotted wheel covers, rear hood molding, rocker panel molding, and C-pillar courtesy lights, among other equipment.

The 429 Cobra Jet was more popular on the high-zoot XR-7 than the standard Cougar: 329 hardtops and 27 convertibles were built. Additionally, one single XR-7 hardtop was built with the 351 Cobra Jet—the only 351 CJ ever installed in a 1971 Cougar.

The luxurious Cougar XR-7 interior surrounded the passengers in leather and vinyl. With the demise of the Dodge Challenger R/T SE, this was the only luxury pony car with this level of performance. (Photo Courtesy American Muscle Car Museum)

Cyclone: The Storm Gets Downgraded

After 1970's redesign, changes to the Montego series were minimal in 1971. However, as in 1970, the 429 Cobra Jet was not available for pedestrian Montego models. And like the Cyclone's Ford cousin, model year changes were subtle, with several downgrades that reflected a reduced emphasis on performance. Nonetheless, the Cyclone series continued to push through the doom and gloom with optional 429 Cobra Jet power, although the Drag Pak was noticeably absent.

The biggest visual changes for the Cyclones were subtle: a bigger barrel in the gunsight grille and amber parking lights. For numbers geeks, the 429 Cobra Jet returned to the identical manner as Fords; the CJ without ram air was C-code and with ram air was J-code.

Cyclone

As the performance model with the strongest price/performance quotient, the standard Cyclone featured an engine downgrade to the 351 4-barrel rated at 285 hp. This was partly due to the discontinuation of the 360-hp 429 that was standard in 1970, but it was also done to increase the appeal of the model in a market that was eschewing high-performance cars.

Standard was a 4-speed with Hurst shifter, uniquely patterned Tourchon vinyl bench seat, scooped hood (an upgrade from 1970), quad taillights with blackened rear panel, Cross County Ride Package, and F70-14 raised white letter tires. The only optional engine was the 429 Cobra Jet, with or without air induction. The authors do not know how many of the 444 standard Cyclones built in 1971 were equipped with the 429 CJ, but it is known that 17 were C-code 4-speeds.

Cyclone GT

Among Cyclone models, the stylish Cyclone GT changed the least, continuing to feature a standard 351 2-barrel. Standard equipment mostly was the same too, including a sextet of taillights with horizontal appliqué in between, hidden headlights, Comfortweave vinyl bucket seats, tone-on-tone paint treatment (in most cases, black, but also in dark blue and dark green depending on the color), pewter instrument panel with gauges canted toward the driver, three-spoke steering wheel, Select Shift automatic, and G78-14 whitewalls on deluxe wheel covers, among other standard features. Most unique, though, was the "GT" script in the gunsight.

Of course, in addition to the availability of the 351 4-barrel was the 429 Cobra Jet. Out of 2,287 Cyclone GTs built, 111 were built with the 429 Cobra Jet.

Cyclone Spoiler

The Cyclone Spoiler returned for 1971, now with a 351 4-barrel standard. Nonetheless, the Cyclone Spoiler looked bolder with longitudinal graphics running along the beltline and dipping at the front end. Other unique identifying Spoiler features included flat black spoilers front and rear plus six taillight pods with a black painted rear panel, G70-14 white letter tires on hubcaps with trim rings, Competition Handling Suspension, Comfortweave vinyl buckets, Instrumentation Group, three-spoke rim blow steering wheel with black accents, and 4-speed with Hurst shifter and Traction-Lok rear. The 429 Cobra Jet option was available with or without ram air—only 196 out of 353 Cyclone Spoilers were built with the 429 CJ.

With My Big-Block Boots On

Ford and Mercury should be commended for hanging in for one more model year before the death knell of low-compression engines. General Motors thought it was creating good public relations by going with low-compression engines a year early, but enthusiasts missed out. FoMoCo, on the other hand, had monsters like the 429 Super Cobra Jet to go out in a blaze of glory. On the other hand, the company from Dearborn could be criticized for restricting the Drag Pack to only the Mustang, which also meant restricting digger gears to the pony car as well. How to compete with Six Packs and Hemis when the best gear for the Torino or Cyclone was 3.50? Sure, it was as close as the Muscle Parts catalog, but it almost sounds like shades of 390 Mustang—close, but not quite enough to be competitive.

The 1971 Cyclone Spoiler looked wilder, but its standard engine was tamer than 1970's standard 429 Cobra Jet. As equipped, performance with the CJ was similar aside from the Drag Pak being MIA. (Photo Courtesy Richard Truesdell)

CHAPTER NINE

1972: THE DEATH KNELL HAS RUNG

The 1972 model year was not good for anyone in Detroit—the inevitable had arrived. All cars sold in the United States were required to run on low-lead or unleaded gasoline. They also had more emissions equipment with more regulations to come. To be a performance enthusiast during this moment was to be a dinosaur but, truth be told, the market was evolving in other ways: personal-luxury vehicles were becoming more popular, and they had begun to move downmarket after years of being upper-middle class vehicles à la Thunderbird. The guy who purchased a 428 Cobra Jet in 1968 was ripe to have something more responsible in 1972—maybe even with a baby seat in the back.

The 1972 Mustang looked the same, but underneath the hood there were many changes. Only 531 convertibles were built with the 351 Cobra Jet. (Photo Courtesy Cris Ferregur)

And when it came to dealing with the lean years, Ford Motor Company may have dealt with it the worst. All Detroit-based competitors offered big-blocks putting out at least 270 net horsepower but, in comparison, Ford and Mercury didn't develop the 429 Cobra Jet for low-compression motoring. Rather, Ford reintroduced a low-compression version of the 429 4-barrel (the former Thunder Jet) for the Torino and Montego. Horsepower was a blink-and-rub-your-eyes 205 net horsepower and 322 ft-lbs of torque, and only with an automatic.

And that was the other thing—horsepower was no longer rated in gross terms, which reflected more perfect conditions on an engine stand. Net horsepower was a more honest method where the measurement was done with both engine and accessories installed in the vehicle. This made the horsepower drop appear much more severe, but it all depended on the engine. In the 429's case, 1972 was somewhat of an apples-to-oranges comparison.

And the 351 Cobra Jet? That ended up being FoMoCo's performance torchbearer. It was rated at 248 horses for the Torino and Montego and 266 horses for the Mustang and Cougar (with another version for Cougars putting out 262 hp—more on that below). In most literature, it was simply referred to as the "351 4V" and horsepower ratings were not listed, as if *horsepower* was a dirty word, although that was not unique in the market.

Ford

Ford was unique in betting its 351 would carry the performance banner. Pontiac continued to exploit the 455 (with the 400 being no slouch), and the rest of the General Motors clan offered strong 454 and 455s. Over in Highland Park, the 440 had plenty of support with the 340 and 400, and even American Motors made do with the 360 and 401. So why no performance version of the 385-series 429 when everyone else was trying to maintain the good times?

Thus, the 351 ended up being the only true performance engine in Dearborn. When the 351 CJ was introduced in May 1971, it was rated at 280 gross horsepower. For 1972, with a slight drop in compression (from 9.0 to 8.6), the drop in horsepower was not too severe, even with the new rating system.

Even in the high-compression days, 5.8L engines were not exactly known as being stormers in midsize cars like the Torino, so you can imagine how rough it was to show up at the local joint in a Gran Torino Sport with a 351 CJ when a 455 HO GTO ran ETs about a second quicker. The lighter Mustang was not as compromised, but for all the reasons to be depressed about the state of high-performance, Ford didn't offer much consolation—the 351 HO was one bright spot, but it was only available for the Mustang and very few were built.

Mustang

After 1971's complete redesign, the 1972's changes were subtle outside of what was under the hood. "Mustang for '72 is a refinement and improvement of the car line which has led the sporty compact league since it was introduced," read the sales manual. As before, five models on three bodystyles continued to characterize the series "designed to meet specific market requirements of the sporty compact market." The Décor Group, a longtime resident of the Mustang option list, was notable for 1972 because it gave the hardtop and convertible Mach I–style lower bodyside paint treatment with bright chrome upper molding, plus the Mach I's honeycomb grille and sports lamps, color-keyed front bumper, hood, moldings, and hubcaps with trim rings. Even the Mach I's optional longitudinal stripe was available for vehicles ordered with the package.

The big-block was discontinued, as was the basic 351 4-barrel. The 351 Cobra Jet became the de facto muscle engine with 266 hp—quite generous for its size. In fact, that was a higher rating than the fabled LT1 that was used in the Camaro Z28. Ford even offered a more powerful 351 called the 351 HO, which was the heir apparent of the Boss 351. The solid lifter-cammed engine was rated at 275 hp (down from 330 gross) and was available for every Mustang model and bodystyle. However, not long after the introduction of the model year, ram air was canceled for the CJ and was restricted to the 351 2-barrel.

The 351 Cobra Jet was available with ram air at the beginning of the 1972 model year and then was quickly discontinued, leaving the 351 2-barrel as the only recipient of the option. (Photo Courtesy Jerry Heasley)

1971 and 1972 Cobra Jet 351 Engines	1971 351 CJ	1972 351 CJ
Carburetor (cfm)	Autolite 750	Motorcraft 750
Compression ratio (:1)	9.0	8.6
Horsepower	280	248/262/266 net
Torque	345	301 net
Block type	Four-bolt mains	Four-bolt mains
Piston type	Cast aluminum alloy	Cast aluminum alloy
Connection rods	Forged steel	Forged steel
Crankshaft type	Nodular cast-iron alloy	Nodular cast-iron alloy
Cylinder head casting number	D1ZE	D1ZE
Combustion chamber type	Open	Open
Combustion chamber size (cc)	73.9–76.9	74.3–77.3
Valve sizes (Intake/Exhaust, inches)	2.190/1.71	2.190/1.71
Valvetrain type	Hydraulic	Hydraulic
Valve lift (inches)	0.480/0.488	0.480/0.488
Camshaft duration (degrees)	270/290	270/290
Overlap (degrees)	46	46

Hardtop

For 1972, the base hardtop received several upgrades with the addition of bright wheel lip and rocker panel moldings, deluxe chrome-plated wheel covers, dual racing mirrors, and deluxe two-spoke steering wheel. A floor-mounted consolette was also a new feature. Mostly everything else was the same as 1971, aside of a shuffling of color and trim options. While the hardtop was not the go-to model for most go-fast enthusiasts, 611 people felt the 351 Cobra Jet was perfect for the hardtop (not including the Grandé).

This 1972 Mustang is one of two identical 4-speed 351 Cobra Jet coupes ordered and modified by Firestone for testing. (Photo Courtesy Barrett-Jackson)

After a short run in 1971, the 351 Cobra Jet received several tweaks to make it compliant with 1972 rules, including a slight cut in compression. For its size, it was a strong runner. (Photo Courtesy Barrett-Jackson)

Grandé

As the Mustang for the sophisticated pony car buyer, the 1972 Grandé featured new, unique dual-colored longitudinal tape stripes plus specially ornamented deluxe wheel covers for even more dash. A full vinyl roof, cloth and vinyl interior trim, upgraded instrument panel with black and wood-tone appliqués, and door panels with integral arm rests plus door-pull handles (shared with the convertible) were among other upgrades that set the Grandé apart from other pony cars, if not other Mustangs. For those who desired their horsepower with luxurious trimmings, 430 people ordered the Grandé with the 351 Cobra Jet.

SportsRoof

Ford considered the base fastback "for the buyer who wants the unique Mustang flair but is concerned about price." Performance looks with economical performance was available with the stroke of a pen, but most buyers ordered the 351 2-barrel, which was a happy medium to the general public. To performance enthusiasts, only the 351 Cobra Jet would do—906 SportsRoofs (not including Mach I) were built with the CJ.

Mach I

As the Mustang for the style-conscious enthusiast, the Mach I continued to come standard with a 302 2-barrel and a flat hood, but any engine upgrade included the NASA hood. Dual racing mirrors, white sidewall Wide Ovals, color-keyed front bumper, honeycomb black grille with sportlamps, black honeycomb rear appliqué, black or argent painted lower body (including front and rear valence panels), rear tape stripe with Mach I decals, Competition suspension, and hubcaps with trim rings, among other features. When the 351 Cobra Jet was ordered, chrome exhaust extensions were also included. A robust 7,771 Mach Is were built with the CJ.

Convertible

Along with its Mercury Cougar cousin, the Ford Mustang was the last pony standing when it came to convertibles, as the Plymouth Barracuda and Dodge Challenger discontinued their ragtops. The Mustang convertible received all the 1972 model year upgrades as the above models plus knitted Comfortweave vinyl trim (formerly optional), unique molded door panels with integral pull handles and armrests, and new black instrument panel

The Décor Group was revised for 1972, now including features inspired by the Mach I: lower body side paint treatment with bright chrome molding, Mach I grille, color-keyed front bumper, color-keyed hood and fender moldings, and trim rings/hubcaps. This 351 Cobra Jet convertible was ordered with the package. (Photo Courtesy Jerry Heasley)

appliqué with courtesy lights. Only 531 convertibles were built with the 351 Cobra Jet.

Torino

The midsize Torino line was completely redesigned for 1972, evolving from unibody to body-on-frame construction. The model line also was shuffled once again, with the series now consisting of nine Torinos within the Torino, Gran Torino, and Gran Torino Sport models—all two-doors were hardtops and all four-doors were sedans, plus three wagons. "[Torino] sports new styling, new ride and handling, new engineering and new options," touted Ford. In particular, Ford was most proud of the LTD-like quiet drive for a big-car ride and comfort in an intermediate size. Two-door hardtops used a 114-inch wheelbase while all sedans and wagons were on a 118-inch wheelbase.

The Torino series featured two grille designs as before, but the model lines were distinguished by more than just grilles. The standard Torino featured a dark argent eggcrate grille made of ABS plastic, with front-end styling an evolution of the previous generation's; the Gran Torino and Gran Torino Sport were distinguished by an extended nose featuring a light argent flattened oval "high series grille" design and hatch-type hood. The difference was profound.

The Gran Torino Sport took the place of the Torino Cobra and Torino GT, available as a SportsRoof and formal roof hardtop. A more prominent hood scoop (newly functional when ordered for the 351 Cobra Jet or 429) was the easy way to identify the Gran Torino Sport. Alas, horsepower choices left little doubt that a new era was upon us: top engine was a 248-hp 351 Cobra Jet, with a 206-hp 429 as a torquey alternative. There still were

The 1972 Gran Torino featured a front end distinct from the base Torino, which added several more inches in length. This is a Gran Torino Sport. (Photo Courtesy Jerry Heasley)

Ram air was a very rare option for Gran Torinos and Gran Torino Sports with the 351 Cobra Jet or the 429. A special air cleaner assembly relied on a vacuum-actuated valve to open a trapdoor at near-full throttle. (Photo Courtesy Jerry Heasley)

sporty options, however, such as the Laser stripe, Instrumentation Group (which included tachometer, trip odometer, engine gauges, and electric clock), and Rallye Equipment Group, which packaged the Instrumentation Group with the 351 Cobra Jet, 4-speed, Competition suspension, and G70-14 Wide Ovals on 6-inch rims; the Rallye Equipment Group was also available with the 429.

Torino

Available as a two-door hardtop and four-door sedan plus wagon, the Torino hardtop was the only way to get the 351 Cobra Jet. Standard equipment included 3-speed manual, manual front disc brakes, high-back all-vinyl bench seat, bright drip moldings, and color-keyed vinyl-coated rubber floor mat. Of the 1972 Torinos built with the 351 CJ, it is known that 57 were built with the 4-speed, but there is no information on how many automatics were built.

Gran Torino

Available in four configurations (including two wagons), the Gran Torino added the fancier front end and added cloth vinyl and seat trim, color-keyed carpeting, lower bodyside molding, wheel lip moldings, decklid lock cover, and rear armrests. While not a performance model, the Gran Torino was available with the scooped hood when ram air was ordered for the 351 Cobra Jet or 429. At the end of the model year, 2,031 Gran Torino formal hardtops had been built with the CJ.

Gran Torino Sport

Ford claimed "each Gran Torino Sport gives you lines that say action and mean it. With emphasis like integral hood scoops. Dual racing mirrors. Deluxe steering wheel. Wide-oval [E70-14] white sidewalls. Sporty trim rings with hub caps. And a jaunty new oval grille." Also

The new Gran Torino Sport evolved the SportsRoof bodystyle from 1970–1971. The backlight angle was less flat, complemented by bulging rear fenders. The Laser stripe was optional. (Photo Courtesy Jerry Heasley)

The stock instrument panel for the 1972 Torino utilized five pods, but order the Instrumentation Group and you'd have three pods plus a cluster of five more. Added were a tachometer, trip odometer, engine gauges (oil, amperage, temperature, and fuel), and an electric clock. (Photo Courtesy Jerry Heasley)

included with the Gran Torino Sport formal hardtop and SportsRoof were 302 2-barrel with floor-shifted 3-speed, plush all-vinyl pleated interior trim, door panels with molded-in armrests, deluxe two-spoke steering wheel with simulated wood-tone appliqué, and bright pedal trim. If there was a model to showcase the 351 Cobra Jet, this was it. In total, 12,844 SportsRoofs were built with the CJ, plus an unspecified number of formal hardtops.

Ranchero

For 1972, the Ranchero was available as Ranchero 500, Ranchero GT, and Ranchero Squire. All featured the front-end styling of the Gran Torino. Powerplants were identical to the Torino's, including the 351 Cobra Jet, although the Ranchero GT was not available with a six. The GT came equipped with color-keyed body side stripes, hood with twin air scoop design, body-colored

The standard Ranchero GT interior featured a unique high-back bench seat incorporating integrated headrests, which mimicked buckets quite nicely. (Photo Courtesy Jerry Heasley)

Like on the Torino, the top-performing engine for the Ranchero (GT or otherwise) was the 351 Cobra Jet. (Photo Courtesy Barrett-Jackson)

racing mirrors, hubcaps with trim rings, and E14-70 whitewall tires, among other items. An interesting option unique to the Ranchero GT was black stripes for the hood that were not available for the Gran Torino Sport. The 351 Cobra Jet was installed in 3,332 Ranchero GTs; no information is available at this time on CJ installation for other Rancheros.

Mercury

The vicissitudes of high-performance affected Mercury the same way as Ford, although the division did not have the 351 HO grace its engine lineup. Mercury's model lineup was also quite similar to Ford's aside from respective variations particular to the brands.

Other than the drop in horsepower, 1972 appeared to be a continuation from 1971 for the Cougar, notwithstanding the usual model year changes for colors and interiors. For the Montego, it was different, as its redesign went with body-on-frame construction for the first time in years. If one squinted, it was apparent how the Cougar's styling influenced the Montego's, but that's where the resemblance ended. The Montego GT replaced the Cyclone as the sporty midsizer, bringing back the fastback bodystyle that had last been seen in 1969; unlike the Gran Torino Sport, the Montego GT was not available as a formal coupe.

Cougar

The Cougar's second year of its third generation reflected minimal changes. "Sleek, sophisticated, in the European Grand Touring manner," Mercury claimed. Improvements to sound insulation and the front and rear suspension made for a cushier ride. Color-keyed dual racing mirrors were initially optional but made standard as a running change during the model year.

Like the Mustang, the big-block was gone; however, unlike the Mustang, there were a pair of 351 4-barrel engines. Available for the Cougar above the standard 351 2-barrel, a buyer could opt for a 242-hp 351 4-barrel with a balanced crankshaft, 2½-inch dual exhausts with "Quiet Exhaust,"

The 1972 Cougar XR-7 only received detail changes, but under the hood the changes were quite profound. Only 137 Cougar XR-7 convertibles were built with the 351 CJ Performance Group.

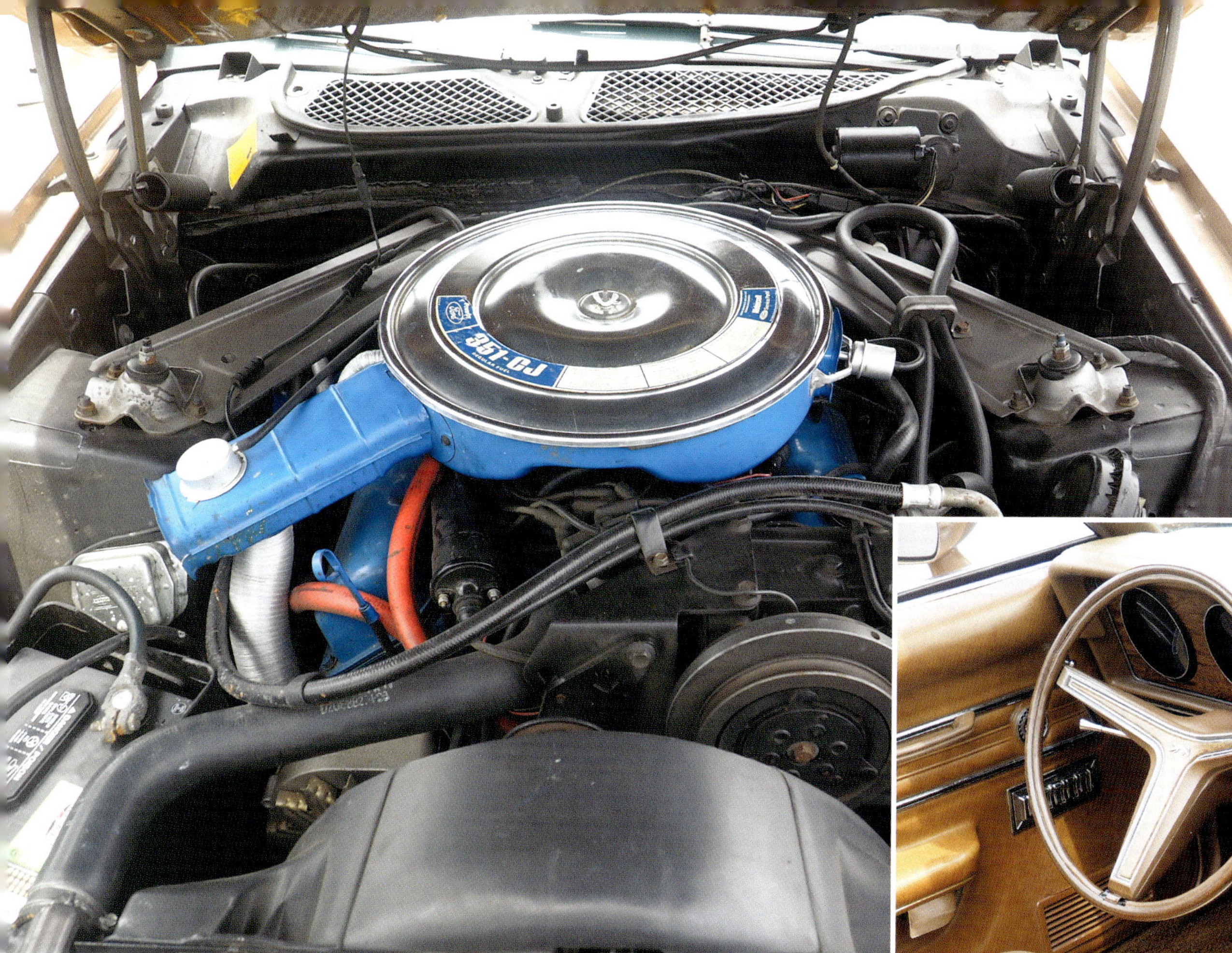

The 4-barrel 351 for Cougars was rated at 262 net horsepower, but when the 351 CJ Performance Group was selected, horsepower increased by 4.

Only 32 Cougar XR-7 convertibles were built in 1972 with the 351 Cobra Jet and 4-speed.

and SelectShift automatic with 12-inch torque converter. In order to receive the 266-hp 351 Cobra Jet, the 351 CJ Performance Group needed to be specified. It included low-restriction dual exhausts, Competition suspension with rear stabilizer bar, and F70-14 whitewall tires. A Hurst-shifted 4-speed or SelectShift was required, with the latter receiving a sportier 10¼-inch torque converter.

Deluxe wheel covers were now standard for the base Cougar hardtop and convertible in 1972. Other upgrades were consistent for the whole Cougar series, as mentioned above. Of the cars built with the 351 CJ Performance Group, 207 were hardtops (including GTs) and 20 were convertibles.

Cougar GT

The GT Package was offered for the standard Cougar hardtop for the last time. Equipment was identical to the previous years, aside from general 1972 Cougar updates. The authors currently do not have information on how many of the 256 Cougar GTs were built with the 351 Cobra Jet Performance Group.

Cougar XR-7

"What others call 'luxury extras' are just standard on the XR-7," Mercury proclaimed in a 1972 brochure. Clearly the XR-7's marketing had evolved even more from Euro-inspired into something more personal-luxury, even though equipment was basically the same as the previous year's. Yet the luxury appointments were not incongruent with whatever semblance of performance was available, as the 351 Cobra Jet Performance Group was more popular on the Cougar XR-7 than the base Cougar—877 XR-7 hardtops and 137 convertibles were built with the CJ.

Montego

"Mercury Montego. A totally new car with a ride that challenges larger cars." With a complete styling makeover, a wider track, and a new suspension system, Mercury's 1972 midsize series added up to what Mercury called "one of the most maneuverable, easy-to-handle cars you've ever had your hands on." The prow that characterized 1971–1972 evolved into an upright rectangular eggcrate grille (no more gunsight) that appeared to be influenced by the Cougar, if not an evolution of the previous-generation Montego. The model line didn't change much: Montego, Montego MX, Montego MX Brougham, plus a pair of wagons.

So, what happened to the Cyclone? It was succeeded by the new Montego GT, a cousin to the Gran Torino Sport SportsRoof. The Montego GT appeared more angular and featured a hood scoop that was a new design not inspired by previous Cyclones. It could be made functional with the Cyclone Performance Package, which was also available on the formal roof Montego and Montego MX. Besides the air induction system, it consisted of 351 Cobra Jet or 429, Traction-Lok axle, wide-oval F70 tires with raised white letters, hubcaps with trim rings, black or argent lower bodyside paint and striping with Cyclone decal on front fender, Cyclone identification on the dashboard, twin racing mirrors, and three-spoke rim blow steering wheel. The package was canceled in the middle of the model year.

The 351 Cobra Jet was only available for two-door hardtops and was the only Montego engine available with a 4-speed.

Montego

Touted as Mercury's least expensive personal-size car, the standard Montego two-door hardtop started off with economy in mind, such as 6-cylinder and 3-speed, cloth and vinyl notchback bench seat, and two-spoke steering wheel; it also featured what would be considered upgrades only a few years before, such as front disc brakes and a sound insulation package. The 351 Cobra Jet was available, but currently the authors do not have statistics on how many were built like that; the number is most certainly low.

Montego MX

As the "right-now intermediate with the big-car ride," the Montego MX featured an upgraded interior with notchback seats in cloth and vinyl or all-vinyl, or with optional high-back buckets. Also included were a deluxe sound insulation package, 100-percent nylon loop carpeting, and rocker panel molding. It is unknown at this time how many Montego MX two-doors were built with the 351 Cobra Jet, but it is known that one single MX was built with the Cyclone Performance Package and the CJ.

Montego MX Brougham

Far from a vehicle used for the stoplight drags, the Montego MX Brougham could still be equipped with the 351 Cobra Jet for decent thrust for the era. Befitting its name, the Brougham started with the same mechanicals as the base Montego but strutted its stuff inside thanks to an abundance of creature comforts and accoutrements: Flight Bench seat with rich fabrics or Valino vinyl (all with center folding armrest), carpeting that extended to the door panels, two-spoke steering wheel with woodgrain appliqué, deluxe wheel covers, left-hand side-view mirror, and bright pedal trim. No information is available on how many were equipped with the 351 Cobra Jet.

Montego GT

As the "one-of-a-kind Mercury with sports car flair and fastback styling," the Montego GT was the only model in the Montego series to feature a standard V-8. Can you imagine the 302 2-barrel with low compression? At least the 3-speed shifter was on the floor and not the column! Other standard equipment included white sidewall tires, dual racing mirrors with driver-side remote control, deluxe wheel covers, lower body side trim, performance instrumentation including tachometer and gauges, color-keyed deep-loop carpeting, choice of Flight Bench or high-back bucket seats, three-spoke sport steering wheel, and special black instrument panel appliqués. This was the perfect vehicle for the 351 Cobra Jet and, indeed, out of 5,820 Montego GTs built, 1,052 were built with the CJ, including 9 with the Cyclone Performance Package.

Ford and Mercury sold a decent number of performance cars, considering they didn't have the strongest lineup in the industry. While big-bore engines were great halo products, sales often amounted to under 1,000 per model. With a solid midsize engine putting out a decent amount of horsepower for the era, combined with strong styling (the Gran Torino Sport SportsRoof in particular, while never having the grace of high-compression, had charms that have already begun to be appreciated by collectors), Ford handled the transition well.

So did Mercury. The demotion in horsepower was not a big deal for the Cougar because it had slowly been targeting a different customer who preferred to be pampered. The Montego GT actually sold more than the previous year's Cyclones—all three models—and it was a looker besides. The promise that the lean years weren't going to be as bad as anticipated would be fleeting when more government regulations began to take hold.

CHAPTER TEN

1973–1974: GASPING FOR BREATH

To enthusiasts, 1973 was even darker than 1972 due to even more emission controls (Transmission Controlled Spark and Exhaust Gas Recirculation), but the big news was new front bumper standards. Posed as protecting consumers from preventable repair costs, the idea was to avoid damage to components related to safety, such as lights and even gas tanks, in 5-mph (front) and 2.5-mph (rear) crash tests. The standard was upped in 1974 to include standardized height for both front and rear bumpers capable of withstanding 5-mph impacts, even at an angle.

The 1973 Mustang experienced the biggest facelift in the final year of its three-year reign. It looked quite good despite the new government bumper regulations. (Photo Courtesy Jerry Heasley)

However, it often looked like the safer bumpers were an afterthought, integrated onto cars that had already been designed.

There was a bright light in the barrage of changes, but not in Dearborn: Pontiac engineers figured out how to extract high-compression performance out of a low-compression 455. Dubbed Super Duty 455, its development was not without its issues but, by the time it was approved by the EPA and ready for a mid-1973 release, the SD gave enthusiasts a way to run solid sub-14-second ETs from the factory. The 455 SD lasted through 1974 after 1,296 Firebird Formula 455s and Trans Ams were produced with the round-port motor.

FoMoCo had nothing to compare in 1973. The 351 HO—Ford's fastest in 1972—disappeared for 1973, leaving the 351 Cobra Jet as the top engine in Ford's portfolio. With 7.9:1 compression, it was rated at 259 hp for the Mustang, 255 hp for the Torino and Montego, and 253 for the Cougar, but good luck finding that information in dealer literature (for any engine, for that matter). For what it's worth, Ford did not call the 351 4-barrel a Cobra Jet, but in the Automobile Manufacturers Association specifications for the 1973 Mustang, it's listed as a CJ (with the character in the VIN remaining Q).

For its Cougar cousin, the 351 4-barrel was rated at 253 hp. And the Ford Torino and Mercury Montego? Now rated at 255 hp. The midsizers were now in their second year of their styling cycle, with the Torino receiving a stronger facelift of the two. Both featured the big, clumsy front bumpers that had affected most of the industry.

And then came 1974. Although the formal hardtop remained, the Gran Torino Sport's SportsRoof bodystyle was discontinued. So was the 4-speed transmission. There was a new 460 that replaced the 429, but it too didn't measure up to the 351 Cobra Jet, which was only available on two-door models, including the all-new Torino Elite, a personal-luxury coupe introduced in February 1974. It shared its body with the Mercury Cougar, which had completely shed its pony car roots and went full-zoot as a midsized personal-luxury car. This was becoming common in the era, as the midsize Dodge Charger too had moved in a more pampered direction.

So, what about the Mustang? It became a Pinto-derived runabout, maintaining several of the styling hallmarks—even a Mach I model—but lacking a V-8 engine. Perhaps it was the right car at the right time, and that would sweeten somewhat as the 302 appeared on the option sheet the following year, albeit in 2-barrel form.

For the 1974 Montego, it too lost the fastback *and* the Montego GT, but Mercury offered a Sports Appearance Package that appeared to use similar striping from the Cyclone package from 1972. Like the Torino, the 351 Cobra Jet was only available for two-door models.

Ford

Ford carried on just like everyone else in Detroit. Much of the horsepower available in 1972 continued into 1973 without drastic changes. The Mustang weathered the updated bumper rules with aplomb, but the Torino series not so much. When 1974 rolled by, the Mustang was reformulated into something that was much closer to the same size as the original 1964½ version, though

Despite being 99 percent the same Q-code engine as in 1972, the 351 4V did not include "CJ" on the air cleaner. (Photo Courtesy Jerry Heasley)

many enthusiasts have been cringing ever since. The Mustang II, as it was christened, was touted as having "exclusive engineering refinements" but, horsepower or not, it didn't feel that way. The bean counters reading the sales reports certainly didn't care since the Mustang II was a big success.

Mustang

"Liberate yourself today with a 1973 Mustang Hardtop, SportsRoof or Convertible. Only Ford has such a wide choice of models in the luxury sporty car field," read the brochure. Among the three years of this generation, the 1973 was the most unique, its most noticeable feature being a new grille with parking lights on the outer ends. All Mustangs received a urethane body-colored front bumper (previously a Mach I item), which actually helped make the new bumper regulations less of a bummer.

The Décor Group once again was given a remix of sorts. Available for the hardtop and convertible, it included the Mach I's grille, black or argent lower body paint with bright chrome molding, and hubcaps with wheel trim rings. An option only available with the Décor Group was a body side tape stripe, which was identical to the one available on 1971–1972 Mach Is.

Ram air induction was still available, but only for the 351 2-barrel. Rumor has it that during Ford's certification process for 1972, a supervisor

Note this 351 4V 4-speed convertible and compare it with the one below. This one does not have the Décor Group, as evidenced by the standard Mustang grille and side trim.

This 1973 Mustang convertible features the Décor Group, as evidenced by the Mach I grille with R/W/B Mustang badge, and lower body paint. It also features the new-for-1973 forged aluminum wheels. (Photo Courtesy Jim Smart)

gave a test car (equipped with the 351 Cobra Jet with ram air) a tune-up, which ended up recalibrating the specs needed to submit to the EPA for compliance. Ford decided it was not worth the time to start the process over, even for the 1973s.

Hardtop

"Bright rocker panel and wheel lip moldings sparkle outside and a rich, durable all-vinyl interior with deep-cushioned High Back bucket seats accentuate the interior," read the brochure. Other standard appearance and comfort features included lower back panel appliqué with bright molding, bright rectangular left-hand mirror, and the usual standard equipment familiar to the Mustang window sticker of years past. As before, the 351 Cobra Jet was available for the hardtop, with 427 (not including Grandés) being built.

Grandé

Just like this was the last year for the Mustang as a proper pony car, the luxury Mustang model was making its final appearance. "A matter of grace, touch and taste . . . and an exceptional escape from the ordinary," claimed Ford, suggesting the Mustang Grandé combined quiet luxury with a beautiful driving experience. Standard equipment included color-keyed racing mirrors, "halo" vinyl roof, unique longitudinal paint stripes, special wheel covers, Lambeth cloth and vinyl interior, deluxe instrument panel with wood-tone appliqué, panel-mounted electric clock, and other items. Interestingly, more Grandés than hardtops were built with the 351 Cobra Jet: 637 in total.

SportsRoof

"Instant Go with handling ease and a whistling crisp profile" was the name of the game for the Mustang fastback. Equipment was identical to the hardtop's, from the standard 250 six and 3-speed manual to the all-vinyl interior with high-back buckets. Only 640 SportsRoofs were built with the 351 Cobra Jet.

Mach I

"Smoothly rambunctious with marvelous road and ride manners" is how Ford characterized the Mach I SportsRoof. The 1973 iteration featured a honeycomb grille that had a badge portraying a pony with a red/white/blue banner in the background. A new stripe design also set the Mach I off from earlier years, now with a simple longitudinal stripe going from the rear wheels to just aft of the front bumper.

The 1973 Mach I featured a grille that was distinct from regular Mustangs (aside of those equipped with the Décor Package). Standard power since 1971 was the 302 2-barrel, but the top option was the 351 Cobra Jet. Unfortunately, ram air was certified only for the 351 2-barrel. (Photo Courtesy Liz Green)

The 1973 Mustang Mach I featured redesigned stripes in either black or argent. The 1971–1972-style stripes were available on other Mustangs with the Décor Package. (Photo Courtesy Liz Green)

Out back, a Mach I tape treatment wrapped around the top of the taillights. A flat hood was standard on the Mach I, but the NASA hood was a no-cost option (and standard with the 351). Other standard features included dual color-keyed racing mirrors, bonded door trim panels with pull-type handles and armrests, and other items. New options included forged aluminum wheels and three-quarter vinyl roof treatment in addition to stalwarts like "tutone" hood (in black or argent) and rear spoiler. The 351 Cobra Jet was most popular in the Mach I, with 9,885 built.

Convertible

The last Mustang convertible until 1983, Ford suggested that "road romance begins with the *only* convertible produced by the Ford Motor Company—and the lowest priced U.S.-built convertible in the personal sporty car field." The Mustang convertible always came equipped with several items not standard on other Mustangs, and 1973 was no different: knitted vinyl seat trim, deluxe molded door panel appliqués, tinted windshield, bright upper back panel molding, and power front disc brakes, among other items. When the final 1973 convertible rolled off the line, Ford had built 968 Mustang droptops with the 351 Cobra Jet.

1973 Torino

The Torino, Gran Torino, Gran Torino Sport, and new Gran Torino Brougham (previously an optional interior package in 1972) "was designed with the idea that you shouldn't have to sacrifice quality, comfort and stability for the convenience of a midsize car." All 11 models featured new energy-absorbing front bumpers that stuck out like a sore bottom lip, but the facelifted Torino series was not alone in that regard. Along with the new bumper, front end styling for both Torino and Gran Torino models was smoothed out.

The Gran Torino Sport continued to carry the performance banner with SportsRoof and formal roof bodystyles, but this would be the last time the SportsRoof and the 4-speed would make an appearance.

The base Torino continued to differentiate itself from Gran Torinos thanks to a unique full-width eggcrate grille, but the softened facelift

The Mustang's rear end styling stayed the same for 1973. Since there was no performance model for the convertible, sporty accoutrements—no matter what engine—could be added via the Décor Package and forged steel wheels. (Photo Courtesy Jim Smart)

appeared more drastic due to the new regulation bumpers. Most noticeable were the parking lights that gravitated to the front fenders, but most everything else was a carryover from 1972, including all-vinyl seat and door trim, rubber floor mat, and manual front disc brakes.

Gran Torino

A step up in trim level scored you a completely different front end. Compared to 1972's nose, the 1973 featured a wide trapezoidal cross-hatch grille with slightly hidden parking lights residing on both ends, beside the inboard headlights. New for 1973 were low-back bench seat with low-profile head restraints. Standard equipment included cloth and vinyl seat and door trim, color-keyed carpeting, deluxe sound package, lower bodyside/wheel lip/valence moldings, and decklid lock cover, among other items.

Gran Torino Sport

"Call it responsive . . . call it rakish . . . call it fun!" While the definition of fun in 1973 may have changed from previous years, Ford tried its darndest to glean the kind of fun enthusiasts wanted (notwithstanding the scooped hood that was no more). As before, the Gran Torino Sport SportsRoof and two-door came with a standard 302 2-barrel with column-mounted 3-speed. Also included were F70-14 Wide Ovals with raised white letters, black bumper pad, dual racing mirrors, hubcaps and trim rings, lower bodyside and wheel lip moldings, pleated all-vinyl bench seat, molded door trim panels, and color-keyed nylon carpet, among other items. The Rallye Equipment Group was again available for the serious performance buff (and available for other Torino two-doors), and a slightly redesigned Laser stripe helped the Gran Torino Sport look the part. Out of 51,853 Gran Torino Sport SportsRoofs, 10,241 were built with the 351 Cobra Jet; there is no information on how many formal roofs featured the CJ.

Gran Torino Brougham

"Where splendor is the inside story," said Ford. That's because the Brougham model shone with its luxurious interior of nylon cloth with leather-like vinyl-trimmed Flight Bench seat with center armrest and door panels. Even the instrument panel was unique among Torinos thanks to wood-tone inserts, plus electric clock and bright pedal pads. Despite the pretensions, the standard engine was a 250-ci six with a 3-speed manual; although, the 351 Cobra Jet was available.

Ranchero

The Ranchero series continued to offer the hierarchy of Ranchero 500, Ranchero GT, and Ranchero Squire, all with the Gran Torino front end. The value-packed Ranchero 500 featured an all-vinyl bench seat, bright left-hand mirror with remote control, and bright metal windshield, rear window, drip rail, and top of cargo body moldings, among other features. The Ranchero GT added Laser stripes, body-colored racing mirrors, black hubcaps with trim rings, F70-14 white-lettered belted tires, unique door

The 1973 Gran Torino Sport continued to carry the torch for the true muscle car enthusiast. The hood scoop may have been gone, but the sleek SportsRoof and optional Laser stripe maintained the image of days passed. (Photo Courtesy Ken MacLean)

Notice the air cleaner? While Cobra Jet branding seemed to be at a deficit in 1973, "CJ" did appear on the Torino's air cleaner, unlike the Mustang's. It was rated at 255 hp, a slight bump from 1972. (Photo Courtesy Ken MacLean)

trim panels, and more. The Ranchero Squire built upon the Ranchero 500's features to include deluxe wheel covers, woodgrain paneling on sides and tailgate, wood-tone trim on the instrument panel, electric clock, plus other features. All were available with the 351 Cobra Jet.

1974 Torino

It may appear to have been a good year for music in 1974—witness Lynyrd Skynyrd, Bad Company, Frank Zappa, and UFO—but automotive enthusiasts continued to scratch their collective heads wondering what was going on in Detroit. Horsepower continued to be deemphasized, and the energy-absorbing bumper system was now able to withstand 5-mph impacts front and rear, plus 3-mph corner impacts. It may be debatable when exactly the low point was, but it had certainly begun.

While the Gran Torino Sport continued, it lost its fastback bodystyle. In an era of padded vinyl tops and opera windows, performance had taken a back seat to pimpin'. Most noticeable with the 1974 facelift was a larger grille for Gran Torino models with larger parking lights. Taillights were also a new design with wide rectangular lenses that included integral side-marker lights.

Standard among all Torinos for the first time was a V-8, as the six was discontinued for midsize vehicles. For enthusiasts, Ford continued to offer the 351 Cobra Jet for one final year. More often referred to as "351 4V," it was only available with an automatic transmission. A 460-ci V-8 replaced the 429, but its horsepower output continued to pale in comparison to the CJ.

The midyear introduction of the Gran Torino Elite was a major (if not overdue) success for Ford. Just like the Mercury Cougar and others creeping into personal-luxury territory, the market exploded after the redesigned 1973 Chevrolet Monte Carlo. In fact, the Monte was first introduced in 1970, but Ford didn't seem interested. With the Gran Torino Elite, Ford was able to slap together a unique personal-luxury coupe based on a modified Gran Torino coupe body (shared with the 1974 Cougar). It was no performer, but the Q-code 351 was available.

Torino

Emphasis continued to be placed on the Gran Torino, clearly overshadowing the base Torino model, which was much like what happened to the Fairlane several years before. As the value leader, the Torino continued to be differentiated by the same "face" as in 1973, including its one-piece plastic eggcrate grille. Despite being the lowest trim level, it was apparent standard trim and features had risen a few notches from just a few years ago. For example, color-keyed loop carpeting was standard, as was an energy-absorbing armrest. Another upgrade from earlier days was the standard V-8, with the 351 Cobra Jet being the only interesting engine worthy of enthusiasts' ardor—as long as you didn't live in California.

Gran Torino

As the first step up, the Gran Torino featured the corrosion-resistant grille and front end that characterized all Gran Torino models. Standard equipment included plush, pleated cloth and vinyl seat trim, rear armrest (for two-door models), deluxe sound package, and luggage compartment mat.

Gran Torino Sport

With the SportsRoof gone, there only was a two-door hardtop left for the Gran Torino Sport. Dual fender peak paint stripes, dual color-keyed outside mirrors with remote control, and wide bright belt and front fender lower moldings did not impart any hint of sportiness, but the "Turbine" wheel covers certainly helped. The standard performance cluster (with engine-turned black appliqué) with tach was another suggestion this was no ordinary Gran Torino; the interior also featured a super-soft vinyl Flight Bench seat, center armrest (with buckets a no-cost option), 25-ounce cut-pile carpeting, deluxe two-spoke steering wheel with simulated wood-tone appliqué, and bright-rimmed pedal pads. As usual, the 302 2-barrel with 3-speed was standard, as were HR78 steel-belted whitewall tires.

Gran Torino Brougham

Somewhat the antithesis of a performance model, the Gran Torino Brougham was nonetheless available with the 351 Cobra Jet. Perhaps the 460 was more at home pushing a 2-ton vehicle to comfortable speeds, but the CJ suited it just fine. Additional features included an opera window and wide body belt moldings (for two-doors), red rear reflective trim, full vinyl roof with color-keyed longitudinal vinyl body side molding, and deluxe wheel covers.

Interior and other features included split bench in luxury Westminster cloth trim (with matching door panels) or no-cost super-soft all-vinyl trim, dual center armrests, simulated woodgrain appliqué, electric clock, soft fiber carpeting and trunk lining, deluxe sound package, and HR78 steel-belted whitewalls, among other features. Only 1,045 Gran Torino Brougham two-doors were ordered with the 351 Cobra Jet.

Gran Torino Elite

The Elite gave the Ford portfolio an easy entry into the personal-luxury market after Ford witnessed the Pontiac Grand Prix and Chevrolet Monte

The 1974 Gran Torino Brougham sat atop the Torino hierarchy, but it was a strange model for which to order a 351 Cobra Jet. More folks chose the 400 2-barrel, among others. (Photo Courtesy Luis Arevalo)

Carlo experience several years of impressive sales. Sure, Ford had the Thunderbird (in fact, the Elite was advertised as a "midsize car in the Thunderbird Tradition"), but it was in a higher price class. The Elite nonetheless shared plenty with the Torino series. With a traditional upright grille surrounded by dual headlights, it was almost a kissing cousin to the Cougar and was also available with the 351 Cobra Jet.

Ranchero

The Ranchero series continued to offer Ranchero 500, Ranchero GT, and wood-paneled Ranchero Squire models. All featured the Gran Torino nose and, in the case of the GT, had a color-keyed side stripe sweeping the full length of the sides and rear hatch. Also included in the GT were remote control "sport style" body-colored mirrors, black hubcaps with bright trim rings, color-keyed seat belts, door armrests, padded instrument panel, and more. At publication, the authors had no information how many of any Ranchero models had the 351 Cobra Jet.

Mercury

As the 1970s took hold, the auto industry fell in love with luxury. Former top-level models like the Torino were superseded by the Gran Torino, then Gran Torino Brougham. Hence, Mercury may have felt the Montego was being crowded out, as it traditionally had been a small step up from the Torino series.

In contrast, Mercury didn't feel that the Cougar was being cannibalized by the Mustang. But when the Gran Torino Elite was introduced midyear 1974, that may have become a problem. By 1975, it was more apparent.

Nonetheless, the Q-code 351 was available for both series for both 1973–74. After that, Ford would have no engine with any semblance of performance.

Cougar

In its final year as a Mustang-based pony car, the Cougar featured one big change shared with every other American car: impact-resistant front and rear bumpers, with the front being a completely new unit able to withstand a 5-mph impact. Bumper guards with black protection strips assisted in protecting the Cougar's new grille too. Out back, the taillights featured a new vertical texture. Less noticeable but still notable were a whole selection of new colors and trim to make the 1973 Cougar seem even more unique from 1971 to 1972.

Automatic transmission became the standard choice for all Cougar models. No 3-speed manual was available for the 351 2-barrel, and if one wanted to do his/her own shifting, the only choice was the 351 Cobra Jet with a 4-speed. Indeed, while the CJ Performance Package was no longer available, the CJ continued on as the de facto 4-barrel engine, now offering 253 hp. For $74.70, the engine also included a 10¼-inch torque converter (when equipped with the automatic), higher-rate springs and heavy-duty shock absorbers, and larger-diameter front/rear stabilizer bars. As part of the Cougar's luxury evolution, the GT package was discontinued for 1973.

1973 Cougar

Aside from the equipment mentioned, the feature list for the standard 1973 Cougar remained similar: color-keyed instrument panel with complementary two-spoke steering wheel, consolette, cut-pile carpeting, and more. Standard for the convertible and optional for the hardtop was the Decór Group, which upgraded the interior to include woven vinyl or cloth seats, deluxe wheel covers, bright rocker panel molding, door pull straps, and more. At the end of the model year, 367 standard Cougars were equipped with the 351 Cobra Jet.

1973 Cougar XR-7

The most luxurious Cougar continued to be the luxury car that also was a sporty car. While sharing the same standard engine as the base Cougar, the XR-7 differentiated itself with special rocker moldings, XR-7-specific wheel covers, vinyl roof (for the hardtop), remote driver-side mirror, bucket seats with leather components, instrument panel and three-spoke rim blow steering wheel with cherry woodgrain inserts, door and instrument panel assist straps, tachometer and other gauges, toggle switch

The Q-code 351 in the 1973 Cougar was rated at 253 hp, which was 6 fewer horses than the Mustang's. (Photo Courtesy Don Quirk)

Despite the government-regulated front bumper, the 1973 Cougar (here a 351 Cobra Jet–equipped XR-7) did not look as if the bumper was an afterthought. The same front end styling would evolve into 1974 attached to a Montego-based midsizer. (Photo Courtesy Don Quirk)

panel, and more. An impressive 2,921 Cougar XR-7s were built with the 351 Cobra Jet in 1973.

1974 Cougar XR-7

"Still retaining its European flair with a long sleek body, it's noticeably roomier on the inside and more luxurious than ever. A fabulous leap upward . . . into a whole new class." In actuality, the new Cougar wasn't redesigned but, rather, its name was applied to a special Montego coupe, so the Cougar was now officially a midsize vehicle. The only model available was the XR-7. Standard features included 351 2-barrel with Select-Shift automatic, power front disc brakes, steel-belted radial tires, impact-resistant bumpers front and rear, power steering, performance instrumentation, bucket seats and console or Twin Comfort Lounge Seats, and more. Engine options included the 460 4-barrel, but the 351 Cobra Jet featured the most horsepower.

Montego

The Montego line received updated front bumpers per federal regulation, which further diminished the angular style that made the 1972 unique. Otherwise, much of the series was the same as in 1972, with the Montego, Montego MX, Montego GT, and Montego MX Brougham making up the series. The 351 Cobra Jet continued to be the top horsepower engine, and it was the only one available with a 4-speed in 1973.

1973 Montego

The standard Montego continued to offer value in the Mercury midsize series. As in previous years, standard was a six and 3-speed manual, plus front disc brakes, and E78-14 black sidewall tires, among other items.

1973 Montego MX

A smooth and stable ride was the hallmark of the Montego MX. According to Mercury, "You've no idea how Montego's wide tread and high-stability suspension can add to your driving pleasure." On top of the base Montego, the MX's standard features included deluxe sound insulation and color-keyed deep-loop carpeting.

1973 Montego GT

The Montego GT presented itself to enthusiasts for the last time as both the model and the fastback bodystyle disappear after 1973. The GT continued to be a looker, even if one had to hold his or her nose because of the new

The 1973 Montego GT's new front bumper disrupted the smooth style of the SportsRoof sportster but, when equipped with the 351 Cobra Jet, it was the heir apparent of the Cyclone. (Photo Courtesy Steve Schrimscher)

From behind, the 1973 Montego GT changed little from 1972. The 1972–1973 Montego GT was the first midsize Mercury fastback since the 1969 Cyclone. (Photo Courtesy Steve Schrimscher)

front bumper. Standard engine continued to be a 302 2-barrel with 3-speed; other standard equipment included front disc brakes, F78-14 white sidewall tires, deluxe sound insulation, hood with dual scoops, dual racing mirrors, deluxe wheel covers or hubcaps with trim rings, full complement of gauges, sports-type three-spoke steering wheel, and color-keyed deep loop carpeting, among others. Out of 4,464 Montego GTs built, 1,120 were built with the 351 Cobra Jets, which was more than the 302, 400 2-barrel, and 429.

1973 Montego MX Brougham

The interior is what made the Brougham different from other Montegos. With the cloth and vinyl Flight Bench seat with the center armrest (or super-soft all-vinyl at no charge) and upgrades in trim and wheel covers, it faked being a Marquis but was a foot less in stature. Interestingly, despite the luxury, standard was a 250 six, but the Brougham also came equipped with E78-14 black sidewall tires, deluxe sound insulation, deluxe wheel covers, deluxe two-spoke steering wheel with woodgrain insert, color-keyed deep loop carpeting, and more.

1974 Montego

The Montego series received a mild facelift for 1974, with the center grille reshaped from a square to a rectangle. Out back, the wraparound horizontal taillights found on the Ford Torino series were used by Mercury as well, but with different trim designs. A V-8 was standard for the first time (all models started with the 302 2-barrel), and the 351 Cobra Jet made its last appearance for all two-door models save the Montego MX Brougham. Only an automatic was available.

A replacement for the Montego GT was the Montego two-door hardtop with the Sports Appearance Group, which was available for the standard Montego and the Montego MX. Included in the package were a scooped hood, dual racing mirrors, black-painted hubcaps with trim rings, lower body paint/tape stripes, black-out rear panel, leather-wrapped steering wheel, tachometer and other gauges, and more.

The 255-hp 351 Cobra Jet, as installed in the 1973 Montego GT, featured plenty of plumbing for emissions purposes. Ram air induction was no longer available. (Photo Courtesy Steve Schrimscher)

1974 Montego

A few years prior, the midsize Comet was quite austere. Its successor, the Montego, gradually became less so. By 1974, the standard Montego appeared upscale in comparison. Aside of the standard 302 2-barrel with 3-speed, the Montego also included front disc brakes, G78-14 black sidewall tires, cloth and vinyl bench seat (or all-vinyl, if preferred), among other equipment. The 351 Cobra Jet was available on two-door Montegos, but it is unknown at this moment how many were built.

1974 Montego MX

The Montego MX continued to be one step up from the base Montego, and it was the top Montego model available with the 351 Cobra Jet. "In blindfold ride comparison tests last year, a majority of owners of competitor's cars rated the 1973 Montego MX . . . superior in ride to their car's," claimed Mercury in the 1974 brochure. Standard equipment on top of the base Montego included deluxe sound insulation, rocker panel molding, and fancier dashboard and seat trim.

CHAPTER ELEVEN

2009–2019: COBRA JETS IN THE MODERN ERA

With the history of the 1968½ Cobra Jet etched in stone, it was time to write the next chapter of the Cobra Jet. That required Ford to build a new CJ Mustang—one that would be delivered with serious track capabilities. Much like the original plan, a strategy was set to develop a high-powered, lightweight, race-ready Mustang devoid of unnecessary street gear, such as sound deadening, airbags, or a stereo.

The return of the Cobra Jet began with the 2008 models. (Photo Courtesy Evan J. Smith)

And with that, the idea for the 2008 Cobra Jet was born. The return of the CJ came with a touch of nostalgia but, more importantly, it also offered owners the chance to compete in NHRA Stock and Super Stock in a late-model factory race car—like they did back in 1968 with the original "135" Mustangs. A small, determined team inside Ford Performance (formerly Ford Racing) with a passion for drag racing and winning set forth a detailed strategy that included selling the idea to management, acquiring bodies, designing a suitable powertrain, selecting components, sourcing parts, creating custom wiring and, finally, building and testing prototypes. That was just the start.

"At the 2005 SEMA show we revealed the FR500-C road race car and the media immediately started asking questions about a drag race version," said Jesse Kershaw, former Drag Racing Parts and Competition manager at Ford Performance. "Having come from SVT and having worked closely with NMRA [National Mustang Racers Association], I knew there was a market for something. The idea at the time was FR500-DR. I pitched it on the spot to Dan Davis [former director at Ford Performance] in the glass room above the Ford booth—a supercharged car based off the upcoming 2007 GT500. Dan didn't see things as I did and said something along the lines that customers wanted naturally aspirated engines and that his 500-hp Cammer should go 9.20s. This shelved the idea for the time being, but I started a PowerPoint presentation and continually refined it over the next several years."

Kershaw continued, "Ford Racing then launched another road race car called the FR500-S and built an initial run of 75 units, with another 50 units to follow. Sales weren't as brisk as they hoped. Making 50 more made no sense, but the bodies and parts were already ordered with a build date scheduled for fall 2008. At some point, Roger Pohlman (who worked at our warehouse) called me and asked if I could help him coordinate a marketing event with NHRA around the 40th anniversary of the Cobra Jet. He owned one of the 50 original lightweight cars and wanted to organize a reunion. He enlightened me to the details on the original Cobra Jet and from there on my PowerPoint was for a Cobra Jet—the FR500-DR idea was gone."

More than just a publicity stunt, the team wanted to ensure Ford racers had a competitive late-model Mustang within the Stock and Super Stock ranks. So, the plan was refined, becoming a combination that would be quick, consistent, and reliable. An added bonus was that it closely represented what the factory was selling in the Shelby GT500—this made it easily relatable to Mustang enthusiasts everywhere.

"Because NHRA [Stock and Super Stock] is HP/weight-based, my thought was that with the electronic throttle, we could make the horsepower whatever we wanted," said Kershaw. "At this point, I thought NHRA might actually test a car on a dyno, which it never did. By closing the throttle [a predetermined percentage], we could dial the horsepower back and give the customers a calibration to open it up. I spoke to journalist and NHRA racer Evan Smith several times about the details of NHRA racing compared to NMRA to help put the idea together. Evan was a sounding board for me during this time and remained a personal consultant for many of my crazy ideas throughout my time working on the CJ. Evan also became a test driver for the Cobra Jet and, along with Jimmy Ronzello, really helped get the car competitive.

"I saw my opportunity to pounce and updated the Cobra Jet presentation to launch with a naturally aspirated 5.0L 3-valve engine because Ford had already ordered all the parts for a 3-valve in the cars. I thought this was my only chance to get the cars built, and if I could show it worked I would move to the 5.4L supercharged engine after Job 1," added Kershaw.

"During the same time frame, Brian Wolfe [a long-time Ford employee and drag racer] was a director outside of Ford Racing. Brian would ask me for input and help on drag stuff from time to time, and I sent him the presentation to get his input. I had failed to get approval so many times that I felt this was my last chance and he could help. Brian responded immediately with a meeting notice for me and my boss, Jamie Allison. Brian loved the idea, but it still wasn't a slam dunk," stated Kershaw. "Brian wasn't in our division [at Ford] so, while he was high-ranking, he didn't have the final say.

"With his encouragement, we built a test mule, but the project was moving slow and it was likely we wouldn't make timing. Dan Davis just didn't think this was a worthwhile program; his exact words to me were, 'You'll be lucky to sell six.' Then Brian Wolfe became the Ford Racing director in summer 2008 and things changed quickly and dramatically. We kicked Cobra Jet into high gear and delivered the cars starting in December.

"Looking back, I know the car would never have been made without Brian's support, and I wonder if he would have come over to run the group had the idea of the car not been on the table. It was a rare occasion where,

Vigorous testing of the original prototypes was necessary to ready the 2008 Cobra Jets for competition. (Photo Courtesy Evan J. Smith)

inside a big company, you can say a small group of people definitely made a big difference."

2008 Cobra Jet

The starting point for the 2008 Cobra Jet was the rigid S197 chassis that already proved to be an excellent racing platform. The body/chassis had been in service since 2005 and there were many drag racing parts already available. A development team was assembled but, before moving forward with another prototype, Kershaw worked with the NHRA to approve the combination.

With specifications approved, development cars were assembled and testing began. When finalized, the 2008 Cobra Jet powertrain consisted of a 5.4L modular V-8 supercharged by a 2.3L Eaton four-lobe TVS intercooled supercharger. It also featured an iron block with aluminum heads, 0.413-inch cam lift, SFI balancer, 80 lb/hr injectors, long-tube headers, twin-bore throttle body, and 123-mm mass air meter.

All engines were assembled at Ford's Romeo, Michigan, engine plant with Manley H-beam rods and Mahle pistons and were similar in many ways to the Shelby GT500 powerplant. NHRA rated the CJ engine at 425 hp, which would allow it to run in the AA class in Stock Eliminator.

Backing the torquey 5.4L modular was a Centerforce clutch, Tremec 6-speed transmission modified by Liberty Gears, and a 9-inch rear with Strange Engineering internals, and 4.11:1 gears. The rear was mounted with a Ford Performance rear suspension consisting of tubular rear trailing arms,

Race prep on the S197 body included removing the front firewall and welding all the remaining holes normally used for air conditioning and heating. (Photo Courtesy Evan J. Smith)

Prior to installation, the fully dressed 5.4L supercharged engines had a Centerforce clutch and Tremec transmission installed. (Photo Courtesy Evan J. Smith)

Roll bars were welded in place and painted black on the 50 2008 Cobra Jets. (Photo Courtesy Evan J. Smith)

Bare bodies await assembly. Note the hole in the hood, which will be covered by a Boss 429–style air induction scoop. (Photo Courtesy Evan J. Smith)

Cobra Jets are hand-built, including the roll bar and entire assembly. (Photo Courtesy Evan J. Smith)

rear anti-roll bar, and Ford Racing adjustable dampers. Drag racing–specific adjustable struts were used in the front, along with a lightweight radiator support, and the anti-roll bar was deleted. Cobra Jet Mustangs were also fitted with a manual steering rack.

Bodies and critical Mustang trim components were sourced from Automotive Alliance Industries (AAI, now Flat Rock Assembly). Assembly, along with welding in the six-point roll bar, was handled by Roush on a niche line in Livonia, Michigan. Affixed to where the VIN would go on a production car, Ford attached a stick-on vehicle serial number with a bar code to identify each of the 50 cars.

A serialized sticker was affixed to the cowl in the location where the VIN normally resides. Cobra Jet FR500CJ018 belongs to Erich and Herb Bollman of Delaware. The car is consistently raced in NHRA Division 1. (Photo Courtesy Evan J. Smith)

Each build would take a few days from start to completion, including the rear axle and suspension, engine, clutch/transmission, and front suspension, which was installed as one unit, with the driveshaft being attached with a driveshaft safety loop. A custom wiring harness was used to eliminate weight, and a single battery was mounted in the trunk along with an NHRA-required on/off switch.

As stated previously, all 50 Cobra Jets were prepared for Stock Eliminator but could be modified to run in Super Stock or, of course, NMRA, NMCA, or bracket racing. "The goal was to run one second under the NHRA AA/Stock class index as-delivered with room for improvement," said Kershaw. "With the 2008 cars, we fell a touch short due to the stock-type manual transmission—it was really a street car transmission and not up to the job. However, the engine and rest of the hardware were spot on, so a trans swap later and the car was breaking records. It became a challenge to slow them down because NHRA hadn't seen anything like it before. The fastest class at the time was 7.5 lbs/hp; now it's 5.5 lbs/hp. We rated the

A worker prepares the instrument panel, which was ultimately fitted with a trio of gauges and a unique tachometer.(Photo Courtesy Evan J. Smith)

A set of 2008 Cobra Jets receive their interior trim. (Photo Courtesy Evan J. Smith)

Rear suspension consisted of Ford Performance control arms, shocks and anti-roll bar. Every Cobra Jet also received a strong 9-inch Ford rear. (Photo Courtesy Evan J. Smith)

Once the rear axle was installed, the front cradle—including the suspension, engine, and transmission—was raised into the chassis. (Photo Courtesy Evan J. Smith)

The completed engine bay of a 2008 Cobra Jet is shown. (Photo Courtesy Evan J. Smith)

A host of 2008 Cobra Jet Mustangs await inspection. (Photo Courtesy Evan J. Smith)

Each Cobra Jet was closely scrutinized before being given the okay for delivery. (Photo Courtesy Evan J. Smith)

Cobra Jet at only 425 hp because we couldn't rate it any higher and still have a class to race in," he added.

Appearance wise, all Cobra Jets were fitted with a Mustang California Special front fascia with black-out grille à la the Bullitt Mustang, and a scoop resembling that of the 1969–1970 Boss 429. The scoop was added to allow racers in Super Stock GT to have fresh air for the carburetor. Also, the side mirrors and rear spoiler were deleted and the CJs were finished with Bogart 15x10- and 15x3.5-inch wheels and Goodyear tires (rear 9x30 inches/front 28x4.5 inches). Other unique parts included CJ hood pins, seat covers, airbag delete cover, snake-logo faux fuel cap, modified Ford GT start button, Ford Racing windshield banner, and gauges for oil, vacuum, and water temperature.

All 50 cars were painted Performance White, and a graphics package was available featuring a swooping red and blue stripe leading to a Cobra Jet snake that climbed the quarter panel, just ahead of the rear Goodyear 9x30-inch slicks. "5.4 COBRA JET" stickers lined each side of the hood, and "COBRA JET" banner logos were placed at the top of each rear quarter. Ford also added a Ford Racing windshield banner, a Powered by Ford fender badge, and a FR500CJ sticker on the rear of the decklid.

The Cobra Jet Mustang was officially introduced at the 2008 SEMA show. Demand was immediate and incredible. Carrying no VIN and not street-legal, Cobra Jet Mustangs were sold through Ford dealer part departments using a specific part number for the entire car. Selling price was $69,995.

"The Cobra Jet was featured at SEMA, PRI [Performance Racing Industry] and Barrett Jackson," said Jesse Kershaw. "There was an event called the Ford Racing Invitational where we let media drive our prepared cars, and everyone got to make a pass in a Cobra Jet. We hosted 'town halls' at NHRA races to show off the car, and there were delivery events for customers to meet the Ford team who created their cars. We had a match race between John Force and Bob Tasca III at Pomona, and Tasca III versus Bill Glidden at Las Vegas. Plus, we circulated lots of social media photos and videos, often shot on my personal camera and emailed to our web guys the same day.

"With help from NMRA, we created the Cobra Jet Showdown and partnered with Roy Hill to help our customers get their NHRA competition license. Sometimes they would do so the day before the showdowns.

Jesse Kershaw (left) chats with champion Cobra Jet racer Bo Butner. (Photo Courtesy Evan J. Smith)

Cobra Jet drivers have set many NHRA records, but only Don Fezell can claim the title of being the first NHRA Stock Eliminator driver to run in the 8s. He has since run in the 8.20s at over 165 mph with his 2008 Cobra Jet. (Photo Courtesy Evan J. Smith)

We went so far as to have Ford engine experts Jimmy Ronzello and Steve Egan on hand at the NHRA US Nationals to help customers with teardown. In fact, Cobra Jet racers got torn down a ton and many weren't familiar with the engines, so the factory support was important and appreciated by the racers. You could win class and never take a spark plug out. We also ran a spread in *National Dragster* after the US Nationals congratulating all our class winners, mostly Cobra Jet owners, but every Ford winner got in," he added.

Return to the Winternationals

Not surprisingly, all 50 Cobra Jets sold out within a week, with the first 10 vehicles going to Brent Hajek of Hajek Motorsports. Hajek, a long-time Ford racer and collector, understood the significance of the 40-year anniversary of the Cobra Jet, and he set out to prepare four of his new cars for action at the upcoming NHRA Winternationals.

"More than anything, I wanted racers to feel like they were part of a Ford team," Kershaw added. "I handed out decals and hats to everyone. I made sure I was at a ton of races from early morning to late at night, because I genuinely cared about their success and wanted them to know that. Grassroots racing isn't about big money and sucking up, so if you're not genuine, you're done."

Historically, something big was about to happen, and energy within the Ford community was building. It was four decades earlier, almost to the day, when the CJ made its debut at the NHRA Winternationals and Al Joniec took one to victory.

Sensing that he could recreate history, Hajek teamed with Ford and champion racer John Calvert (who has a rich history racing his own original 4-speed 1968 Cobra Jet) to get the new Cobra Jets ready. Hajek had each of his four CJs lettered with a retro theme to honor four of the Cobra Jets driven at the 1968 Winternationals by Joniec, Hubert Platt, Randy Ritchey, and Gas Ronda. This time, the drivers were Jim Waldo, Gary Stinnett, Jimmy Ronzello, and John Calvert.

"Miraculously, it all fell together with a 2008 Cobra Jet winning its first race in 2009 at the Winternationals. John Calvert was driving, and the car had a livery to match the 1968 Winternationals-winning Cobra Jet piloted by Al Joniec. You couldn't buy the publicity we got from history repeating itself," explained Kershaw. "This deal came together because, while promoting the new Cobra Jet, I arranged a shoot for the cars at Pomona and it fell through last minute, so friends at Source Interlink Media [now TEN The Enthusiast Network] rented Fontana and agreed to let me tag along with the cars.

"Jerry Pitt at Source asked if I could get Brent Hajek to bring his Tasca Super Boss to the shoot as well. Brent agreed, and I had also called John Calvert to bring his 1968 Cobra Jet for the shoot. Brent already ordered the first 10 Cobra Jets. He and John got talking at this photo shoot and hatched a plan to work together at the upcoming Winternationals. Brent took delivery of his first four cars and immediately sent two to Calvert, who thrashed to get them ready for NHRA competition. Had Pomona not crashed out for photos, had Source Interlink not let me tag along to Fontana, had Jerry not asked for the Super Boss, had Brent not agreed to bring it, had John not agreed to bring his car, the 2009 Winternationals victory wouldn't have happened. It was a very cool ripple effect to have the privilege to watch."

"When we rolled out the cars, we realized they lacked the disclaimer plates like the old Thunderbolts, so they made the stickers that went on all the cars," said Brent Hajek. "We took delivery on December 29, and they couldn't go faster than 10.0, so we had to extend the cages and [continued] were testing [in the] middle of January. There was only like 20 working days until the Winternationals. The drivers pulled up and there was Gas Ronda, Al Joniec, Hubert Platt, and Randy Ritchey, and all these legends were watching Stock at 8:00 am. It wasn't about us—we wanted to make the old legends proud. We didn't want to stink in front of them, and there was so much general media there [besides].

"Brian Wolfe pulled off a lot to get it done, and there was a lot of pressure on us—it was a new experience for everybody. When you're on a roll, you get that feeling, and then we wanted to win. It's like a dream—history will repeat itself. That's what got this thing going in the first place. When we went to Bonneville and we were running E85 in C/BFA, we set the record with a 325 mph run with Danny Thompson driving. We got a lot of media coverage for that, and Ford loved it. That really helped with the Cobra Jet deal.

Test drivers Ronzello and Evan J. Smith were instrumental in ensuring Cobra Jet Mustangs performed well and were easy to drive. (Photo Courtesy Evan J. Smith)

Every automatic-equipped Cobra Jet was delivered with a Hurst shifter. (Photo Courtesy Evan J. Smith)

Jimmy Ronzello's own 2008 convertible Cobra Jet is a one-off model that has been raced in Stock and Super Stock competition. (Photo Courtesy Evan J. Smith)

Michelle Bongiovanni is one of several female Cobra Jet drivers. The Penn State student from New Jersey has multiple wins, including the NMRA 2016 Cobra Jet Showdown in Bradenton, Florida. (Photo Courtesy Evan J. Smith)

Charlie Downing has done well with his stick-shift three-valve Cobra Jet. Downing has set NHRA national records and has scored a few wins. (Photo Courtesy Evan J. Smith)

There are several naturally aspirated combinations for Cobra Jet Mustangs. This CJ runs a 5.0 Coyote that is similar to the base 5.0 Mustang GT engine. (Photo Courtesy Evan J. Smith)

Erich Bollman owns 2008 Cobra Jet number 18. Bollman has run his CJ with both stick shift and automatic. (Photo Courtesy Evan J. Smith)

"So, I realized, after a few rounds, that we had a shot at winning this thing [the Winternationals], but there was rain and we kept having delays. John kept going rounds and it was so crazy and so cool. I had to load the other Cobra Jets, so I wasn't even there for the final. John called me, and I immediately called Brian [Wolfe] and everyone at Ford who was involved—we really enjoyed the moment."

2010 Game On

The raging success of the 2008 Cobra Jet ensured the continuation of the program and set the stage for the 2010 CJ. Now, with a year of racing and development, Ford was able to add content, improve performance, and make the Mustang more turnkey and thus race ready from the factory. While solid performers, the 2008s suffered on track from a street-style clutch and transmission, and only featured a six-point roll bar rather than a full cage. Serious NHRA racers swapped these parts immediately for parts more suitable for NHRA competition.

Jimmy Ronzello heats the tires on a 2010 prototype Cobra Jet during development testing. (Photo Courtesy Evan J. Smith)

"The 2010/2012 cars were more complete race cars," stated Kershaw. "We added Strange brakes, put 19 mm of travel into the front shock, thrifted the wiring, and put in true race-prepped transmissions. We also tweaked the rear suspension geometry. It was basically all the things we wanted to do on the 2008 but didn't have time for. We also offered several engine and transmission options including a few pushrod engines for racers who were turned off by overhead cams.

"For the price, the car was untouchable, and even Chevy racers started to convert. Chevy tried to match us, but they had engine trouble and eventually gave racers new cylinder heads as a fix. All the Ford guys had to do was add fuel and wipe it down between runs," Kershaw stated.

The 2010 Cobra Jet took on a new look with the updated 2010 Mustang styling that was enhanced by a lightweight raised-cowl hood. Ford also installed a full NHRA roll cage legal to 8.50 ET and, as Kershaw stated, there was a variety of engine options. The sophomore year for the modern Cobra Jet was unique in that Ford offered a choice of manual 5-speed transmission or 3-speed automatic. The manual consisted of a Liberty Gears 5-speed transmission manipulated by a vertigate "in-line" shifter. The auto was a C4 with a Hurst shifter. Ford also switched from Goodyear to Hoosier rubber mounted on Weld wheels.

Ford also provided a strong engine lineup including two supercharged 5.4L engine options, two naturally aspirated 4.6L three-valve options, and two small-block Windsor-based engines—one with 352 ci and one with 428. And those displacements were no accident. The base engine was the 435-hp Eaton supercharged 5.4L. Owners could upgrade to the 4.0L Whipple supercharger, which came with a rating of 500 hp and was listed as a

Here's a look at a 4.6L (281-ci) CJ three-valve engine. (Photo Courtesy Evan J. Smith)

Engine teardown inspection is part of the NHRA game. Here, NHRA's Ryck Campbell checks the size of a combustion chamber on the Cobra Jet cylinder head. It is the responsibility of the racers to complete the teardown and reassembly. (Photo Courtesy Evan J. Smith)

Super Cobra Jet. At the time, the CJs equipped with the 4.0L blower were only legal for Super Stock, but they are now allowed in Stock Eliminator. It should also be noted that the 4.0L Whipple-equipped CJs have run in the 7s in the quarter mile, making them some of the fastest Super Stockers in the world.

Ford also offered a base 4.6L at 235 hp, which was a hot-rodded 2010 Mustang GT engine with improved heads, Ford Performance intake, larger throttle body, and a few other options; the NHRA rated it at 270 hp. It should be noted that all Cobra Jets were fed by electronic fuel injection.

As delivered, the 2010 Cobra Jets ran well into the 9s at 140-plus mph. According to Kershaw, "Kevin Cour, who currently works for Ford, was an executive at Toyota at the time, and his family bought a 2010 Cobra Jet just before the NHRA Seattle event. He flew in on Wednesday and was holding up a Wally on Sunday. The 2010 let the world know that the car was race-ready as received, and Kevin proved it."

2012: Getting Serious

Building on the success of the 2010 platform, Ford Performance unveiled the 2012 Cobra Jet Mustang in December 2011 at the Performance Racing Industry (PRI) show in Orlando. Ford announced the intention to build another 50 turnkey drag race cars using a production body with a lightweight hood. For first time, the Cobra Jet Mustang was available in three colors including Race Red, Grabber Blue, and Winner White—coordinated graphics were also available.

Gone from the engine lineup was the naturally aspirated 4.6L three-valve, which was replaced with a larger Coyote 5.0L, available in two different configurations. Like the 2010 Cobra Jet and the Mustang FR500S road race car, the 2012 Cobra Jet was built on the Mustang production line at the Auto Alliance International (AAI) assembly plant in Flat Rock, Michigan.

George Goddu, former business manager of Ford Racing Performance Group, is quoted from the original Cobra Jet press release saying, "Ford Racing is proud to build the 2012 Cobra Jet and continue the tradition of delivering turnkey competitive race cars to Ford drag racing enthusiasts. With every Cobra Jet build we strive to carry the spirit of the original Cobra Jet while developing the next generation of drag racing icon. The enthusiast who races the 2012 Cobra Jet can be competitive at virtually any event, from their local track up through NHRA Stock or Super Stock classes."

The release also stated "The goal for the 2012 Cobra Jet is to build a turnkey race car ready to take its own place in NHRA history. Like its predecessors in 2008 and 2010, it's a factory-built race car intended for NHRA Stock and Super Stock racing that can also be campaigned in other racing sanctioning bodies such as NMRA, NMCA, PSCA, and IHRA." The evolution continued, however, as the 2012 CJ featured a full race-prepared automatic transmission, drag race–specific shocks and springs, manual steering and brakes, 8.50 certified roll cage, and an Aeromotive return-style fuel system with trunk-mounted fuel cell.

And, like 2010, there were supercharger options: a 2.3-liter TVS unit or a 4.0-liter Ford Racing Whipple supercharger. Weight savings came from an aluminum engine block, and durability was ensured with a double-keyed crankshaft and Manley H-beam connecting rods. Ford also installed low-drag racing brakes and suspension development continued that resulted in improved spring rates for the front and rear. The Cobra Jet sported new-look wheels from Weld Racing and a new compound tire with unique Cobra Jet branding from Goodyear.

In addition, the entire 50-car run was built on the production line that produced the 2012 Ford Mustang production car. MSRP for the 2012 M-FR500-CJ was $91,900, with a fully loaded Cobra Jet priced at $103,980. Plus, Ford offered a Mustang Competition Roller kit based on the Cobra Jet that was serialized and complete, minus the powertrain. This was the perfect option for anyone wanting to build his or her own Cobra Jet. Even with the kits available, many racers started from scratch, building their race cars using a Mustang Body-In-White or a donor car since nearly all of the CJ components can be found in the Ford Performance Parts catalog found at fordracingparts.com.

Shown here are the 2013 development "Spy vs. Spy" Cobra Jets. The black car sported the all-motor 5.0, and the white car was supercharged. (Photo Courtesy Evan J. Smith)

The 2013 5.0 engine was a stout piece, capable of pushing the Cobra Jet deep into the 10s. (Photo Courtesy Evan J. Smith)

With a Whipple supercharger, the 2013 blown car was capable of 8s in the quarter mile. (Photo Courtesy Evan J. Smith)

2013/2014: Enter Coyote

For 2013, Cobra Jet took another leap forward. The DOHC modular served as a formidable soldier, but the 5.0L Coyote had many clear advantages so it was chosen to replace the 5.4L powerplant. The Coyote was lighter, had improved cylinder head flow, and was topped with a potent 2.9L Whipple twin-screw intercooled supercharger. Cobra Jet production/assembly also was transferred from AAI to Watson Engineering in Brownstown, Michigan.

Available engines included three 5.0L Coyotes plus a pair of Windsor-based pushrod engines: a 363 ci and a 427 ci rated by NHRA at 330 and 425 hp, respectively. Like prior Windsor Cobra Jet engines, these used a Ford Performance block; FP aluminum heads; and single-plane, carburetor-style intake

Cobra Jet testing was not without drama, as the engineering team learned to expect the unexpected. After struggling with traction, the team made changes that led to this 300-foot wheelie. Test driver Evan J. Smith kept his foot on the gas and landed without any damage. (Photo Courtesy Evan J. Smith)

Anthony Bongiovanni often finds the winner's circle with his 2016 Cobra Jet. (Photo Courtesy Evan J. Smith)

with a single EFI throttle body. Two of the 5.0 engines were naturally aspirated and rated at 350 and 380, while the Whipple supercharged variant was rated at 500 hp.

According to Kershaw, "2013 and 2014 was another step up—this time with the new Coyote engine. Overall, these cars were excellent refinements to the brand and, as-delivered, were capable of 8-second ETs in Stock Eliminator trim, which was insane for the time.

"I was fortunate enough to have driven a Cobra Jet for Anthony Bongiovanni's Micro Strategies race team," said Evan Smith. "We won the first Cobra Jet Invitational in his 2008 CJ and then the following week won Class eliminations at Indy. I was pretty new to those cars, so it was an honor to be teamed with Jimmy Ronzello and serve as a factory Ford test driver on the Cobra Jet program. There is so much that goes into developing any race car, and there are even greater challenges when a major manufacturer is selling such a high-powered track car. I learned a lot from Ronzello and, in 2013, I drove both the naturally aspirated and supercharged cars, making dozens of runs. We worked on everything typical racers work on, but we did so on a compressed time schedule.

"The engineering team was relentless, testing calibrations plus loads of

A multitude of components were brought to the track during testing. (Photo Courtesy Evan J. Smith)

Lead engine calibrator Dev Saberwal works his magic on the all-motor combination. It was not uncommon to rev this beast past 8,000 rpm. (Photo Courtesy Evan J. Smith)

Drag racing legend Roy Hill currently runs a fleet of Cobra Jet Mustangs. Hill's Super Stocker has run in the 7s at 175 mph. (Photo Courtesy Evan J. Smith)

New Jerseyan Anthony Bongiovanni owns a fleet of Cobra Jet Mustangs. Bongiovanni has multiple wins in NHRA competition, dozens of Class wins, and his 2014 (near lane) has won the NHRA's coveted "Best Engineered" award. He competes with daughters Michelle and Genna, along with drivers Steve Ficacci, Ken Miele, and Evan J. Smith. (Photo Courtesy Evan J. Smith)

Bongiovanni's Cobra Jet team is backed by Micro Strategies and Resource1. (Photo Courtesy Evan J. Smith)

components in order to make the car fast, safe, and reliable. And none of the models were released before a series of durability tests was completed. That really puts the car through a lot, but it ensures racers will get a car that's fast and can last. Test driving can be challenging because there are times when I can change my driving style to make the car fast, and other times when we have to be spot-on consistent in order to bring back the desired data for the engineers. We're also providing input that helps the engineers deliver a car that's comfortable and easy to drive," Smith added.

Performance for the 2013 Cobra Jet came from the wickedly powerful 5.0L with CNC-ported heads, custom cams, tuned headers, and a big mono-blade throttle body. The engine was fed by an Aeromotive fuel system and controlled by a custom calibration in the Copperhead ECU. Ford also traded the manual rack for factory power steering with electronic assist. Those wanting a naturally aspirated engine could select the all-motor CJ, which featured more compression, different cams, and a unique Cobra Jet intake manifold. The lone transmission option was a C-4 3-speed automatic prepared by Joel's on Joy. Available colors were black or silver.

Most Cobra Jets are white or black, but in 2014 Ford Performance offered Gotta Have It Green as an option. (Photo Courtesy Evan J. Smith)

Looking for improved performance, Ford kept evolving the Cobra Jet, its 5.0L powerplants, and the drivelines. "The 2014 car offered the Reid SFI case T4 [Turbo 400] transmission," said Kershaw. "In my opinion, the 2014 is still the best Cobra Jet we ever made and, at the time, the competition had no answer for it. Really, 2010 to 2014 models were always a step ahead of the competition, and racers made us look good. Without teams willing to go the extra mile we would have never had that level of success, but we gave them a solid foundation."

Anthony Bongiovanni goes wheels-up with his 2014 Cobra Jet. (Photo Courtesy Evan J. Smith)

Ford worked with the engine calibration and boost levels to pick up over 100 hp from 2013 to 2014, and that made a big difference on the track. Changes to the transmission gearing also helped improve 60-foot times and quarter-mile elapsed times. Improvements were also made to the launch control and two-step, and after some R&D time, Cobra Jets were solidly in the 8s at close to 160 mph. Available colors for 2014 were Flat Black, White, and Gotta Have It Green.

All 50 2014 Cobra Jets have proven to be very successful race cars, winning in NHRA, NMCA, and NMRA competition, and Ford utilized the on-track accomplishments to its advantage.

"Internally, we promoted it heavily," said Kershaw. "I would send emails to parts of the company that helped when we had success. SVT gave me test engines, and when a racer would win with parts from an engine that SVT had donated to the cause, I would send them pics of that. The engine lab brought its high-speed camera that is used to monitor accessory drive belts to the track to shoot our cars slow motion for promotional videos. We found a way to pinch budgets to get photos done, too," he added. "There was a party at the plant for building the cars and everyone would sign a hood (with the snake on it) for the wall. The rapid prototype lab was sent updates pictures whenever one of our 429 'Ninja' cars won with the intake they produced. I handed out hundreds of Cobra Jet stickers to Ford employees and thanked them for being on the Cobra Jet team.

"In big companies, people have a job and often could have said no to my requests. But there was a true One Ford spirit to the program—

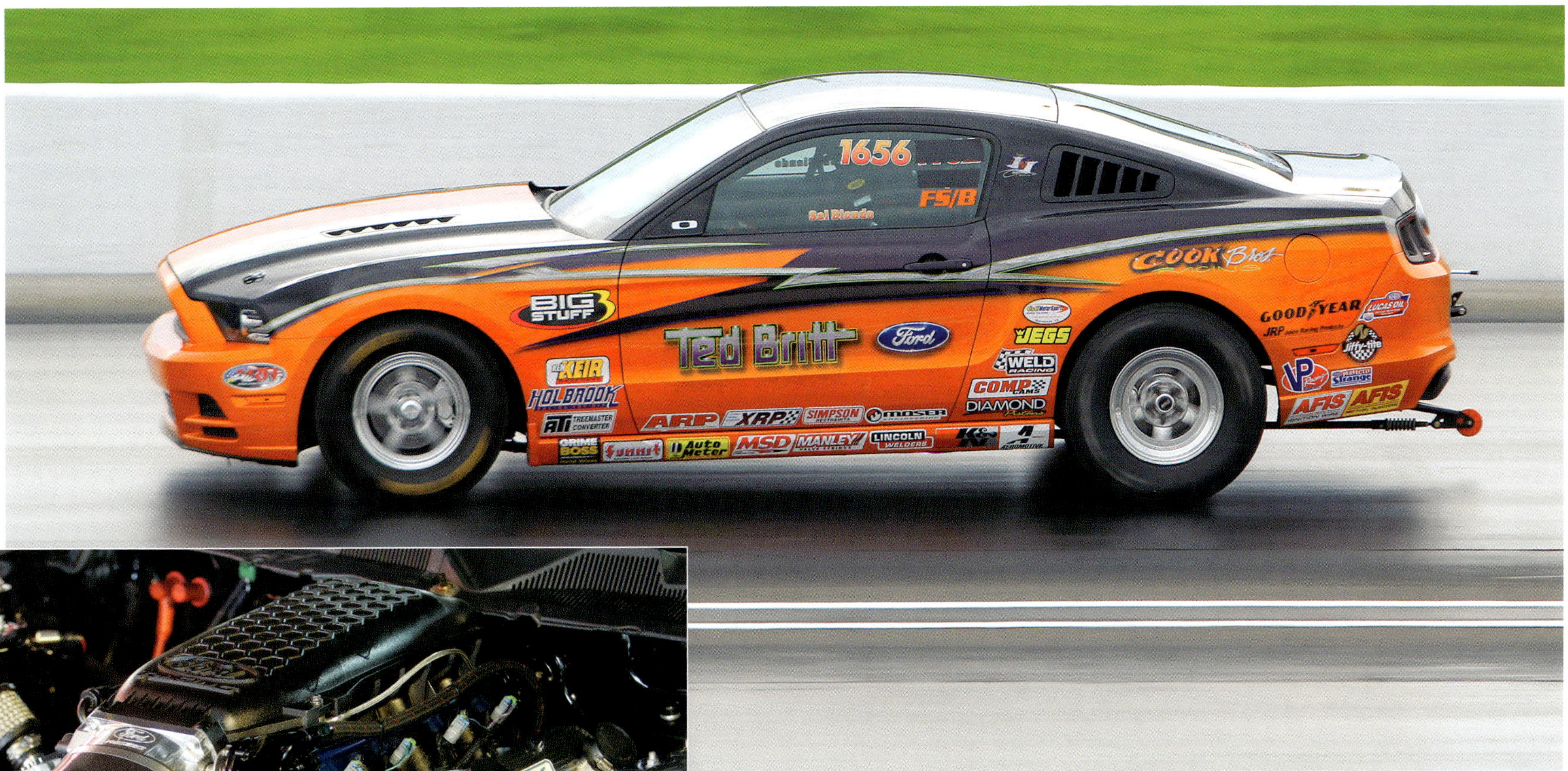

The Cook Brothers run a Ninja in their 2014 Cobra Jet that has run well into the 8s. The colorful CJ has been wheeled by national event-winning drivers Sal Biondo and Ken Miele. (Photo Courtesy Evan J. Smith)

The hottest all-motor engine is the 429-ci "Ninja," which features Yates-style heads, 14.9:1 compression, a 0.650-inch lift cam, and a special composite intake manifold. Rated at 455 hp by NHRA, a well-built Ninja can develop upward of 900 hp. (Photo Courtesy Evan J. Smith)

Gary Richard of New York takes on a classic 1968 Hemi Barracuda in Super Stock action. (Photo Courtesy Evan J. Smith)

Mike Delahanty, product manager driveline and power/drag racing program manager. (Photo Courtesy Evan J. Smith)

especially at the beginning—and people wanted to help," said Kershaw. "The Cobra Jet embodied the One Ford motto that Alan Mullaly brought to Ford. It knocked down barriers internally, and people wanted to be involved and help. It was also a huge success with customers. I'm immensely proud of what we accomplished and, if imitation is the sincerest form of flattery, I'm very flattered."

2016: S550 Shootout Warrior

Major changes were in store for 2016. Production Ford Mustangs were now being built on the new S550 chassis with IRS rear suspension, and that presented a new challenge to the Cobra Jet engineers. A solid "live" axle is the best choice for all-out drag racing, and NHRA rules allow for a straight-axle conversion, so Ford developed a unique four-link rear suspension and attached a typical 9-inch Ford housing with Strange aftermarket axles, spool, and gearing suited for the best performance with the supercharged Coyote engine.

"The 2016 uses the latest bodystyle, and the IRS posed some issues," said Kershaw. "It was originally supposed to be a 2015 model, and there were plans to show it at the 50th Anniversary of Mustang celebration in April of 2014, but those fell through. The performance targets for the car were set for a summer 2014 build, but the cars weren't produced until December 2015."

There was no denying the aggressive looks of the 2016 Cobra Jet, and the performance was strong thanks to engine upgrades including the improved cylinder heads and upgraded front-entry Whipple 2.9L supercharger. Ford also listed a 5.2L variant for the CJ that utilized Shelby GT350 cylinder heads for improved flow and more power. Performance, more than ever before, was critical—in addition to running in Stock and Super Stock, Cobra Jet Mustangs now competed head-to-head with the Chevrolet COPO Camaro and the Dodge Drag Pak Challenger in the NHRA Factory Stock Showdown and NMCA Holley EFI Factory Super Cars classes.

"The 2016 Cobra Jet program took the car to a new level of race readiness with a new four-link rear suspension," said Mike Delahanty, product manager driveline and power/drag racing program manager. "We had another new group of CJ owners that would take the car as delivered and put it in the 8s at over 150 mph. These are happy owners and racers

Ford Performance displayed the 2016 Cobra Jet at the Performance Racing Industry (PRI) show in Indianapolis. (Photo Courtesy Evan J. Smith)

The 2016 engine features a 2.9L Whipple supercharger. Ford also offers a "Shootout" engine designed for action in the School of Automotive Machinists (SAM) Tech Factory Stock Showdown. This engine utilizes larger 5.2L displacement and Shelby GT350 cylinder heads. (Photo Courtesy Evan J. Smith)

who continue to be amazed with the performance of the CJ." Adding to the raciness were Sparco race seats, steering wheel, and Weld wheels with Hoosier tires.

Ford Performance revealed the 2016 Cobra Jet Mustang at the SEMA show in Las Vegas. The modern program started with 50 cars for the 2008 model year, continuing with 50-unit limited builds in 2010, 2012, 2013, and 2014. For 2016, the car was available in Oxford White or Deep Impact Blue, with each color limited to 25 examples.

"The modern Cobra Jet has performed for our customers and put Ford in the winner's circle consistently since 2008," said Dave Pericak, director of Ford Performance. "The new car is the first Cobra Jet built off the all-new 2015 Mustang and the only factory 2016 Mustang with a solid axle rear suspension."

Keeping with the production theme, Cobra Jet's 5.0L engine was made up of 75 percent production Mustang GT components and was boosted by an efficient front-inlet Whipple supercharger. The T4 transmission remained, although gearing had been altered to optimize performance with the upgraded engine.

"It was important to use production hardware wherever possible to ensure parts are readily available and reasonably priced for racers," said Jesse Kershaw. "The production parts are also incredibly durable in passing our rigorous dyno and drag strip testing."

Since that glorious win at the 2009 Winternationals, Cobra Jets have added to the legacy with a multitude of wins and national records in many forms of drag racing. The 2016 Cobra Jet featured such enhancements as drag race–specific coilover shocks and springs and lightweight racing brakes by Strange Engineering. Ford has kept the Cobra Snake graphics as well.

Ford Performance engineers tapped many internal and external resources, utilizing technology and adapting it for racing. For instance, the Cobra Jet now uses an electric water pump from the Ford C-MAX Hybrid that allows cool-down without the engine running. This is advantageous in expediting the cooling process between runs and aiding in consistency via improved management of engine temperature. Ford also used dyno cells calibrated to simulate drag strip burnouts, and quarter-mile runs were used to prove out engine durability.

The M-FR500-CJ Cobra Jet was sold through any

In addition to building Cobra Jets, Watson Racing is well known for fielding its own competitive cars. In 2017, Chuck Watson Sr. dismantled a field of serious players to win the NHRA SAM Tech Factory Stock Showdown in Norwalk, Ohio. (Photo Courtesy Evan J. Smith)

Don Carson has the distinction of owning the quickest 5.0L Coyote Cobra Jet. His JDM Engineering–built and –tuned CJ has run 9.30s in NHRA trim and as quick as 9.06 at 147 mph with weight removed. Amazingly, the little 302 has pushed the 2014 CJ to sub-1.20-second 60-foot times! (Photo Courtesy Evan J. Smith)